LONDON RECORD SOCIETY
PUBLICATIONS

VOLUME XXXIII
FOR THE YEAR 1996

CHELSEA SETTLEMENT AND BASTARDY EXAMINATIONS, 1733–1766

EDITED BY
TIM HITCHCOCK AND JOHN BLACK

LONDON RECORD SOCIETY
1999

© *London Record Society*
ISBN 0 90095233 4

Dedicated to
Nadia and Emilio

Typeset by
The Midlands Book Typesetting Company, Loughborough, Leicestershire
Printed and bound in Great Britain by
Quorn Selective Repro Ltd, Loughborough, Leicestershire

CONTENTS

INTRODUCTION

Hannah Elliett and her infant daughter Mary were abandoned by her husband and Mary's father, George, in the Spring of 1749. Destitute, she applied to the parish of Chelsea for poor relief and was examined in the committee room of the parish workhouse as to her legal settlement by two justices of the peace on Friday, 6 June. Hannah was asked about her age, the circumstances of her marriage, details of her daughter's birth, her husband's, her own and her father's employment history, and whether she, or they, had ever rented a house of £10 per year, paid any parochial taxes or served as a parish officer. The details of her answers were then transcribed into a large bound volume kept for this purpose by the attending clerk. The entry was then signed by Hannah with a mark, and by the two attending justices, Peter Elers and Henry Fielding. A note was later appended to the entry stating that she was passed by an order to the parish of St John Southwark – the place of her legal settlement, and the parish now responsible for her support (**207**). It is the contents of the volume this information was entered into, along with that of a subsequent volume, which are reproduced here. Some 466 examinations were entered between 1733 and 1766, and they record both enquiries into the legal settlement of paupers (settlement examinations) and the paternity of illegitimate children (bastardy examinations). In the first case, the information recorded is concerned with the issues addressed to Hannah Elliett; and in the second, in the bastardy examinations, the sexual behaviour of the mother, the name, date of birth or likely delivery date of the child, and the name, occupation and behaviour of the father were all scrutinised.

These examinations bring into sharp focus the meeting point between the poor and the system of relief, the Elizabethan Poor Law, upon which the majority of the eighteenth-century population relied at some point during their lives. In the case of the settlement examinations, although they were recorded as a means of establishing who was entitled to relief from which parish, they likewise provide an insight into the ambivalent, ambiguous, and often contradictory relationship between the recipients of relief and those who administered the system. At first sight the settlement examinations would appear to reflect the dominant concerns and views of the parish officers, magistrates and clerks – the interlocutors who elicited and recorded the responses of the examinees. But at the same time the documents produced reflect the admittedly limited choices made by the poor, and illuminate the strategies the poor could adopt in order to influence the outcome of the interviews to their own advantage. By judicious self-censorship the apparent victim of the process could, within limits, effectively control its result. And, while the system of legal settlement,

which tied individual paupers to a single parish (see below), has traditionally been criticised, from the eighteenth century onwards, for its oppressive role in the lives of the poor, more recent work has helped to remind
us that the eighteenth-century poor believed their legal settlement in a
particular parish represented the possession of a positive claim on that
parish, and a 'right' to relief from it.[1] The frequent references within the
examinations themselves to discussion of individual legal settlements
between parents and children and husbands and wives, suggest it was a
matter of no small consequence, and self-conscious concern, to the poor
themselves (**36, 51, 69**). And indeed, the answers recorded in these examinations frequently suggest that the individuals involved had a very clear idea
of the legal requirements for a settlement, and likewise that they were in a
position to manipulate the system to their own ends.

The same ambiguity apparent in settlement examinations is present
within the bastardy examinations. Unmarried mothers and their illegitimate
children are often viewed by historians as the section of early modern
English society most vulnerable to ill treatment by the parish and legal
system.[2] Nevertheless, bastardy examinations taken under oath before one
or two magistrates were a powerful means by which the mothers of
illegitimate children could establish the parish and/or the putative father
responsible for the physical well-being of their child or children. In many
ways the parish was in effect enforcing the rights of the mother and child
against the father. It was acting as a powerful coercive mechanism directed
in part by one of the least powerful groups within society.[3]

In some very important ways, therefore, these examinations reflect the
working out of the power relationships amongst paupers and administra-
tors. At the same time they also contain a great deal of information about
the lives and experiences of the poor. Patterns of apprenticeship and of
service, employment and matrimonial histories are each recorded here. The
examinations give new insight into the nature of family relationships among

1 Perhaps the best known eighteenth-century critic of the law of settlement is Adam Smith
   who claimed 'There is scarce a poor man in England of forty years of age ...who has not
   in some part of his life felt himself most cruelly oppressed by this ill-contrived law of
   settlements.' Adam Smith, *An Inquiry into the Nature and Causes of the Wealth of Nations*
   (Everyman Edition, 1926), I, p. 128. For an analysis of development of idea of a 'right'
   to relief see T.Hitchcock, P.King and P.Sharpe, eds., *Chronicling Poverty: The Voices and
   Strategies of the English Poor* (Basingstoke, 1996), pp. 1–18.
2 For an example of the ill-treatment that could be meted out to bastard-bearers, and their
   lovers, see the bastardy examination of Ann Spond, whose child died as a result of the
   criminal negligence of the parish officers of Fulham, London Metropolitan Archive
   (henceforth LMA), Chelsea, P74/LUK/15 May 1794. For a general discussion of this and
   other such cases see J. S. Taylor, ' The impact of pauper settlement 1691–1834', *Past and
   Present* 73 (1964), pp. 61–2.
3 For a discussion of the roles of parish relief in the lives of poor women and 'bastard
   bearers' see Tim Hitchcock, ' "Unlawfully begotten on her body": illegitimacy and the
   parish poor in St Luke's Chelsea' in T.Hitchcock et al., eds., *Chronicling Poverty*, pp. 70–
   86. See also Nicholas Rogers, 'Carnal knowledge: illegitimacy in eighteenth-century
   Westminster', *Journal of Social History*, XXIII, 2 (1989) pp. 355–75; A. Wilson,
   'Illegitimacy and its implications in mid-eighteenth-century London: the evidence of the
   Foundling Hospital', *Continuity and Change* 4 (1989) pp. 103–64.

the least articulate members of eighteenth-century society. Likewise, patterns
of sexual behaviour are recorded, as are indications of the resources available
to the poor and the nature of the communities within which they lived.
In a whole range of ways the material reproduced here adds a new level of
complexity to our understanding of eighteenth-century London and its
environs, and the experiences of the approximately fifty per cent of the
population who were likely to need relief from the parish at some point
during their lives. In relation to migration, patterns of courtship, and the
experience of working and living within the rapidly changing social welfare
provision of mid-eighteenth century London, all areas of recent interest to
modern historians, this material provides a new perspective.[4]

The legal context

To use these examinations effectively we need to understand the legal
context within which they were created. The precept that each person had
a place of settlement, or home parish, was not new to the eighteenth
century. It had been implicit in the series of vagrancy laws passed between
the late fourteenth and early seventeenth centuries, and was likewise implicit
in the Elizabethan Poor Law itself, 43 Elizabeth c.2.[5] But, it was with the
passage of the Act of Settlement in 1662 (13 & 14 Car. II c.12.) that the
legal requirements for gaining a settlement were explicitly defined. The 1662
Act was principally concerned with restricting migration, and providing
the basis for the exclusion of outsiders from a given parish. Those
immigrants thought 'likely to be chargeable' to a parish could be removed
under the Act's auspices by order of two justices of the peace, if a complaint
was brought against them within 40 days of their arrival, and always
providing that they had not married someone with a settlement, rented a
house or land worth £10 per year or more, or provided a certificate from
their parish of previous legal settlement accepting responsibility for the
relief of the individual and his or her dependants.[6]

In the period following the passage of the Act of Settlement, its provisions were adapted and modified. In addition to the £10 property qualification, later legislation ensured that settlement could be earned through the
payment of local rates, serving as an unpaid parish officer, by being bound
an apprentice or hired as a servant for a year. Acts were passed ensuring
that those with 'certificates' could only be removed if they became chargeable to the parish of residence. And finally, if no other settlement could be

---

4   For the best overview of the changing pattern of voluntary and charitable provisions for
    the poor in mid-eighteenth century London, see Donna Andrew, *Philanthropy and Police:
    London Charity in the Eighteenth Century* (Princeton NJ, 1989).
5   For a complete list of poor law statutes up to and including this period, see Paul Slack,
    The English Poor Law, 1531–1782 (Basingstoke, 1990), pp. 59–64. See also J.S. Taylor,
    Poverty, Migration, and Settlement in the Industrial Revolution (Berkeley CA, 1989), p. 19;
    Sidney and Beatrice Webb, *English Local Government: English Poor Law History*: Part 1 :
    The Old Poor Law (1927), pp. 315–6.
6   See Slack, *English Poor Law*, pp. 35–7; Paul Slack, *Poverty and Policy in Tudor and Stuart
    England* (London, 1988), pp. 194–5; Taylor, *Poverty, Migration, and Settlement*, pp. 9–10,
    19; Webb, *Old Poor Law*, pp. 314–43.

determined, or if the individual was illegitimate, the settlement would be established in the place of birth.[7]

During the same period case law came to modify significantly the workings of the settlement system. Of particular importance was the development of the idea of derivative settlements, established by lawyers at the Courts of King's Bench during the eighteenth century, which ensured that if a person did not form a new settlement for themselves they would then derive their settlement from that of their parents, or even their grandparents.[8]

All of these aspects of the system of legal settlement can be seen reflected in the examinations reproduced here. It is these provisions which explain the inclusion of the formulaic statement found in many of the examinations, that an individual 'never has rented a house of £10 a year, or paid any parochial taxes' (e.g. **261**). These provisions also explain the large amounts of information elicited about marriage, place of birth (particularly in relation to illegitimate children), parentage, apprenticeship and employment in service for longer than a year. They likewise explain the detailed information provided in some examinations about the location where individuals spent their last 40 days in service (**93, 104, 397**).

The legal context in which bastardy examinations were conducted was, of course, somewhat different. Illegitimate children gained their settlement from their parish of birth. To protect the ratepayers the law allowed the parish officers either to persuade the putative father to marry the mother of the illegitimate child, this being especially attractive if the father was from somewhere else, or to force the father to indemnify the parish against any expenses incurred for the delivery and later maintenance of the child (**29, 425, 433**).[9] Because, in this instance, it was place of birth and paternity which were at issue, it is information relating to these points which were recorded.

Inevitably, these examinations were conducted to the specific end of determining either the settlement or paternity of an individual. As a result, they represent the outcome of a single-minded pursuit of the answers to just a few questions which revolve around the limited concerns of the poor relief system as to the birth, family, marriage, and employment of each pauper as far as they affected the place of settlement of the pauper concerned. Similarly, the sexual history of the mother of an illegitimate child and the putative father was only of interest in as far as it shed light on who would be answerable for the maintenance of that child.

Practice

While there was a well-established set of legal requirements which an examination needed to satisfy if it was to be used to remove an individual

---

7 Legislation significantly modifying the 1662 Act of Settlement includes: 3 William & Mary c.11, and 8 & 9 William III c.30. See Slack, *English Poor Law*, p. 62; Taylor, *Poverty, Migration, and Settlement*, pp. 19–22; Webb, *Old Poor Law*, pp. 327–9.
8 See Slack, *English Poor Law*, pp. 36–8; Taylor, *Poverty, Migration, and Settlement*, p. 20; Webb, *Old Poor Law*, p. 334.
9 See Taylor, 'Pauper Settlement', pp. 43–66.

– it had, for example, to be given under oath before two justices – the actual circumstances under which settlement and bastardy examinations were recorded could vary greatly from one part of the country to another, and even from one month to the next.[10] In Chelsea there is substantial evidence that normal practice varied widely depending on factors such as the character of the presiding magistrate, the type of examination being transcribed, and the experience of the clerk.

In the majority of cases, settlement examinations were heard at petty sessions – the regular meetings held by the magistrates of each division within a county.[11] At the same time, however, the Chelsea examinations reflect a wide variety of practice.[12] For instance, although statute law suggested that examinations had to be heard before two justices of the peace, a substantial minority of the examinations reproduced were heard by a single justice, even though any removal orders which resulted from such examinations would, under a strict construction of the law, be legally void.[13] The volumes themselves suggest that the examinations were conducted under relatively formal conditions. They are clearly and expertly drafted, suggesting that they were written up by the parish clerk from notes. At the same time they are invariably marked or signed by the pauper and the examining magistrates, suggesting in turn that the process of entering the text in the volume was undertaken while the examinee and justices waited. The poor condition of the bindings imply that the examinations were consulted regularly, while the marginal notes on the outcome of particular cases reflect the use of these documents as a part of a larger legal system. Chelsea frequently appealed against the removal of paupers from other parishes, and was itself frequently the object of an appeal. Many of the individuals whose examinations are recorded here also turn up in the petitions and orders contained in Middlesex county session papers, as various parishes used the courts to dispute their responsibility.[14]

10 There is in fact some debate between K.D.M. Snell and Norma Landau as to where, when, by whom, and in the presence of which county officials settlement and bastardy examinations were recorded. For details of this debate see K.D.M. Snell, *The Annals of the Labouring Poor: Social Change and Agrarian England, 1660–1900* (Cambridge, 1985); K.D.M. Snell, 'Pauper Settlement and the right to poor relief in England and Wales', *Continuity and Change* 6 (1991) pp. 375–415 and Norma Landau's reply in the same volume, pp. 417–39; Norma Landau, 'The Laws of Settlement and the surveillance of immigration in eighteenth century Kent', *Continuity and Change* 3 (1988) pp. 391–420; Norma Landau, 'The regulation of immigration, economic structures and definitions of the poor in eighteenth-century England', *Historical Journal* 33 (1990) pp. 541–72. For a more accessible discussion of the role of justices at this period see Ruth Paley, ed., *Justice in Eighteenth-Century Hackney: The Justicing Notebook of Henry Norris and the Hackney Petty Sessions Book* (London Record Society, 28, 1991), 'Introduction'.
11 For a discussion of general practice see Norma Landau, 'Immigration in eighteenth-century Kent'.
12 Landau herself freely acknowledges the wide variety of practice found in collections of examinations. See Norma Landau, 'The eighteenth-century context of the Laws of Settlement', n.40, pp. 436–7.
13 Ibid, n.15, pp. 433–4.
14 John Tallent was examined in 17 August 1751 (**238**) and passed to the parish of St Martin in the Fields. St Martin appealed against the pass warrant, and the October Sessions ordered that Chelsea undertake the support of John and his wife. LMA MJ/SP/1751/10/

Indeed the timing, location, and administrative props employed by the Middlesex magistrates who sat in Chelsea reflected and encouraged a combination of both inflexible propriety and sloppy disregard for the requirements of the law. In part, this variety of practice resulted from the workaday necessities involved in the operation of parish poor-law administration. These examinations contain numerous instances where the logical legal outcome of a given examination is eschewed in favour of more humane treatment of the pauper involved, or occasionally a result significantly advantageous to the parish of Chelsea.[15]

This variety of practice is also tied to the circumstances in which the examinations were taken. The size of the two bound volumes involved would seem to suggest that they were intended to remain in one location, while their inclusion in the archive associated with the parish workhouse would at least imply that the meeting room integral to the design of the house built in 1737 was used both to hear the examinations and to stockpile the resulting manuscripts. Because the workhouse was in most respects the centre of parochial administration in eighteenth-century Chelsea, a wide variety of personnel, both parish officers and magistrates, inevitably had access to these volumes, and would have expected to contribute to them.

An analysis of the timing of the petty sessions would further suggest that pauper examination by the local Chelsea magistrates was inextricably bound up with the rhythms of parish administration. The practice of holding petty sessions in order to hear examinations once a month was the norm, but this was regularly varied when the numbers of pregnant women and paupers demanded it.[16] Indeed, an analysis of the numbers of examinations recorded and the number of times petty sessions met (occasionally three times a month: **9, 10, 11**), provides evidence to suggest a seasonal pattern which matches voluntary entry into the workhouse – a dramatic leap in the numbers of examinations in October followed by a further peak in January and a gradual subsidence in business during early April. In part this pattern must be ascribed to changing cyclical unemployment patterns of the sort examined by K.D.M. Snell, but it must likewise result from the self-conscious policy decisions of parish officers. And as Norma Landau has suggested, it must reflect an active process of parochial and magisterial surveillance of both indigent and non-indigent migration.[17] The balance

---

58–59. Information from the examination reproduced here was used as part of the case. Other examinees who were the subject of appeals which can be traced through the Quarter Sessions records include Ephraim Hilary (**227**), LMA MJ/SP/1751/01/31; Ann Williamson (**378**) LMA MJ/SP/1758/12/31; Sarah Baldwin (**418**), LMA MJ/SP/1762/09/55–56; and Ann Whitesides (**413**), LMA MJ/SP/1762/04/24–25.

15 For an example of more benign treatment of paupers by Chelsea parish officers see Taylor, 'Pauper Settlement', p. 61.

16 For a discussion of the timing and administration of petty sessions in relation to hearing examinations see Landau, 'Immigration in eighteenth-century Kent', p. 393.

17 See Snell, *The Annals of the Labouring Poor*; Norma Landau, 'The eighteenth-century context of the laws of settlement'. The pressures on the system in Chelsea can be traced by analysing the contemporaneous workhouse register which is available as a database on CD-ROM. See Tim Hitchcock and Robert Shoemaker, *Economic Growth and Social Change in the Eighteenth-Century English Town* (Glasgow, Core Resources for Historians, 1998).

between these two factors, unemployment and surveillance, is almost impossible to determine with any certainty, but it is clear that both the economic choices of the poor, i.e. their decision to apply to enter the workhouse, and the policy decisions of parish and magistracy, contributed to the seasonal patterns of examinations found in these volumes.

The Middlesex Bench

Besides the poor themselves, the people most intimately concerned with the creation of these examinations were the magistrates of the Middlesex Bench. Derided in the eighteenth century for their low social status, mercenary approach to the law, and corruption, the magistrates whose signatures appear in these volumes seem to belie this reputation.[18] Certainly, these examinations contain little evidence of gross or extreme cruelty beyond what one would expect in the normal run of eighteenth-century poor law administration. Similarly, these manuscripts provide no evidence of peculation or corruption. At the same time, however, it must be admitted that many of the people who heard the examinations recorded here were possessed of somewhat unsavoury reputations. For example, Thomas Cotton, a relatively active Chelsea magistrate, was among the 75 justices removed from the Middlesex Bench by Lord Chancellor Hardwicke in 1738 in response to various charges of corruption, gross misconduct, and abuse of office (**2, 37, 47**).[19]

If there is some evidence to justify the low esteem in which the justices of Middlesex were held, we must likewise be careful not to allow eighteenth-century snobbery to colour our perceptions. The Middlesex Bench was synonymous with the character of the 'trading justice',[20] the tradesmen, manufacturers, merchants, retailers, and professionals whom contemporaries believed to be colonising the role of magistrate, traditionally reserved to the supposedly more virtuous and independent members of the gentry. Contemporary contempt for the low social status of Middlesex justices was based on the belief that people of this modest status would necessarily be open to bribery and corruption. And although these expectations were not necessarily fulfilled, many observers, both amongst their contemporaries and historians, have viewed the members of the Middlesex Bench with a jaundiced and disapproving eye.[21] Edmund Burke's characterisation of 1780 will suffice to record the vitriol occasionally

---

18 Modern scholars have viewed the Middlesex Bench in a much more positive light. See Robert B. Shoemaker, *Prosecution and Punishment: Petty Crime and the Law in London and Rural Middlesex, c. 1660–1725* (Cambridge, 1991); Norma Landau, *The Justices of the Peace, 1679–1760* (Berkeley CA, 1984). The only comprehensive overview of the Middlesex Bench is still E.G. Dowdell, *A Hundred Years of Quarter Sessions: The Government of Middlesex from 1660–1760* (Cambridge, 1932).

19 Landau, *Justices of the Peace*, pp. 126–7.

20 See Landau, *Justices of the Peace*, pp. 143,316–7; S. and B. Webb, *English Local Government* Part 1: *The Parish And The County* (1906), pp. 327, 330, 332–5, 337–8, 553; Ruth Paley, *Justice in Eighteenth-Century Hackney* (London Record Society, 28, 1991), pp. xii-xiv.

21 See Landau, *Justices of the Peace*, pp. 126–7, 162, 184–8, 190, 202–5; and Webb, *Parish and the County*, pp. 326–47, 558–61.

thrown in their direction: 'The justices of Middlesex were generally the scum of the earth – carpenters, brickmakers, and shoemakers; some of whom were notoriously men of such infamous characters that they were unworthy of any employ whatever, and others so ignorant that they could scarcely write their own names'.[22]

It is very difficult to know the extent to which these stereotypes can be applied to the magistrates active in Chelsea. It is certainly true that the genus 'trading justice' can be easily found operating in these two volumes. Sir Thomas de Veil, the most famous of all trading justices, periodically attended the Chelsea petty sessions. Other famous names such as Henry Fielding, and his half-brother Sir John Fielding, both of whom have ambiguous reputations which include a propensity to bribery, are also to be found managing the business of poor relief in Chelsea.[23] However, the bulk of parochial business was undertaken by more obscure personalities. Perhaps the most active justice whose name is recorded in these volumes is Peter Elers. He was the 'quorum' or lead justice at almost all of the petty sessions recorded from 1736 to 1752,[24] and appears to be closely related to a family of Dutch merchants whose fortune was based on the pottery industry in Staffordshire with a related retail outlet in London. In the early eighteenth century the family became involved in the manufacture of glass and porcelain in Chelsea. Peter Elers appears to have been the son of merchants, rather than a merchant himself.[25] Trained in the law, he adopted a punctilious and responsive approach to petty session business, and, at least in relation to the financially non-remunerative business of settlement, seems to have behaved in an exemplary manner. The same could be said of the majority of the justices who sat at petty sessions in Chelsea. Indeed, what is remarkable about the administration of parishes like Chelsea is precisely the care and apparent honesty with which it was conducted. Neither magistrates nor parish officers were paid for their troubles, and yet they were expected both to give up a substantial proportion of their time to the business of the parish, and to handle large sums of money, in a variety of contexts, on the parish's behalf.

The parish
While the peculiarities of the Middlesex Bench provide one factor contributing to the creation of the records reproduced here, the parish of Chelsea – its economic and social makeup, its location and the nature of

22 Quoted in Webb, *Parish and the County*, p. 325.
23 For De Veil see Landau, *Justices of the Peace*, pp. 185–7; and Webb, *Parish and the County*, pp. 326–8, 338–41. For Thomas Cotton see Webb, ibid., p. 560n. For Henry and Sir John Fielding see Webb, ibid., pp. 32, 326n, 329, 333n, 336, 341, 342, 344, 345, 349, 360, 378, 448n, 556n, 574, 579.
24 For a justice to be described as 'of the quorum' meant they had a working knowledge of the law. This was an assumption contained in many of the statutes which referred to the powers and duties of the members of the bench from 13 Richard II st.1 c.7 (1389) until 1689. By this time it had become a formality as all justices were referred to as quorum justices. For a fuller discussion of the quorum justice, see Webb, *Parish And The County*, pp. 302–3.
25 See *Dictionary of National Biography*, 'Elers, John Phillip'.

its population – provide an equally significant variable in the process. Chelsea in the eighteenth century had perhaps as diverse a population as any parish in the country. While still predominantly agricultural, the parish had already acquired its modern reputation as a resort for the well-heeled and socially advantaged. It was also one of the many rapidly urbanising parishes which circled the metropolis. By the start of the nineteenth century Chelsea had a population of twelve thousand people, its housing stock having mushroomed from a mere 350 buildings in 1717 to 2,300 in 1809.[26]

Despite its growing urban character, the economy of the parish continued to be dominated by agriculture, and in particular market gardening. Even in the early nineteenth century, Chelsea was one of four districts which supplied half the produce sold in Covent Garden. At the same time, however, the parish was becoming a significant site of manufacture. The Chelsea Porcelain Works opened in 1745, and gained substantial success in the decades of mid-century, employing one hundred workers and one hundred charity trainees. By 1810 Chelsea had two large brewhouses, a stained paper factory, a floor cloth manufacture, and a melting pot and crucible factory. It also played a significant role in the transport industries to be found along the Thames.[27] And if this kaleidoscope of activity was not enough, the parish was also home to the Royal Hospital at Chelsea, opened in 1692. With its 476 pensioned soldiers, or 'in pensioners', and perhaps one thousand 'out pensioners', who took up temporary residence half yearly as they converged on the area to receive their allowances and medical attention, the Hospital ensured that elderly soldiers and their families would be heavily represented among the examinees.[28] The combination of a wealthy population employing large numbers of servants, the demand for labour in agriculture, manufacturing and transport, along with the impact of the Royal Hospital ensured the objects of these examinations was a peculiar and unique sample of the eighteenth-century poor – made up of the urban, and the rural; including but not dominated by those employed in service, agriculture, manufacture and transport, and some military men and their families.

While its economy and the make-up of its population set Chelsea apart, it shared many characteristics with other eighteenth-century parishes. Its administration and governance, while rather more complex and sophisticated than most, was conducted within the same legal framework, and provided the same services as the other 15,000 or so parishes up and down the country. The legal duties of the parish towards the relief of the poor were based on the statute 43 Elizabeth, c.2. Under its auspices the

---

26 William Gaunt, *Chelsea* (London, 1954), pp. 37–61; Thomas Faulkner, *A Historical & Topographical Description of Chelsea and its Environs* (London, 1810), p. 11; R.G. Clark, *Chelsea Today* (London, 1991), pp. 37–41.

27 Faulkner, *Description of Chelsea*, pp. 13–15, 34–8.

28 For a fuller account of the history of Chelsea in this period see Gaunt, *Chelsea*, pp. 39, 49, 53, 59, 85, 178–80; Faulkner, *Description of Chelsea*, pp. 11, 14, 36, 37; Clark, *Chelsea*, pp. 37–41; C.G.T. Dean, *The Royal Chelsea Hospital* (London, 1950), pp. 216, 228; Thea Holmes, *Chelsea* (London, 1972), pp. 61–74.

parish was responsible for the provision of work for the unemployed, the apprenticeship of pauper children, and the relief of the 'lame, impotent, old, blind, and such other among them being poor and not able to work'.[29] By the eighteenth century, through their own extra-legal decisions and actions, successive parish administrations had greatly extended their obligations to the pauper population, so that by the 1730s, when this series of examinations begins, the parish had come to resemble what might, without hyperbole, be described as a welfare state in miniature. Maintenance of and free medical attention for the ill; the payment of funeral expenses; the supply of clothes, fuel, food, furniture, and household equipment, and the payment of rents and the maintenance and supply of 'social housing'; the payment of supplementary allowances to families on low wages; as well as extraordinary payments to the casual poor, and the maintenance of illegitimate children, all came within the ambit of the parish.[30]

The extreme localism proverbially associated with parochial government ensured that eighteenth-century poor relief would be made up of a patchwork of good and bad practice. In the case of Chelsea, the system was dominated by the parish workhouse which was built as a result of a series of decisions of the vestry made between 1727 and 1733. The actual house was sited on land donated by Sir Hans Sloane and was opened in 1737. The house could accommodate up to seventy people, and like most eighteenth-century institutions it housed predominantly the 'impotent' poor. The population was made up of the sick and disabled, widows and their families, children and spouses deserted by parents and partners; illegitimate children and their mothers, the old and infirm, and deserted or orphaned children.[31] In a large minority of the examinations included here the workhouse figures as either the site of the birth of an illegitimate child, or the current residence of the examinee (e.g. **45, 440**). Indeed, it is clear there is a strong relationship between policies pursued in the governance of the house, and the peculiar mix of individuals brought before the magistrates for examination. And because, in common with all eighteenth-century workhouses, Chelsea's institution served a multitude of purposes – from hostel to infirmary, sheltered housing for the elderly to orphanage

---

29 Dorothy Marshall, *The English Poor in the Eighteenth Century: A Study in Social and Administrative History* (London, 1926), p. 2.
30 Hitchcock et al., eds., *Chronicling Poverty*; G. Boyer, *An Economic History of the English Poor Law, 1750–1850* (Cambridge, 1990); Taylor, *Poverty, Migration, and Settlement*, pp. 116–167; G. Oxley, *Poor Relief in England and Wales, 1601–1834* (Newton Abbot, 1974); Marshall, *English Poor in the Eighteenth Century*, pp. 3–4.
31 For a general discussion of the early eighteenth-century parochial workhouse movement see Tim Hitchcock, 'Paupers and preachers: the SPCK and the parochial workhouse movement' in L. Davison et al., eds., *Stilling the Grumbling Hive: The Response to Social and Economic Problems in England, 1689–1750* (Stroud, Gloucestershire, 1992), pp. 145–66. For detailed information on the paupers of this particular parish see the workhouse registry reproduced as a database and included in Hitchcock and Shoemaker, *Economic Growth and Social Change*. For a near contemporary description of the workhouse and its inmates see Faulkner, *Description of Chelsea*, II, pp. 24–5.

– the vast majority of paupers relieved by the parish received that relief in the form of workhouse accommodation.[32]

While eighteenth-century social policy is frequently seen as oppressive and controlling, it is clear that the workhouse at Chelsea was relatively well run. Its accounts suggest a good diet was provided, while the mortality rate among inmates was certainly lower than most London workhouses in the same period.[33] Indeed, Chelsea produced one of the most comprehensive and sophisticated archives of parochial administration of any parish in the country. The volumes reproduced here are part of a complex set of records that encompass the whole range of interactions between the parish and the individual pauper. Account books, vestry minutes, workhouse committee minutes, outdoor relief accounts, pauper apprenticeship records, a substantial workhouse register, along with a plethora of miscellaneous documents survive for Chelsea for the mid-eighteenth century, making it the best parochial archive of materials relating to poor relief in the broader metropolitan area. This level of survival also suggests, at the very least, that its administration was relatively professional, and, more generously, that it was relatively efficient.

The poor
While the magistrates may have provided the theatrical focus of the process of examination, and the parish its stage set, the leading role in the drama which produced these documents was taken by the examinee. The process whereby they ended up swearing to the father of their child, or to their place of settlement, was a complex one, which necessarily resulted in the creation of an awkward text. Having said this, it is possible to generalise from these examinations about the lives of the poor in eighteenth-century Chelsea, and in the process to comment on the extent to which their analysis can contribute to modern debates surrounding a variety of elements of eighteenth-century society, and in particular those relating to migration, employment, gender and sexuality.

By their very nature, settlement examinations shed a remarkable light on the migratory history of those whose lives are recorded. They reveal a highly mobile population, with a variety of migratory patterns. Many came from areas in the south and east of England. Counties such as Surrey (**6, 117**), Kent (**92**), and Hampshire (**158, 173, 210**) feature strongly in these

---

32 The balance within the system of relief in Chelsea changed several times over the course of the period covered by these examinations. Obviously the opening of the workhouse in 1737 had a significant impact, but there was also a substantive change in policy in 1749, when demand for ongoing residential relief outstripped the accommodation available in the workhouse. From this date onwards the parish granted outdoor relief to between ten and thirty paupers per month.

33 For statistics on infant mortality in London workhouses at this period see Jonas Hanway's figures reproduced in M. Dorothy George, *London Life in the Eighteenth Century* (2nd edn, Harmondsworth Middx, 1965), p. 401. Hanway suggests that 46 per cent of workhouse children who entered a house before the age of four, or were born there, died in the house. The equivalent figure for a sample of 558 children who entered the workhouse at Chelsea between 1743–69 and 1782–99, was 23.3 per cent. For the workhouse at Chelsea see Hitchcock and Shoemaker, *Economic Growth and Social Change*.

pages. This pattern seems to reinforce K.D.M. Snell's suggestion that changing agricultural employment in these areas resulted in the increasing casualisation of waged male labour, and the gradual elimination of yearly farm service and substantive female employment in agriculture, and that this in turn resulted in a growing stream of migrants to the capital and its environs.[34]

What is more surprising is the significant numbers who travelled longer distances. Particularly prominent are those who migrated from the counties of the south-west, from Dorset (**21, 195**), Devon (**213**), and Somerset (**127**), and from the Midlands (**201, 207**). These examinations also confirm the presence in London of large numbers of Irish (**27, 127, 144, 164, 192, 205**), Scots (**19, 141**), and Welsh (**139**) migrants. Of the Scottish and Irish samples almost all had been soldiers who ended up in Chelsea because of their association with the Royal Hospital. A typical example of these was Hugh Wise who was born in Scotland and became first a soldier in the Horse Guards for 28 years, and later an in-pensioner of the Hospital. His death in the hospital ensured that his wife and three children would become, in the first instance at least, the responsibility of the parish, and that his migratory and employment history would be recorded in this volume (**19**).

But the migratory patterns evident in this material are not restricted to those travelling to London. Within the metropolis itself there appears to have been a significant internal movement within and on the periphery of the capital westwards to its outer fringes. For example, Penelope and John Otway were born in Southwark and Wapping respectively and lived with their children in Chelsea until John's death. At this point Penelope Otway was forced to apply for relief, and consequently she and her daughter were passed on to her husband's parish of birth in Wapping (**10**).

The sexuality and sexual behaviour of the poor of Chelsea is also illuminated by these records. As would be expected, they reveal much about the relationships which led to illegitimate pregnancies and births. For the most part these relationships were conducted between men and women who lived and worked in close proximity to each other. Fellow servants, master-servant, servant-lodger, servant and member of the family of the employer; these were the relationships from which the majority of illegitimate births recorded here resulted.[35]

The women who bore illegitimate children in Chelsea were mainly young, unmarried, migrant servants. While the majority of the fathers came from the large proportion of the population employed as male servants and household workers. In addition, roughly a quarter of the fathers were skilled artisans and construction workers, including apprentices, young journeymen and older master tradesmen. A significant further minority, approximately ten per cent of the total, could be classified as coming from the middling sort, most of these being employers, or their friends, who fathered bastard children on their servants.

34 Snell, *Annals of the Labouring Poor*.
35 For a discussion of these issues based on an analysis of a set of examinations for the parishes of Westminster see Rogers, 'Carnal knowledge'.

While birth outside of marriage could cause social and financial difficulty for the parents, marriage itself was not always as secure as it might have been. Desertion by one or other spouse, but usually the husband, was frequent. Mary Andrews was deserted by her husband James after eight years of marriage, even though she was ill at the time and there were two young children from the marriage still living (**269**). Bigamy was likewise a serious possible danger for married couples. Isabella Askin alias Willett was a 34-year-old widow from Herefordshire when her examination was heard in August 1737. Thirteen years earlier she had married a saddler named Henry Askin in the liberty of the Fleet in London. Two years later Isabella gave birth to a daughter named Elizabeth, and it was only then that she seems to have discovered that her marriage was invalid. Henry Askin was already legally married with one child. After her discovery Elizabeth was declared a bastard, and Isabella was forced back into service in order to maintain herself and her daughter (**50**).[36]

If desertion and bigamy reflected the insecurity of plebeian marriage, the clandestine nature of the majority of the unions recorded here is also significant. Of the 190 marriages cited in the examinations where the place of marriage is specified, just over fifty per cent were conducted in 'the liberty of the Fleet'. These were, at least technically, 'clandestine', and as such, although binding in canon law, took place in circumstances which placed them largely outside the oversight of parents and friends. Some occurred without banns being read, others were conducted without a licence being obtained, or were staged in a location other than a church, or outside canonical hours, or in a forbidden season of the year, or outside the diocese of the couple concerned. One major reason why pauper couples took advantage of such marriages was the relative cheapness of the fees attached to such a ceremony. But the impact of clandestine and 'Fleet' marriages was to undermine peer and family oversight of the process of family formation. The high percentage of such marriages recorded here suggest that couples married in this way were particularly susceptible to the poverty and insecurity of metropolitan life.[37]

---

36 For material on plebeian marriage and its breakdown see John Gillis, 'Married but not churched: plebeian sexual relations and marital nonconformity in eighteenth-century Britain' in R.P. Maccubbin, ed., *'Tis Nature's Fault: Unauthorized Sexuality During the Enlightenment* (Cambridge, 1987) and D.A. Kent, ' "Gone for a Soldier": family breakdown and the demography of desertion in a London parish, 1750–91', *Local Population Studies*, 45 (1990) pp. 27–42.

37 Hardwicke's Marriage Act (26 George II c.32) of 1753 tightened the legal definition of marriage and closed down such extra-parochial marriage sites as the liberty of the Fleet. The closure of the Fleet half-way through the period covered by these examinations makes the high proportion of Fleet marriages recorded in this volume all the more spectacular. The literature on clandestine and 'Fleet' marriages has grown tremendously in recent years. For the most recent and comprehensive work on the subject see R.B. Outhwaite, *Clandestine Marriage in England, 1500–1850* (London, 1995). See also Jeremy Boulton, 'Clandestine marriages in London: an examination of a neglected urban variable', *Urban History*, XX, 2 (1993); John Gillis, *For Better, For Worse: British Marriages 1600 to the Present* (Oxford, 1985), pp. 95–8; R.L. Brown, 'The rise and fall of Fleet Marriages' in R.B. Outhwaite, ed., *Marriage and Society: Studies in the Social History of Marriage* (London, 1981).

Sexual violence also figures in the lives of the poor as they are captured in these documents. One case of violent rape, and one of possible rape come to light in these pages. The common factor in both of these episodes is that the perpetrator was the male master of the household in which the victims lived. Sarah Powell was the victim of the possible rape which was committed by James Silvester at about two o'clock on a June morning in 1754 while her mistress had gone to sell her produce at the local market. It is not clear whether sex was taken by physical force, but it is certain that sex took place under compulsion, as Sarah feared she would lose her place in service if she refused the sexual advances of her master (277). Perhaps the most harrowing account of sexual violence reproduced here is contained in the examination of Elizabeth Bussell. In it, she describes a protracted series of incidents in which she endured extensive sexual abuse, under the threat of death, at the hands of her employer Samuel Firmin. She also recounts how the father-in-law of her employer, a Mr Stammers, also subjected her to sexual harassment and rape whilst she lay drugged by a sleeping potion he had surreptitiously administered. As a result of this succession of events Elizabeth suffered serious eye injury, a miscarriage, and psychological breakdown (224).[38]

Even a cursory glance at these examinations will reveal the powerful interaction of the life-cycles experienced by plebeian women, and the poor law. Widows and their families, single mothers and deserted wives comprised some of the most economically vulnerable sections of eighteenth-century English society, and were among the main recipients of parish welfare resources. Thus, while these groups were perhaps more likely than many others to apply to the parish for relief, it was also these groups whom parish officers were most anxious to have examined, particularly if their place of settlement was not in Chelsea.[39] In a very real way, therefore, the system of relief and settlement which ensured the creation of these records affected and was largely directed at women.[40]

The image that emerges from these documents in many ways supports the model of metropolitan society found in the historiography of eighteenth-century London. The occupations and characters who emerge from these pages are familiar from the works of M. Dorothy George and Peter Earle, and reinforce the sense of change and excitement which characterise the

38 For discussions of sexual aggression and rape in this period see Tim Meldrum, 'London domestic servants from depositional evidence, 1660–1750: servant-employer sexuality in the patriarchal household' in Hitchcock et al., eds., *Chronicling Poverty*, pp. 47–69; and for a more general view A. Clark, *Women's Silence, Men's Violence: Sexual Assault in England, 1770–1845* (London, 1987).
39 For the interrelationship between life-cycle and the working of the poor law see B. Stapleton, 'Inherited poverty and life-cycle poverty: Odiham, Hampshire, 1650–1850', *Social History* 18 (1993) pp. 339–55; T. Sokoll, *Household and Family among the Poor* (Bochum, 1993); and Tim Wales, 'Poverty, poor relief and life-cycle: some evidence from seventeenth-century Norfolk' in R. Smith, ed., *Land, Kinship and Life-cycle* (Cambridge, 1984).
40 The population of the Chelsea workhouse between 1743 and 1766 was composed of 50 per cent adult women; 31 per cent children and 19 per cent adult men. See Hitchcock, ' "Unlawfully begotten on her body" ', p. 84, n.12.

period.[41] But, overall, what this source reflects is that complex conflict between the poor majority of the population and the local political nation, encompassing justices and parish officers. It exemplifies the relationships between power and poverty; between the need for order, felt by local elites, and the possibility for violence and disorder, represented by unwed mothers, abandoned children, and the unemployed.

Note on editorial method and acknowledgements

The originals of both volumes reproduced here are held at the London Metropolitan Archive. The first volume is catalogued as MS. P74/LUK 121, and the second as MS. P74/LUK 122 . Both are unavailable for consultation owing to their poor condition and can only be used on microfilm. The text reproduced here is taken from the microfilm copies held at the LMA. These materials form part of the extensive collection of St Luke, Chelsea parish records, and can be cross-referenced to vestry and workhouse committee minutes, a very complete workhouse register, and a volume of apprenticeship records, all covering much of the period between 1733 and 1766 and currently held at the LMA.

Spelling and punctuation, capitalisation, place names (parishes, towns and counties) have been modernised. Personal and street names have been left in their original form, although they have been standardised to conform with the most frequent usage, and signatures, where available, have determined the reading of personal names. Where possible eighteenth-century usage has been allowed to stand without comment, even when it is ungrammatical in modern English. Abbreviations have been expanded, except in the cases where this would inhibit readability, as in 'vizt' (the preferred form in the original). Dates have also been modernised and made consistent in the form '25 Dec. 1997'. Up to the end of 1751, when New Style was introduced, all dates between 1 January and 24 March have been updated to the form '1745/6'. Monetary sums have been expressed in the form £6 13s. 4d, although where the original expresses a large amount in shillings, as in 50s., this usage has been retained. This edition is essentially a transcript, but occasionally additions and elisions of not more than a few words have been made in order to clarify the original text. These have been indicated by the use of square brackets for additions and ellipses for elisions. Round brackets, { }, have been used to indicate marginal comments which have been interpolated into the text at their referenced location. One repetitive formulation has been replaced throughout: the expression 'one of his majesty's justices of the peace of and for the county of Middlesex', which normally follows the names of the justices in bastardy examinations, has been eliminated whenever it appears. Scribal errors corrected in the original manuscript have been amended without comment. Each successive entry has been given a separate number, in bold, and the indexing of this volume is to those numbers. The layout has been modified to eliminate unnecessary 'white space', but the material has been ordered to conform

---

41 George. *London Life*; Peter Earle, *A City Full of People: Men and Women of London, 1650–1750* (London, 1994).

with the original as closely as can conveniently be done. Page numbers in the original volumes are inconsistent and erratic, but been put in square brackets where appropriate. Where signatures are taken from the original, they are reproduced without comment. Where the examinee marked rather than signed the deposition, this has been indicated by the reproduction of the statement from the original, in the form, 'Joan Lester, her mark'.

We would like to thank the Revd. Derek Watson, the incumbent at Chelsea, for permission to reproduce this material. We would also like to thank the staff at the London Metropolitan Archive for their help and support.

CHELSEA SETTLEMENT AND BASTARDY EXAMINATIONS, 1733–50

1. [fol.1–3 A very incomplete contemporary names index.]

2. [p.1] Middlesex, to wit. Elizabeth Davis, single woman, aged about thirty years, upon oath saith that she was born at Trysull in Staffordshire. And that about three years since she quitted the service of one Mr Snow who then kept the Turks Head Coffee House in the Strand, which is in the parish of St Martin in the Fields in the said county of Middlesex and liberty of Westminster, with whom she lived as a cook for the space of three years and half, and received of her said master her full wage for the said time at the rate of £5 a year, meat, drink, washing and lodging. And further saith that since she quitted the said service of Mr Snow [she] has not rented a house of £10 a year, or paid any parochial taxes, or done any act or thing (to her, this examinant's knowledge) whereby to gain a legal settlement elsewhere. The mark of Elizabeth Davis. Sworn before us, 3 Sept. 1733, Peter Elers, Thomas Cotton. Passed to the parish of St Martin in the Fields in Middlesex.

3. [p.2] Middlesex, to wit. The examination of Martha Foss, widow, taken upon oath before me, Peter Elers esq. . . . . Who saith that she is now pregnant of a bastard child or children, which was unlawfully begotten on her body by one John Sills of Burton upon Trent in Staffordshire, innholder. Who had carnal knowledge of her body for the first time about June last, was twelve months, in the dwelling house of the said John Sills (known by the sign of the George in Burton upon Trent, aforesaid), and several times after in the said house, and other places. And further saith, that the said John Sills is the true and only father of the said bastard child or children. And further saith not. Martha Foss. Sworn at Chelsea, 8 Sept. 1733, before me, Peter Elers.

4. [p.3] Middlesex, to wit. Margaret Abbott, widow, upon oath saith that Sarah Norton, a girl aged about sixteen years, was born at a little house at Avery Farm, then in the parish of St Martin in the Fields, and now in the parish of St George Hanover Square in the said county of Middlesex. And that she was present at the birth of the said girl, who was born of the body of Sarah Norton, deceased. And saith that one William Norton, a soldier in the Scotch Guards, was the reputed father of the said girl. But [she] does

1

not know [if] the said William Norton was ever married to the said Sarah Norton (though she went by his name). The mark of Margaret Abbott. Sworn before us, 3 Oct. 1733, Peter Elers, Thomas Cotton.

5. [p.4] Middlesex, to wit. The examination of Anne Mackenny, single woman, taken before me, Peter Elers esq. . . . Who saith that she is now pregnant of a bastard child or children which was unlawfully begotten on her body by one James Sparks of the Custom House, Tidewater. Who had carnal knowledge of her body the first time about the month of March last in the dwelling house of this examinant's master (John Guerney), known by the sign of the Old George in the parish of Chelsea in the county aforesaid. And several times after in the said house, where the said James Sparks at that time lodged. And this examinant further saith that the said James Sparks is the true and only father of the said bastard child or children. And further saith not. The mark of Anne Mackenny. Sworn at Chelsea, before me, 31 Oct. 1733, Peter Elers. [See **39**].

6. [p.5] Middlesex, to wit. Barbara Tiser, single woman, aged about 24 years, born in the parish of St Margaret, Westminster, upon oath saith that about two years since she quitted the service of Mr Fisher, a farmer at the Ferry House at Molesey in the county of Surrey, with whom she lived as a hired servant by the year for about the space of 8 years at the rate of 50s.wages for the first year. And for the remainder time, her wages was advanced yearly. And this examinant further saith that since she left the said service of Mr Fisher, [she] has not lived a year in service, or done any act or thing (to the best of her, this examinant's, knowledge) whereby to gain a legal settlement elsewhere. The mark of Barbara Tiser. Sworn before us, 29 Nov. 1733, Peter Elers, John Williams. Passed to Molesey.

7. [p.6] Middlesex, to wit. Joannah Chapman, widow, aged about 58 years, born in the city of Exeter, upon oath saith that about 39 years since she married her late husband, Christopher Chapman, staymaker at Exeter. By whom she had six children, one of which is living, named Elizabeth Chapman, now a servant. And saith that her said husband, about fourteen years since, quitted a home in Tinkers Alley near Bear Street in the parish of St Anne [Soho] within the liberty of Westminster in the county of Middlesex, where he lived about the space of five years, and paid £10 a year rent for the same, and all parochial taxes. Since which he lived in lodgings only. And afterwards [he] entered himself in the army where he continued till he was admitted a pensioner in Chelsea College, and died about five months since. And further saith not. The mark of Joannah Chapman. Sworn before us, 29 Nov. 1733, Peter Elers, John Williams. Passed to St Anne [Soho] within the liberty of Westminster.

8. [p.7] Middlesex, to wit. Margaret Bailey (alias Game, widow) aged about 40 years, upon oath saith that she was born at Market Drayton in Shropshire. And about eighteen years since she lived a servant hired by the year with one Mrs Tuck of the parish of Chelsea in the county of Middlesex in the station of a cook, where she continued about the space of two years and received her full wages for the said time (meat, drink, washing and lodging) at the rate of £4 per annum. And that about sixteen years since she was married at Drogheda in Ireland to one John Game, an Irishman who came afterwards to England and entered himself a soldier in the First Regiment of Foot Guards, by whom she had three children, two of which are living. One named Mary Game aged about 15 years, and John Game aged about 12 years (which said children were maintained by the parish of Chelsea for several years). And also saith that about 18 months after the death of her said husband, John Game, she married one Joseph Blunt, by whom she had four children. One of which is living, named Sarah Blunt aged about 7 years, born in the house now in possession of one Nelson, in Newkner's Lane in the parish of St Giles in the Fields in the said county of Middlesex. And further saith that her said same husband, Joseph Blunt deceased, was at the time she married him married to another woman who is now living at Kettering in Northamptonshire. And this examinant also further saith that since the time she quitted the said service of Mrs Tuck's [she] has not rented a house of £10 per annum or done any act or thing (to the best of her knowledge) to gain a legal settlement elsewhere. The mark of Margaret Bailey alias Game. Sworn before us, 2 Jan. 1733/4, Peter Elers, Thomas Cotton. Passed to St Giles in the Fields.

9. [p.8] Middlesex, to wit. The examination of Elizabeth Simonds, single woman, taken upon oath this 5 Jan. 1733/4, before me, Peter Elers esq. . . . Who saith, that on or about 3 Dec. last past she was delivered of a female bastard child in the workhouse belonging to the parish of St Margaret, Westminster in the said county of Middlesex. Which [child] is baptised and named Sarah Prosser, and was unlawfully begotten on her body by one William Prosser of the parish of Kensington in the said county, shoemaker, who had carnal knowledge of her body the first time, on or about the month of March last in the dwelling house of one Mr Orchard in Church Lane, Kensington (where the examinant was a lodger) and at several times after in the said house. And this examinant saith that the said William Prosser is the true and only father of the said child. And further saith not. The mark of Elizabeth Simonds. Sworn at Chelsea, 5 Jan. 1733/4, before me, Peter Elers.

10. [p.9] Middlesex, to wit. Penelope Otway, widow, aged about 48 years, born in the parish of St Mary Overey in Southwark, upon oath saith that about 22 years ago she was married to her late husband John Otway in the liberty of the Fleet. By whom she has two children now living, vizt, Richard Otway aged about 19 years, bound apprentice to a carman, and Anne, aged about 12 years now with this examinant. And further saith that her said husband was born in the parish of St John at Wapping in the said county. And [he] was only a sailor, and never rented a house of £10 per annum, or paid any parochial taxes, or done any act or thing (to the best of her, this examinant's, knowledge) to gain a legal settlement since his birth. The mark of Penelope Otway. Sworn before us, 16 Jan. 1733/4, Peter Elers, John Williams. Penelope Otway and Anne, her daughter, were passed to St John, Wapping.

11. [p.10] Middlesex, to wit. John Royde, aged about 21 years, born in London, upon oath saith that on 20 May 1732 he became a servant hired by the year to Captain James Mitford of Little Chelsea (being that part that is in the parish of Chelsea in the county of Middlesex). With whom he has continued to this time and he has received his wages from time to time of his said master at the rate of £5 per annum, meat, drink, washing and lodging. And further saith that on 14 Dec. last, he was married in the liberty of the Fleet to Grace, his wife. And saith that has not done any act or thing (to the best of his, this examinant's, knowledge) to gain any other settlement. The mark of John Royde. Sworn before me, 28 Feb. 1733/4, Peter Elers.

12. [p.11] Middlesex, to wit. The examination of Catherine Price, single woman, taken upon oath, 15 Mar. 1733, before us, John Williams and Peter Elers esqs . . .Who saith that on 1 Feb. last, she was delivered of a female bastard child in Chelsea in the said county (which child is baptised and named Mary). And was unlawfully begotten on her body by one Richard Williamson now a footman to Mrs Anne Fielding, a lady that lives at Odiham near Farnham, in Hampshire. Who had carnal knowledge of her body the first time in the dwelling house of Mrs Evers in Hanover Square in the said county, where this examinant lived in the station of a cook. And twice afterwards on or about the month of May last in the dwelling house of Mrs Bucketts in Swallow Street in the parish of St James, Westminster, where this examinant lodged (when out of place). And this examinant further saith that the said Richard Williamson is the true and only father of the said female bastard child. And further saith not. The mark of Catherine Price. Sworn at Chelsea, 15 Mar. 1733/4, before us, John Williams, Peter Elers.

13. [p.12] Middlesex, to wit. Jane Loveday, widow, aged about 59 years, upon oath saith that she was born at Hammersmith in the said county of Middlesex. And that on or about 42 years since she, this examinant, was married to her late husband, John Loveday, at the parish church of Clerkenwell in the county Middlesex, aforesaid, by whom she hath four children now living and provided for. And saith that her said late husband rented a house in Little Chelsea in the parish of Kensington in the county aforesaid, wherein he continued for the space of twenty five years and upwards, and paid all parochial taxes there. And further saith that since she quitted the said house (which is about seven years since) has not rented a house of £10 a year, or paid any parochial taxes, or done any act or thing to the best of her, this examinant's, knowledge whereby to gain a legal settlement elsewhere. The mark of Jane Loveday. Sworn before us, 25 Mar. 1734, Peter Elers, John Williams. Passed to Kensington.

4

14. [p.13] Middlesex sessions. Elenor Denman, aged about 30 years, the wife of John Denman, upon oath saith that about five years since she was married to her said husband at the parish church of St Margaret, Westminster, by whom she hath two children now living, vizt, Anne, aged about 4 years, and Edmund, aged about 3 years. And saith that her said husband has two more children now living with this examinant by Mary, his first wife, vizt, Thomas, aged about 14 years, and John, aged about 7 years. And further saith that her said husband, about eighteen years since, was bound apprentice to the worshipful Charles Medlycott esq., deceased, who then lived in the parish of St Martin in the Fields, and now St George Hanover Square in the said county, with whom he continued till he listed himself a soldier in the Foot Guards. In which station he has been ever since and is now recruiting in the country. So that this examinant is not capable of subsisting her said family without relief. The mark of Elenor Denman. Sworn before us, 21 May 1734, John Williams, Peter Elers. Passed to St George Hanover Square.

15. [p.14] Middlesex sessions. Hannah Holloway, aged about 52 years, upon oath saith that she was born at Chichester in Sussex. And that about 21 years ago she became a servant hired by the year to one Mr Piles, a surgeon who then lived in Fountain Court in the Strand in the parish of St Clements Danes in the county aforesaid, where she stayed about five years, and received her full wages for the said time at the rate of £4 a year, meat, drink, washing and lodging. And after she quitted the said service she hired herself to one Mr Eyres, a woodmonger, in the same Court, where [she] lived about four years, at the rate of £4 a year, meat, drink, washing and lodging. Soon after she quitted the said service she married John Holloway, labourer, at the Fleet, with whom she lived a week only. And saith that she has not seen her said husband since. Neither can she give an account of him or his settlement. And also saith that after her said husband left her she lived again with the said Mr Piles about a year. And further saith that since she quitted the said service [she] has not done any act or thing (to the best of her knowledge) whereby to gain a legal settlement elsewhere. The mark of Hannah Holloway. Sworn before us, 21 May 1734, . . . John Williams, Peter Elers. Passed to St Clement Danes.

16. [p.15] Middlesex sessions. The examination of Mary Neal, single woman, taken before me, [Peter Elers]. . .Who saith that she is now pregnant of a bastard child or children which was unlawfully begotten on her body by one Francis Potts, footman to Mr Gallerday at Fulham in this county. Who had carnal knowledge of her body the first time on or about eight months since in the dwelling house of the said Mr Gallerday, and never but once after in the same house (which was about two months after). And this examinant saith that the said Francis Potts is the true and only father of the said bastard child or children, and that no other person whatsoever hath had carnal knowledge of her body. And further saith not. The mark of Mary Neal. Sworn at Chelsea, 21 May 1734, before me, Peter Elers.

17. [p.16] Middlesex sessions. Miles Rains, aged about 31 years, upon oath saith that he was born at a place called Avery Farm, then of the parish of St Martin in the Fields but now of St George Hanover Square in the said county. And that about fifteen years since he was a servant hired by the year to Mr Large of Chelsea College, whetster. With whom he continued the first time two years and a half at the rate of 50s. a year, and received of his said master his full wages for the said time. The last year and half of the said time he had meat, drink, washing and lodging. After he quitted his said place he lived with his mother and then returned to the said place and continued upwards of four year. And lived twice more in the said place. And this examinant saith that since he quitted the said service of Mr Large, [he] has not been a servant hired by the year, or done any act or thing whereby to gain a legal settlement elsewhere. And also saith he has not been a servant hired by the year in any other place but that of Mr Large. And further saith that about eight years ago he was married to Barbara, his present wife, in the Fleet, by whom he hath had three children, two of which is living, vizt, William Rains, aged 5 years, and Miles, aged 2 years. Miles Rains. Sworn, 13 June 1734, before me, Peter Elers.

18. [p.17] Middlesex sessions. The examination of Elizabeth Newman, single woman, taken upon oath this 10 July 1734, before me, Peter Elers esq. . . .Who saith that she is pregnant of a bastard child or children which was unlawfully begotten on her body by one John Huggett jr, the son of John Huggett of Chelsea in the county of Middlesex, farmer, who had carnal knowledge of her body the first time in the dwelling house of Mr William Burchett of Little Chelsea, farmer, where this examinant lived a hired servant. And several times after in the said house and other out houses belonging to the said Mr Burchett. And this examinant further saith that the said John Huggett jr is the true and only father of the said bastard child or children and that no other person hath had carnal knowledge of her body but the said John Huggett jr. The mark of Elizabeth Newman. Sworn before me at Chelsea, Peter Elers. [See **20**].

19. [p.18] Middlesex sessions. Mary Wise, widow, aged about 40 years, upon oath saith that she was born in Abingdon in Berkshire. And that about twelve years since she married Hugh Wise, her late husband, in the liberty of the Fleet, by whom she had three children, two of which are living, vizt, Mary, aged about 10 years, and Elizabeth, aged about 4 years. And this examinant saith that her said late husband, at the time she married him, was an in-pensioner of Chelsea College, and that he was a Scotsman, and belonged to General Lumley's Horse for the space of 28 years till he was admitted a pensioner. So that this examinant does not know or believe he ever gained any settlement in England by renting a house of £10 a year, or paying any parochial taxes, or any act whatsoever, to the best of her knowledge. And this examinant further saith that on or about fifteen years ago (which was before her marriage) she lived a servant hired by the year with the Right Honourable the Countess of Darlington and Baroness of Blandford in the courtyard of St James's in the parish of St Martin in the

Fields in the county aforesaid for about the space of two years at the rate of £6 a year wages, meat, drink, washing and lodging. And has not lived a year in service since. The mark of Mary Wise. Sworn before us, 15 July 1734, John Williams, Peter Elers. Passed to St Martin in the Fields.

20. [p.18 *sic*] Middlesex sessions. The examination of Elizabeth Newman, single woman, taken upon oath before us, John Williams and Peter Elers esqs . . . Who saith that on the 14th day of this instant, September, she was delivered of a male bastard child in the house of Mrs Doyley in Mealman's Row in the parish of Chelsea in the county aforesaid. And was unlawfully begotten on her body by one John Huggett the younger of the parish of Chelsea aforesaid, husbandsman, who had carnal knowledge of her body the first time in or about the month of October last, was twelve month, in the dwelling house of Mr William Burchett of Little Chelsea, yeoman (where this examinant lived as a hired servant). And several times after in the said house and other out houses belonging to the said Mr Burchett. And this examinant further saith that the said John Huggett the younger is the true and only father of the said bastard child. And further saith not. The mark of Elizabeth Newman. Sworn at Chelsea, 10 Oct. 1734, before us, Peter Elers, John Williams. [The child is] dead. [See **18**].

21. [p.20] Middlesex sessions. William Hewett, silk weaver, aged about 90 years, born in Dorsetshire, upon oath saith that about 43 years since (being some little time after King William came to the crown) he rented a house in Pepper Street in the parish of St Saviour Southwark in the county of Surrey, where he continued upwards of five years and paid for the said house the yearly rent of £7 and all parochial taxes. And saith that after he quitted the said house he listed himself in the army and has not rented a house of ten pounds a year, or paid any parish taxes, or done any act or thing (to the best of his knowledge) whereby to gain a legal settlement elsewhere. But [he] is now an in-pensioner of Chelsea College. And further saith that about 20 years since he married Charity Hewett, his present wife, aged about 50 years, at the Fleet, by whom he has had only one child, since dead. And saith that he is not capable of providing for his said wife. The mark of William Hewett. Sworn before us, 21 Oct. 1734, Henry Barker, Peter Elers. Passed to St Saviour Southwark.

22. [p.20] Middlesex sessions. The examination of Sarah Randall, single woman, taken upon oath before us, John Williams and Peter Elers esqs . . . Who saith that on 24 Sept. last she was delivered of a female bastard child in the house of Mr Gardner, a brazier near the horse ferry at Chelsea in the said county (which is baptised and named Susannah). And was unlawfully begotten on her body by one William Answorth then servant to Mr Green, a brewer near Sand End near Chelsea aforesaid, who had carnal knowledge of her body the first time in or about the month [of] December last in the dwelling house of Mr Jonathan Wood at the Bull Ale House at Sand End, where this examinant lived a hired servant and where the said William Answorth at the same time lodged. And several times after

7

in the same house. And this examinant further saith that the said William Answorth is the true and only father of the said child. And further saith not. Sarah Randall, her mark. Sworn at Chelsea, 18 Nov. 1734, before us, John Williams, Peter Elers.

23. [p.21] Middlesex sessions. Abell Bird, husbandman, aged about 65 years, upon oath saith that about 26 years since he, this examinant, lived a servant hired by the year with the Right Honourable the Countess Dowager of Winchelsea, at Richmond in the county of Surrey, with whom he continued for the space of five years in the station of a coachman, and received his full wages for the said time, meat, drink, washing and lodging. And after he quitted the said service he rented a house in Richmond, aforesaid, wherein he continued three years and paid all parish taxes. And after he quitted the said house he entered himself a trooper in Lumley's Horse. And this examinant further saith that from the time he quitted the said house at Richmond [he] has not rented a house of £10 a year, or paid any parochial taxes, or done any act or thing (to the best of his knowledge) whereby to gain a legal settlement elsewhere. Abell Bird, his mark. Sworn before us, 30 Oct. 1734, Peter Elers, John Williams. Passed to Richmond.

24. [p.22] Middlesex sessions. The examination of Mary Handbrooke, single woman, taken before me, Peter Elers esq. . . . Who saith that she is now pregnant of a bastard child or children which was unlawfully begotten on her body by one John Evans, an apprentice to Mr John Ross of Chelsea in the county of Middlesex aforesaid, shoemaker. Who had carnal knowledge of her body the first time in the month of March last in the dwelling house of Captain Tanner in Chelsea aforesaid, where this examinant at the same time lived a hired servant. And twice after in the said house. And this examinant further saith that the said John Evans is the true and only father of the said bastard child or children. And further saith not. The mark of Mary Handbrooke. Sworn at Chelsea, 18 Nov. 1734, before me, Peter Elers. [See **25**].

25. [p.23] The examination of Mary Handbrooke, single woman, taken upon oath before us, John Williams and Peter Elers esqs . . . Middlesex sessions. Who saith that on 13 Jan. last, she was delivered of a female bastard child in the house of Mrs Brierly in Church Lane at Chelsea in the said county. Which [child] is baptised and named Mary, and was unlawfully begotten on her body by one John Evans, an apprentice to Mr John Ross of Chelsea, shoemaker, who had carnal knowledge of her body the first time in the month of March last, was twelve month, in the dwelling house of Captain Tanner in Chelsea, aforesaid, where this examinant at the time lived a hired servant. And twice after in the said house. And this examinant further saith that the said John Evans is the true and only father of the said child. And further saith not. The mark of Mary Handbrooke. Sworn before us, 1 Apr. 1735, Peter Elers, John Williams. [See **24**].

26. [p.24] Middlesex sessions. Mary Sadler, aged about 34 years (the wife of John Sadler, gardener) upon oath saith that she was married about ten

8

years since at the church in Blackfriars in the city of London to her said husband, John Sadler. By whom she had three children, one of which is living, named Anne, aged about 10 years. And this examinant saith that her said husband was bound apprentice for seven years to one Mr Heater of the hamlet of Kew in the parish of Richmond in the county of Surrey, gardener, with whom he served his full time. And after marriage her said husband rent[ed] a little house at Turnham Green in the county of Middlesex at the yearly rent of £3, where they continued upwards of one year, but did not pay any parochial taxes for the said house. And also further saith that since her said husband quitted the said house [he] has not rented a house of £10 a year or paid any parochial taxes, or done any act or thing (to the best of her knowledge) to gain a legal settlement since her said husband served his said apprenticeship. And further saith not. The mark of Mary Sadler. Sworn before us, 1 Apr. 1735, John Williams, Peter Elers. Passed to Richmond.

27. [p.25] Middlesex sessions. Abigale Nuttall (alias Richardson) aged about 30 years, born in St Werburghs parish in Dublin, upon oath saith that on or about nine years since she was married to Richard Nuttall, her present husband, in the said parish of St Werburghs, by whom she hath two children now living, vizt, Thomas, aged 4 years, and Elizabeth, aged 14 months. And saith that her said husband was born in Ireland. And also saith that since he came to England [he] has not rented a house of £10 per annum, or paid any parochial taxes, or done any act or thing (to the best of her, this examinant's, knowledge) whereby to gain a legal settlement. [Blank]. Sworn at Chelsea, [blank] Dec. 1735, before me [blank].

28. [p.26] Middlesex sessions. Jane Willis, aged about 32 years, upon oath saith that about six years since she was married to her husband, John Willis, at the parish church at Enfield in the said county of Middlesex. And that before such her marriage, her said husband was a servant hired by the year to Mr Goodyer in Church Lane in this parish, where he continued about the space of two years and half, meat, drink, washing and lodging. And further saith that her said husband after marriage rented a little cottage at Enfield, aforesaid, and paid 45s. a year for the same, but did not pay any parochial taxes during his continuance there. Nor has [he] . . . done any act or thing (to the best of this examinant's knowledge) whereby to gain any settlement since he quitted the service of the said Mr Goodyer's. And also saith that her said husband is a soldier in the Earl of Orkney's Regiment of Foot, now in Ireland, and that he is at this time raising recruits for the said regiment at Bristol. And that she has two children by her said husband living, vizt, George, aged about 7 years, and Edward, about 6 months, and is not capable of supporting them without relief. Jane Willis. Sworn at Chelsea, 18 Dec. 1735, before me, Peter Elers.

29. [p.27] Middlesex sessions. Sarah Johnson, widow, upon oath saith that Mary Wadman, alias Collain, a child aged about seven years (the daughter of Mary Collain, deceased) was born in the dwelling house of one Mr

Blunt in Bull Yard in Windmill Street, in the parish of St James, in the liberty of Westminster, in the said county of Middlesex. And that the said child is a bastard, and was baptised in the said parish of St James, when, this examinant saith, security was given to indemnify from the said bastard child. And further saith not. Sarah Johnson. Sworn, 6 Feb. 1735/6, before us, Peter Elers, John Godfrey. [Mary Wadman] passed to St James, Westminster.

30. [p.28] Middlesex sessions. Esdras Clennick of the parish of St James, Westminster, in the county of Middlesex, chandler, upon oath saith that Mary Edlin, a child aged about six years, the daughter of Mary Edlin, was born in the dwelling house of this examinant, who then lived in Shug Lane in the said parish of St James, Westminster. And saith that he cannot give any account whether the said Mary Edlin, the mother, was ever married. And further saith not. Esdras Clennick. Sworn, 10 Feb. 1735/6, before us, John Mercer, John Godfrey. [Mary Edlin] passed to St James, Westminster.

31. [p.29] Middlesex sessions. Jane Good, the wife of Richard Good, maketh oath that she was married to her first husband John Tredaway on or about seventeen years since in the liberty of the Fleet; by whom she had several children, one of which is still living, vizt, Elizabeth Tredaway, aged about 9 years. And saith that her said first husband was born at Chiswick in the said county of Middlesex, where he served his apprenticeship to a gardener. And [he] has not gained any other settlement since (to the best of this examinant's knowledge) by renting a house of £10 a year, or paying any parochial taxes, or any other act whatever. And this examinant further saith that she received from the said parish of Chiswick several weeks allowance for the maintenance of her said child, Elizabeth Tredaway. And further saith not. The mark of Jane Good. Sworn, 10 Feb. 1735/6, before us, John Mercer, Peter Elers. Passed to Chiswick.

32. [p.30] Middlesex sessions. The examination of Sarah King, widow, taken upon oath, 13 Mar. 1735/6, before us, Peter Elers and James Cardonnel esqs . . . Who saith that on Monday, 16 Feb. last, she was delivered of a female bastard child in a cottage of Mr Coles in Chelsea Park (baptised and named Anne). And was unlawfully begotten on her body by one John Ash of Chelsea in this county, gardener, who had carnal knowledge of her body the first time in his dwelling house at Chelsea on Whitsun Tuesday last. And several times after in other places. And this examinant further saith that the said John Ash is the true and only father of the said female bastard child. And further saith not. The mark of Sarah King. Sworn before us this day and year as above, James Cardonnel, Peter Elers.

33. [p.31] Middlesex sessions. John Johnson, labourer, aged about 28 years, born at Chelsea in the county of Middlesex, upon oath saith that about thirteen years since he was bound apprentice for seven years to Joseph Cook of Mills Street, then of the parish of St Martin in the Fields, but now of the parish of St George Hanover Square in the said county, butcher. And that after serving about four years of his said time, his master and he, this examinant, having some words, his indenture was delivered up. And saith that since the time of leaving his said master (who at that time was a housekeeper in the said parish, and paid about £20 per annum rent) [he] has not rented a house of £10 a year, or paid any parochial taxes, or done any act or thing, to the best of his, this examinant's, knowledge, to gain a legal settlement. And further saith that about four years since he was married to Mary, his wife (aged about 32 years) in the liberty of the Fleet; by whom he has one child now living, named Mary, aged about 3 years. And he is not capable of supporting his said wife and child. And further saith not. John Johnson. Sworn, 27 Mar. 1736, before us, Peter Elers, Robert Mann. Passed to St George Hanover Square. Brought a certificate from thence.

34. [p.32] Middlesex sessions. The examination of Priscilla Howard, single woman, taken before me, Peter Elers esq. . . . Who saith that she is now pregnant of a bastard child or children which was unlawfully begotten on her body by one Edward Lynn, now a servant (as she, this examinant, is informed) to Mr Turner, a seed man, near Durham Yard in the Strand, London. Who had carnal knowledge of her body the first time in the month of August last in the dwelling house of Mr Canum in the parish of St George Hanover Square, victualler, near Chelsea. And several times after in the said house, where this examinant and the said Edward Lynn lived fellow servants. And further saith that the said Edward Lynn is the true and only father of the said bastard child or children (when born). And further saith not. The mark of Priscilla Howard. Sworn at Chelsea, 29 Apr. 1736, before me, Peter Elers. Child died in the workhouse.

35. [p.33] Middlesex sessions. Mary Poulton of Chelsea in the said county, widow, upon oath saith that her son Henry Poulton, aged about 41 years, was bound apprentice about 24 years since to one Richard Brown of the parish of Christ Church in the county of Surrey, waterman, for the term of seven years, with whom he continued for the space of about four years and was afterwards turned over to one Mr Samuel Hills of the parish of Lambeth in the said county of Surrey, waterman, with whom he served the remainder of his apprenticeship, being about three years. And further saith that since her said son left the said Samuel Hill he has not rented a house for £10 a year, or done any act or thing (to the best of her, this examinant's, knowledge) to gain a legal settlement. Mary Poulton. Sworn before us, 28 June 1736, Thomas de Veil, Peter Elers. [Henry Poulton] passed to Lambeth in Surrey.

36. [p.34] Middlesex sessions. Catherine Martin, single woman, aged about 19 years, upon oath saith that she was born in the parish of St Margaret, Westminster, in the county of Middlesex, but now the parish of St John the Evangelist. And that her father, Daniel Martin, deceased, was bound apprentice to one Mr Perry in Wood Street in the said parish of St John the Evangelist, paviour, with whom he served his time (as she, this examinant, is informed). And further saith that since the said servitude of her father she cannot give any account of his renting a house of £10 a year, or paying any parochial taxes, or doing any act or thing (to her knowledge) to gain a settlement elsewhere. And this examinant also saith that she herself has not lived a hired servant a year, or done any act or thing (to the best of her knowledge) to gain a settlement since her birth. Catherine Martin her mark. Sworn before us, 6 Sept. 1736, Peter Elers, Richard Farwell. Passed to St John the Evangelist.

37. [n.p.] Middlesex sessions. James Latham, a pensioner of Chelsea College, maketh oath (to the best of his knowledge and belief) that Cornelius Dowse, a child aged about 2 years, was born in the parish of St Margaret, Westminster, in the said county of Middlesex, as appears by a certificate of birth from the register book of the said parish, under the hand of Thomas Wood, the parish clerk. And also saith that the said child is a bastard, and that one Cornelius Dowse in Church Lane by St Anne's Church in the said liberty of Westminster is the reputed father of the said child, and hath paid this examinant for his wife's nursing of the said child at times £2 17s. But the said Dowse now refusing to continue his payments for the said child's nursing, [James Latham] is not capable of maintaining it. The mark of James Latham. Sworn, 22 Sept. 1736, before us, Peter Elers, Thomas Cotton. [Cornelius Dowse] passed to St Margaret, Westminster.

38. [n.p.] Middlesex, to wit. The examination of Martha Cleasdon, single woman, taken upon oath before us, Peter Elers and Thomas de Veil esqs . . . Who saith that on 8 July last, she was delivered of a male bastard child in the dwelling house of one Mrs Bradgate of Drury Lane, in the parish of St Giles in the Fields in the said county of Middlesex (which is baptised and named Robert Littlejohn). And was unlawfully begotten on her body by one Richard Littlejohn, who was then servant to Mr Chipperfield of Chelsea in the said county, farrier. Who had carnal knowledge of her body for the first time on or about three years since in the dwelling house of Mr Russell in Chelsea, aforesaid, and several times after in the said house, and other places. And this examinant further saith that the said Richard Littlejohn is the true and only father of the said male bastard child, and further saith not. Martha Cleasdon her mark. Sworn at Chelsea, 4 Oct. 1736, before us, Peter Elers, Thomas de Veil. Passed to St Giles in the Fields. [See **44**].

39. [n.p.] Middlesex, to wit. The examination of Anne Mackenny, single woman, taken upon oath before me, Peter Elers esq. . . . Who saith that she is pregnant of a bastard child or children which was unlawfully begotten on her body by one Francis Ricketts, lately a servant to Mr Large, in Chelsea College. Who had carnal knowledge of her body the first time about a year since in the dwelling house of Mr Guerney at the sign of the Old George in Chelsea in the said county. And several times after in the said house, where this examinant lived a servant. And further saith that the said Francis Ricketts is the true and only father of the said bastard child or children when born. And further saith not. Anne Mackenny, her mark. Sworn at Chelsea, 5 Oct. 1736, before us, Peter Elers, Thomas de Veil. [See **5**].

40. [n.p.] Middlesex sessions. Elizabeth Mayhow, aged about 40 years (the wife of Samuel Mayhow) upon oath saith that about nineteen years since she was married to her said husband in the island of Jersey, by whom she hath four children living, vizt, Elizabeth, aged about 13 years, Samuel, aged about 11 years, Mary, aged 9 years, and Sarah, aged about 2 years. And saith that her said husband is a soldier in Brigadier General Barrett's Regiment of Foot, now quartered at Edinburgh. And further saith that her said husband was born at Chelsea in the said county Middlesex, and that he has not gained a settlement since by renting [a] house of £10 a year, or paying any parochial taxes, or by living a hired servant a year, or by doing any other act or thing (to the best of her, this examinant's, knowledge). And further saith not. The mark of Elizabeth Mayhow. Sworn at Chelsea, 8 Oct. 1736, before me, Peter Elers. Passed to Lambeth in Surrey. Vide, exam of J. Holmes, overleaf [See **41**].

41. [n.p.] Middlesex sessions. John Holmes of Chelsea in the county of Middlesex upon oath saith that it appears by the register book of the Waterman's Company, London, that on 17 July 1713 Samuel Mayhow was bound an apprentice for seven years to one Elizabeth Beck (by the name of Elizabeth Beck of St Margaret, Westminster, waterman's widow). And that it also appears by the said register book, on 24 Sept. 1714 the said Samuel Mayhow was turned over to one Seth Banford of St Mary, Lambeth in the county of Surrey, waterman, to serve the remainder of his term. Of which a certificate is given under the seal and signed by the clerk of the said company. And further saith not. John Holmes. Sworn at Chelsea, 26 Oct. 1736, before us, Peter Elers, Thomas de Veil. [See **40**].

42. [n.p.] Middlesex, to wit. Stephen Coney, husbandman, aged about 44 years, upon oath saith that he was born at Chelsea in the said county of Middlesex. And that on or about 22 years since he, this examinant, lived a servant hired by the year with one John Bond of Brompton in the parish of Kensington, in the said county, where he continued about the space of one year and half, and received his full wages of his said master for this said time after the rate of £7 a year, meat, drink, washing and lodging. And saith that at the time of quitting the said Bond, he married Susannah, his late wife, in the liberty of the Fleet, by whom he hath had four children (one of which only is living, vizt, Richard Coney, aged about 18 years). And further saith that his said son having lately fractured his arm by a cart wheel in Hogmore Lane in the parish of Kensington, aforesaid, and now under the care of a surgeon, [he] is not capable of paying the charge of the cure, or maintaining him without subsistence. And further saith that since he quitted the said service of the said Mr Bond he, this examinant, or his said son has not rented a house of £10 per annum, or paid any parochial taxes, or done any act or thing (to the best of his, this examinant's, knowledge) whereby to gain a legal settlement. The mark of Stephen Coney. Sworn, 26 Oct. 1736, before us, Thomas de Veil, Peter Elers. [Richard Coney] passed to Kensington.

43. [n.p.] Middlesex sessions. Jane Purchase, single woman, aged about 21 years upon oath saith that she was born at Battersea in the county of Surrey, and that about four years since she lived a servant hired by the year to Dr Smartt of Chelsea College, where she continued upwards of one year and half, and received her full wages for the said time. The first year £3, and the remainder of time after the rate of £4 a year, meat, drink, washing and lodging. And saith that she has not lived a whole year in any service but the said Dr Smartt since her birth, or done any act or thing, to the best of her, this examinant's, knowledge, to gain a settlement. [The mark of] Jane Purchase. Sworn at Chelsea, 2 Nov. 1736, before me, Peter Elers. Came with a pass from Battersea. [See **45**].

44. [n.p.] Middlesex sessions. Martha Cleasdon, single woman, aged about 23 years, born in St George Yard in King Street in the parish of St Margaret, Westminster, in the said county of Middlesex, upon oath saith that on 3 Jan. last, twelve month, was she, this examinant, became a hired servant to one Mrs Hunt of the parish of Fulham in the county aforesaid, widow. With whom she continued till the Monday before Lady Day last, being a year and upwards. And [she] received of her said mistress her full wages for the said time (meat, drink, washing and lodging) at the rate of £4 a year. And further saith that since she quitted the said service, [she] has not done any act or thing to gain a settlement. The mark of Martha Cleasdon. Sworn before us, 11 Nov. 1736, Peter Elers, Robert Mann. Passed to Fulham. [See **38**].

45. [n.p.] The examination of Jane Purchase, single woman, taken upon oath before us, Peter Elers and William Miller esqs . . . Middlesex, to wit. Who saith that on 1 Dec. last she was delivered of a male bastard child in the workhouse belonging to the parish of Chelsea in the said county, which is baptised and named Andrew Purchase. And was unlawfully begotten on her body by one Walter Goldsmith of Battersea in the county of Surrey, blacksmith, who had carnal knowledge of her body in or about the month of March last in his dwelling house at Battersea aforesaid, where this examinant lived a hired servant. And at no other time or place. And this examinant further saith that the said Walter Goldsmith is the true and only father of the said male bastard child. And further saith not. The mark of Jane Purchase. Sworn, 25 Jan. 1736/7, before us, Peter Elers, William Miller. [See **43**].

46. [n.p.] Middlesex, to wit. Rachel Miles, widow, aged about 34 years, upon oath saith that she was born in Chelsea in the said county, and that on or about sixteen years since was married to her late husband, Michael Miles, at the Tabernacle or Chapel belonging to the parish of St Martin in the Fields in the said county. And that her said husband served his apprenticeship to Mr Robert Abbott, painter, late of Chelsea, deceased. And saith

14

that her said late husband, since such his servitude with Mr Abbott, has only lived in ready furnished lodgings, and has not done any act or thing, to the best of her knowledge, to gain a settlement elsewhere. Rachel Miles. Sworn at Chelsea, 29 Jan. 1736/7, before me, Peter Elers.

47. [n.p.] Middlesex sessions. William Fry, single man, aged about 70 years, upon oath saith that he was born in a village called Sandhurst in Berkshire, and that about the year 1683 he was bound apprentice for seven years to one Mr James Herring, in Tuttle Street in the parish of St Margaret, Westminster in the said county, basket maker, with whom he served out his full time and had meat, drink, washing and lodging. And that since the time of serving such his apprenticeship has not done any act or thing to the best of his knowledge to gain a settlement elsewhere. The mark of William Fry. Sworn, 18 June 1737, before us, Peter Elers, Thomas Cotton.

48. [n.p.] The examination of Margaret Maver, single woman, taken upon oath before me, Peter Elers esq. . . . .Middlesex, to wit. Who saith that she is now pregnant of a bastard child or children, which was unlawfully begotten on her body by one James Ogilvie, peruke maker, now living at Mrs Harrison's, a peruke maker in St Martin Le Grand in the city of London who had carnal knowledge of her body sometime before Christmas last at the house of Mr Gordon's in New North Street. And several times after in the said house. And further saith that the said James Ogilvie is the true and only father of the said child or children (when born). And further saith not. Margaret Maver. Sworn at Chelsea, 6 Aug. 1737, before me, Peter Elers. [See **54**].

49. [n.p.] Middlesex, to wit. Charles Rider, gardener, aged about 40 years, upon oath saith that he was born (as he is informed) at Battersea in the county of Surrey. And that about 25 years since he became a servant hired by the year to one Robert Peek, a baker at Battersea aforesaid, where he continued about the space of 1 year and upwards. And that he received for the said time, at the rate of £5 a year wages, meat, drink, washing and lodging. And saith that since he quitted the said service [he] has not rent[ed] a house of £10 a year, or paid any parochial taxes, or done any act or thing (to the best of his knowledge) whereby to gain a legal settlement elsewhere. And further saith that about fourteen years since he was married to Mary, his present wife, in the parish church of Battersea, aforesaid. By whom he hath four children living, vizt, Charles, aged about 11 years, William, aged about 4 years, Anne, aged about 2 years, and [blank], an infant aged about [blank] months. And also saith that being out of business, [he] is not capable of supporting his said family without relief. [Blank]. Sworn, [blank] Aug. 1737, before us, [blank]. [See **65, 82, 230, 243**].

50. [n.p.] Middlesex sessions. Isabella Askin, alias Willett, widow, aged about 34 years, born at Kington in Herefordshire, upon oath saith that about thirteen years since she was married to one Henry Askin, saddler, deceased, in the liberty of the Fleet, by whom she hath one child now living, named Elizabeth, aged about 11 years. And saith that at the time she married the said Askin, he had a wife and child unknown to her. And also saith that about 2 years since she quitted the service of one Mrs Brown, a widow in Tuttle Street in the parish of St Margaret, Westminster in the said county, with whom she lived upwards of a year and received of her said mistress at the rate of £4 per annum, wages, meat, drink, washing and lodging. And further saith that since she quitted the said service [she] has not done any act or thing, to the best of [her] knowledge, to gain a settlement elsewhere. The mark of Isabella Askin. Sworn, 20 Aug. 1737, before us, Peter Elers, James Cardonnel.

51. [n.p.] Middlesex, to wit. Anne Wiatt, widow, aged about 57 years, born at Brompton in the parish of Kensington in the county of Middlesex, upon oath saith that 32 years since she was married to John Wiatt, her late husband, deceased, in the liberty of the Fleet, by whom she hath one son living, named John, aged about 22 years. And saith that her said husband (as she, this examinant, hath been informed) before her marriage with him, lived a hired servant by the year to one Robert Severe of Brompton, in the parish of Kensington aforesaid, gardener, and that he continued in the said service a year and upwards. And this examinant further saith that since such her marriage, her said late husband, or this examinant has not rented a house of £10 a year, or paid any parochial taxes, or done any act or thing (to the best of her knowledge) to gain a legal settlement elsewhere. The mark of Ann Wiatt. Sworn, 29 Aug. 1737, before us, Peter Elers, James Cardonnel. [See **52**].

52. [n.p.] Middlesex, to wit. Edward Woodhouse of the parish of Kensington in the county of Middlesex, gardener, upon oath saith that John Wiatt, gardener, deceased, about 36 years since became a servant hired by the year to one Robert Severe of Brompton in the parish of Kensington aforesaid, gardener, with whom he continued the space of a full year and quarter (being at the time impressed into the sea service). And that he received of his said master for the said time his full wages, at the rate of £5 a year, meat, drink, washing and lodging. And this examinant saith that he lived at the same time a fellow servant with the said John Wiatt. Edward Woodhouse. Sworn, 29 Aug. 1737, before us, Peter Elers, James Cardonnel. [See **51**].

53. [n.p.] Middlesex, to wit. Elizabeth Bracett, single woman, aged about 36 years, upon oath saith that she was born in the hamlet of Hammersmith in the parish of Fulham in the county of Middlesex aforesaid. And that her father (John Bracett, gardener) about 15 years since quitted a house and about seven acres of land which he had rented in the said hamlet for . . . about the space of 30 years, and paid parochial taxes for the same. And this examinant also saith that since the time of her living with her father, [she] has not rented a house of £10 per annum, or done any act or thing (to the best of her knowledge) whereby to gain a settlement elsewhere. The mark of Elizabeth Bracett. Sworn, 8 Oct. 1737, before us, James Cardonnel, Peter Elers.

54. [n.p.] The examination of Margaret Maver, single woman, taken upon oath before us, [blank] esqs . . . Middlesex, to wit. Who saith that on 9 Sept. last she was delivered of a female bastard child in the workhouse belonging to the parish of Chelsea in the said county, which is baptised and named Elizabeth [blank]. And was unlawfully begotten on her body by one James Ogilvie, peruke maker, now or lately living at Mr Harrison's, a peruke maker in St Martin Le Grande in the liberty of the Westminster in the said county. Who had carnal knowledge of her body some short time before Christmas last, in the house of Mr Gordon's, in New North Street and several times after in the said house. And this examinant further saith that the said James Ogilvie is the true and only father of the said child. And further saith not. [Blank]. Sworn, [blank] Nov. 1737, before us, [blank]. [See **48**].

55. [n.p.] Middlesex, to wit. Edward Griffith, aged about 88 years, born at a place called Oswestry in Shropshire, upon oath saith that about 70 years since he, this examinant, was bound an apprentice for 7 years to one John Parry, a tailor, who then lived near the Axe and Gate in Aldermanbury, in the parish of St Mary Aldermanbury, London, with whom he continued and served 4 years and upwards (at which time his said master died). And about 2 years after the death of his said master he, this examinant, rented a house in Grubstreet in the parish of St Giles Cripplegate, London, for the space of eight years and upwards, and paid £8 per annum rent for the same and all parochial taxes. And saith that since he quitted the said house, [he] has not rented any other house of £10 per annum, or paid any parochial taxes, or done any act or thing (to the best of his, this examinant's, knowledge) whereby to gain a legal settlement elsewhere. And this examinant further saith that about 8 years since he married Anne, his present wife, aged about 40 years, in the liberty of the Fleet. And further saith not. [Blank]. Sworn, [blank] Dec. 1737, before us, [blank]. He has a son-in-law in Grubstreet in Maidenhead Court, named Minton Bayley.

56. [n.p.] Middlesex sessions. Robert Hardy, labourer, aged about 33 years, upon oath saith that seven years since he lived a servant hired by the year with one Mr John Akerman at the corner of Birchin Lane in the parish of St Michael Cornhill, London, cheyney man, where he continued and served for the space of two years and upwards, and received of his said master his full wages for the said time (one part of the time at the rate of £5 a year, and the other part of the time upwards of £5 a year) meat, drink, washing and lodging. And saith that since he quitted the service of the said Mr Akerman, [he] has not rented a house of £10 a year, or paid parochial taxes, or done any act or thing to the best of his, this examinant's, knowledge whereby to gain a legal settlement elsewhere. And further saith that about 6 years since he was married to Mary, his wife, in the liberty of the Fleet, London, by whom he hath two children living, vizt, William, aged about 5 years, and Joseph, an infant, aged about 2 months. And also saith that being afflicted with the rheumatism, [he] has not been able to work for a considerable time past to support his family, and that they cannot subsist without relief. The mark of Robert Hardy. Sworn, 21 Jan. 1737/8, before us, Peter Elers, Robert Mann.

57. [n.p.] Middlesex, to wit. Susanna Garlick, aged about 46 years (the wife of John Garlick, butcher) upon oath saith that on 18 Dec. 1723 she was married in the liberty of the Fleet to her said husband (John Garlick) by whom she has one child living named Sarah Garlick, aged about seven years. And saith that her said husband before her marriage was bound an apprentice for seven years to one Thomas Livintharp, a butcher in Hungerford Market in the parish of St Martin in the Fields in the said county of Middlesex, with whom he continued and served between 3 and 4 years of his time and then went to sea. And this examinant further saith that since marriage her said husband has not rented a house of £10 a year, or paid any parochial taxes, or done any act or thing (to the best of her knowledge) to gain a settlement elsewhere. And also saith that her said husband having absconded and left her for about a 12 month past, and [she] being very lame and infirm, [is] not capable of subsisting herself and child without relief. Susanna Garlick. Sworn, 6 Feb. 1737/8, before us, Peter Elers, Richard Farwell.

58. [n.p.] Middlesex sessions. Mary Jones, aged about 41 years (the wife of Daniel Jones, a gardener), upon oath saith that about 7 years since she, this examinant, was married to her said husband in the liberty of the Fleet, by whom she hath had three children, all living, vizt, Edward Jones, aged about 5 years, Bartholomew Daniel Jones, aged about 3 years, and Hester Jones an infant aged about 15 weeks. And saith that her said husband, about 15 or 16 years ago (which was before he married) lived a servant hired by the year to one Alexander Brand, a gardener at Brompton in the parish of Kensington in the county of Middlesex aforesaid, and continued in the said service for the space of one whole year and upwards, meat, drink, washing and lodging. And also saith that since her said husband quitted the said service of Mr Brand, [he] has not rented a house for £10 a year, or paid any parochial taxes, or done any act or thing (to the best of this examinant's knowledge) whereby to gain a legal settlement elsewhere. Mary Jones. Sworn, 28 Feb. 1737/8, before us, Peter Elers, Robert Mann.

59. [n.p.] Middlesex, to wit. Martha Ratcliff, single woman, aged about 69 years, born at Hendon in the said county of Middlesex, upon oath saith that about 26 years ago she became a hired servant by the year to one Mr Samuel Clark (afterwards Sir Samuel), merchant, in Mincing Lane in the parish of St Dunstan in the East, London, where she continued and served as cook for the space of 1 year and half, and received her full wages for the said time at the rate of £5 per annum, meat, drink, washing and lodging. And saith that since she quitted the said service [she] has not rented a house of £10 a year, or paid any parochial taxes, or done any act or thing, to the best of her knowledge, to gain a settlement. Martha Ratcliff. Sworn, 20 May 1738, before us, Peter Elers, Robert Mann.

60. [n.p.] Middlesex, to wit. June Davies, the wife of John Davies, fisherman, maketh oath that she, this examinant, was married about two years since to her said husband in the liberty of the Fleet, by whom she hath two children, both living: vizt, Elizabeth Davies, aged about 15 months, and Anne Davies, aged about 11 weeks. And saith that her said husband was bound out an apprentice by the parish of St George Hanover Square in the said county to William Pearce of the parish of Chiswick in the said county, fisherman (as appears by the counterpart of his indenture). And further saith that since she, this examinant has been married, her said husband has not rented a house of £10 a year, or paid any parochial taxes, or done any act or thing (to the best of her knowledge) to gain a settlement since the time he quitted and left his said Master, William Pearce at Chiswick. And also saith that her said husband being entered in the sea service is not capable of supporting herself and the said two children without relief. Jane Davies, her mark. Sworn, 31 August 1738, before us, Peter Elers, George Abbott. Passed to Chiswick.

61. [n.p.] Middlesex, to wit. Mary Milliard, the wife of William Milliard, waterman, upon oath saith that on 2 July last, was twelve month, she was married to her said husband in the liberty of the Fleet, by whom she has one child now living, named William Milliard, aged about 14 weeks. And saith that her said husband has also a child by Anne Milliard, his first wife (named also Anne Milliard), aged about 7 years. And also saith that it appears by an indenture of the Waterman's Company, bearing date 20 Sept. 1723, that her said husband (William Milliard) was bound apprentice to Charles Roberts of the parish of Barnes in the county of Surrey, waterman, for seven years. And it also appears by an endorsement on the said indenture, bearing the date 8 March 1727 (his said master, Charles Roberts, being dead), that he was turned over to Robert Parker of the parish of Ealing in the said county of Middlesex, waterman, with whom he continued and served out the remainder of his time. And this examinant further saith that since the time of her said marriage, her said husband has not rented a house for £10 per annum, or paid any parochial taxes, or done any act or thing (to the best of her knowledge) whereby to gain a settlement since his apprenticeship. Mary Milliard, her mark. Sworn, 4 Sept. 1738, before us, Peter Elers, George Abbott. Passed to Ealing. [See **95**].

62. [n.p.] The examination of Elizabeth Bicknall, single woman, taken voluntary upon oath before me, Peter Elers esq. . . . Middlesex, to wit. Who saith that she is now pregnant of a bastard child or children which was unlawfully begotten on her body by one John Boulton the younger who lives with his father, Mr John Boulton of Chelsea in the said county, attorney, who had carnal knowledge of her body in the month of April last in the dwelling house of his said father, where this examinant then lived a servant. And several times after in the said house and once at Kennington in the said county. And saith that the said John Boulton the younger is the

19

true and only father of the said bastard child or children (when born). And further saith not. The mark of Elizabeth Bicknall. Sworn at Chelsea, 13 Jan. 1738/9, before me, Peter Elers.

63. [n.p.] Middlesex, to wit. John Acco, aged about 34 years, born at Navestock in the county of Essex, upon oath saith that about 22 years since he, this examinant, was bound apprentice to Mr Henry Bayley, vintner, deceased (who then kept the St Paul's Head Tavern, gill-house, in Laurence Lane in the parish of St. Mary Le Bow, in Cheapside, London), for the term of seven years, with whom he continued and served his full time of apprenticeship. And that about 5 months after he, this examinant, was out of his time, he married to Catherine, his present wife (who is now in service), by whom he hath only one child, since dead. And saith that since the time of his apprenticeship, [he] has not rented a house of £10 a year, or paid any parochial taxes, or done any act or thing (to the best of his, this examinant's, knowledge) whereby to gain a legal settlement. The mark of John Acco. Sworn, 29 March 1739, before us, Peter Elers, Richard Farwell.

64. [n.p.] Middlesex, to wit. Charles Larchin, one of the churchwardens of the parish of Chelsea in the county of Middlesex, saith upon oath that he, this examinant, when overseer of the poor of the said parish in the year 1730, delivered up Anne Alfree, single woman, with an order, or pass warrant, date[d] 4 Nov. 1730, under the hands and seals of James Cardonnel and Jobson Webster esqs . . . to one Mr John Wilson, then churchwarden of the parish of St Giles in the Fields in the said county, who accepted the said order and received the said Ann Alfree into his care. And the said Anne Alfree (who is now a lunatic), having been for a long time returned to the said parish of Chelsea, is again likely to become chargeable thereto. And further saith that since the time the said Anne Alfree was passed to the said parish of St Giles in the Fields as aforesaid, she the said Alfree, has not rented a house of £10 a year, or done any act or thing, to the best of his, this examinant's, knowledge, to gain a settlement elsewhere. Charles Larchin. Sworn, 30 April 1739, before us, Peter Elers, Michael Margettson.

65. [n.p.] Middlesex, to wit. Mary Rider, widow, aged about 80 years, born near Stourbridge in Worcestershire, upon oath saith that about 60 years since she, this examinant, was married to William Rider, her late husband, at the parish church of St George in the borough of Southwark, by whom she hath had five children, three of which are now living, vizt, William Rider, aged about 45 years, Charles Rider, aged about 43 years, and Emanuel Rider, aged about 42 years. And saith that her said husband before marriage lived a servant hired by the year to one Mr Pedder, a farmer at Battersea in the county of Surrey, with whom he continued and served for the space of four years and upwards at the rate of £7 a year wages, meat, drink, washing and lodging. And further saith that since the time of this examinant's marriage with her said husband they have not rented a house of £10 a year, or paid any parochial taxes, or done any act or thing (to the best of this examinant's knowledge) whereby to gain a settlement. The mark of Mary Rider. Sworn, 24 July 1739, before us, Peter Elers, Richard Farwell. [See **49**, **82**, **230**, **243**].

66. [n.p.] The examination of Elizabeth Barham, single woman, taken voluntary upon oath before us, Pater Elers and Richard Farwell esqs. . . . Middlesex, To wit. Who saith that on 5 Aug. she, this examinant, was delivered of a male bastard child in the dwelling house of Peter Jones near the horse ferry at Chelsea in the said county of Middlesex, waterman, which is baptised and named George. And was unlawfully begotten on her body by one George Guilford, an apothecary, who had carnal knowledge of her body the first time a little while before Christmas last in the dwelling house of Mr Potts, an apothecary, then at Chelsea aforesaid, where the said George Guilford and this examinant lived fellow servants. And at several times after in the said house. And this examinant further saith that the said George Guilford is the true father of the said child. And further saith not. Elizabeth Barham. Sworn, 29 Aug. 1739, before us, Peter Elers, Richard Farwell.

67. [n.p.] The examination of Mary King, single woman, taken voluntary upon oath before me, Peter Elers esq. . . . Middlesex, to wit. Who saith that she is now pregnant of a bastard child or children, which was unlawfully begotten on her body by one Evan Muspratt, servant to Mrs Carey of Chelsea in the county of Middlesex aforesaid. Who had carnal knowledge of her body the first time on Thursday night in Easter week last, in the dwelling house of the said Mrs Carey (where this examinant now lives fellow servant with the said Evan Muspratt). And that he had carnal knowledge of her body twice after in the said house. And this examinant also saith that the said Evan Muspratt is the true and only father of the said bastard child or children (when born). And further saith not. The mark of Mary King. Sworn at Chelsea, 10 Oct. 1739, before me, Peter Elers.

68. [n.p.] Middlesex, to wit. Thomas Hathaway, mariner, aged about 33 years, born at Walham Green in the parish of Fulham in the county of Middlesex, upon oath saith that about nine years since he, this examinant, was married to Frances, his present wife, in the liberty of the Fleet in London; by whom he hath three children now living, vizt. Frances Hathaway, aged about 7 years, Thomas, aged about 4 years, and Mary, an infant, aged about 3 months. And saith that about seventeen years since he lived a servant hired by the year with one William Clark of Earls Court in the parish of Kensington in the said county, farmer, where he continued and served about three years. And from thence he became a servant hired by the year to one William Burchett jr of North End in the parish of Fulham in the county of Middlesex aforesaid, farmer, where he continued and served about the space of one year and three quarters, and received of his master his full wages for the said time (at the rate of £8 10s. a year) meat, drink, washing and lodging. And further saith that since the time he quitted the said service of Mr Burchett he has not rented a house of £10 per annum, or paid any parochial taxes, or done any act or thing (to the best of his, this examinant's, knowledge) whereby to gain a settlement. Thomas Hathaway. Sworn, 15 Oct. 1739, before us, George Tarry, Peter Elers.

69. [n.p.] Middlesex, to wit. Catherine Trussell (the wife of Charles Trussell, gardener), aged about 23 years, upon oath saith that about 5 years since she, this examinant, was married to her said husband at the parish church of St Bridgette alias St Bride, London, by whom she hath two children now living, vizt, John Trussell, aged about 4 years, and Mary Trussell, aged about 2 years. Both born in the parish of Fulham in the county of Middlesex aforesaid. And saith that her said husband's father and mother (as she has heard and been informed) lived in the said parish of Fulham many years and paid all parochial taxes there. And that her said husband was born in the said parish of Fulham and bred up to the business of a gardener there. And further saith that her said husband both before and since marriage (to the best of her, this examinant's, knowledge and belief) has not rented a house of £10 per annum, or paid any parochial taxes, or done any act or thing to gain a settlement since he lived at Fulham as aforesaid. Catherine Trussell, her mark. Sworn, 22 Oct. 1739, before us, William Morice, Peter Elers.

70. [n.p] Middlesex, to wit. Edward Arding of Chelsea in the county of Middlesex, shoemaker, maketh oath that it appears by a certificate dated 20 Apr. 1736 under the hand of one Edward Ashwell, minister, that John Andrews was married to this examinant's daughter, Elizabeth Andrews, in the liberty of the Fleet, London. And his said daughter hath one child now living by her said husband, named Mary, aged about 2 years and half. And this examinant also saith that it appears by an indenture bearing date 29 Dec. 1731 that the said John Andrews was bound apprentice for seven years to his father, John Andrews, late of Kensington in the said county of Middlesex, plumber. And this examinant further saith and believes that the said John Andrews since the time of being bound an apprentice as aforesaid, has not rented a house of £10 a year, or paid any parochial taxes, or done any act or thing (to the best of his, this examinant's, knowledge) to gain a settlement. Edward Arding. Sworn, 9 Nov. 1739, before us, Peter Elers, Richard Farwell.

71. [n.p.] Middlesex, to wit. John Hooper, tailor, aged about 54 years, born near Exeter in Devon, upon oath saith that about fifteen years since he, this examinant, rented a house in Axe Yard in the parish of St Margarets in the liberty of Westminster in the said county of Middlesex, where he continued about seven years and paid £12 per annum rent for the same, and all parochial taxes. And saith that since the time of quitting the said house he, this examinant, has not rented a house of £10 a year, or paid any parochial taxes, or done any act or thing whereby to gain a settlement (to the best of his knowledge) elsewhere. John Hooper. Sworn, 19 Nov. 1739, before us, William Morice, Peter Elers.

72. [n.p.] Middlesex, to wit. Hester Cooke, aged about 30 years, the wife of John Cooke, waterman, upon oath saith that she, this examinant, was married about eleven years since to her said husband, John Cooke, in the liberty of the Fleet, London, by whom she hath five children all living; vizt, William, aged about 9 years, Mary, aged about 7 years, John, aged about 5 years, Hester, aged about 3 years, and Edward, an infant aged about 13 months. And saith that her said husband (as she, this examinant, has been informed) about nineteen years since was bound apprentice for seven years to one Thomas Layton of the hamlet of Kew in the parish of Richmond in the county of Surrey, waterman. With whom he continued and served his time, excepting the two last years which was on board one of his late Majesty's ships. And this examinant further saith that since the time of her marriage her said husband has not rented a house of £10 a year, or paid any parochial taxes, or done any act or thing, to the best of this examinant's knowledge, to gain a settlement. The mark of Hester Cooke. Sworn, 4 Dec. 1739, before us, Peter Elers, William Miller.

73. [n.p.] Middlesex, to wit. Elizabeth Mitchell maketh oath that her sister, Judith Brooks, single woman (a lunatic), aged about 32 years, lived a servant hired by the year with one Mrs Eggelsfield in Delahaye Street in the parish of St Margaret in the liberty of Westminster in the county of Middlesex aforesaid about thirteen years since. Where she continued and served a year and upwards, and received her full wages of her said mistress for the said time at the rate of £5 per annum, meat, drink, washing and lodging. And saith that since the time of such her said sister's living a yearly servant, her said sister (Judith Brooks) has not rented a house of £10 a year, or paid any parochial taxes, or done any act or thing (to the best of this examinant's knowledge) to gain a settlement. The mark of Elizabeth Mitchell. Sworn, 6 Dec. 1739, before us, Peter Elers, William Miller.

74. [n.p.] The voluntary examination of Elizabeth Ellis, widow, taken upon oath before me, Peter Elers esq. . . . Middlesex, to wit. Who saith that she is now pregnant of a bastard child or children, which was unlawfully begotten on her body by one Richard Spragg, now a carter living with one Mr Randall at Uxbridge in the county of Middlesex aforesaid. Who had carnal knowledge of her body the first time in a barn opposite to the sign of the Hogs Brought to a Fair Market at a place called Shepherds Bush near Acton in Middlesex aforesaid, and several times after in the said barn. And this examinant also saith that the said Richard Spragg is the true and only father of the said child or children (when born). And further saith not. The mark of Elizabeth Ellis. Sworn at Chelsea, 6 Dec. 1739, before me, Peter Elers.

75. [n.p.] Middlesex sessions. Ruth Dobson, aged about 26 years, the wife of George Dobson, upon oath says that she, this examinant, was married to her said husband in Jan. 1732 at the parish church of St Brides, London. And says that in the year 1733 her said husband rented a house in King Street in the parish of St Margaret, Westminster, in the county of

Middlesex, at the rate of £20 (and upwards) rent a year. Where they continued about three quarters of a year. And says that she believes her said husband paid the parochial taxes for the said house. And further says that since her said husband quitted the said house [he] has not rented a house of £10 a year, or done any act or thing (to her knowledge) to gain a settlement. Ruth Dobson. Sworn, 24 Dec. 1739, before us, Peter Elers, George Abbott. Passed.

76. [n.p.] Middlesex sessions. Elizabeth Bevin, aged about 32 years, the wife of George Bevin, upon oath saith that about nine years since she, this examinant, was married to her said husband in the liberty of the Fleet in the city of London, by whom she hath had eight children, four of whom are living; vizt, George, aged about 8 years, Evan, aged about 4 years, Mary, about 2 years, and Elizabeth, aged about 15 months. And saith that her said husband (as she, this examinant, has been informed) was bound an apprentice about 20 years since to one James Patterson, a shoemaker, who then lived at the sign of the White Horse and Horseshoe in Queen Street in a place called the Mint in the parish of St George in the borough of Southwark in the county of Surrey, for seven years. With whom he continued and served four years of his apprenticeship. And this examinant further saith that she has been informed that her said husband, since the time of his being an apprentice, has not rented a house of £10 per annum, or paid any parochial taxes, or done any act or thing (to the best of her knowledge) to gain a settlement. Elizabeth Bevin, her mark. Sworn, 24 Dec. 1739, before us, Peter Elers, George Abbott. Passed.

77. [n.p.] Middlesex, to wit. Thomas Davis, aged about 50 years, upon oath saith that about 33 years ago he, this examinant, was bound apprentice for seven years to one John Rogers, the beadle of the Company of Joiners in the city of London, and was soon turned over as an apprentice to James Spikeman of the parish St Gregory by St Paul's, London, caner of chairs, with whom he continued and served seven years. And saith that since the time of serving his apprenticeship he has not rented a house of £10 a year, or paid any parochial taxes, or done any act or thing (to the best of his knowledge) whereby to gain a settlement. And further saith that about 20 years ago he married Anne, his present wife, in the liberty of the Fleet by whom he hath had ten Children, of which six are living; vizt, Aramena, aged about 15 years, Mary, aged about 11 years, Anne, aged about 9 years, Thomas, aged about 7 years, Jane, aged about 5 years, and Elinor, an infant, aged about 1 year. Thomas Davis. Sworn, 21 Jan. 1739/40, before us, Peter Elers, George Abbott. Passed to St Gregory by St Paul's.

78. [n.p.] Middlesex, to wit. Stephen Pewsey, labourer, aged about 28 years, upon oath says that about twelve years ago he, this examinant, was bound apprentice to one Edward Pinner of the parish of Richmond in the county of Surrey, waterman, with whom he continued and served about four years of his time, and was then discharged by his master. And saith that about seven years since he married Anne, his present wife, in the liberty of the

24

Fleet, by whom he hath three children now living; vizt, Anne, aged about six years, Elizabeth, aged about 3 years, and Stephen, an infant, aged about 7 months. And also saith that since the time of serving part of his apprenticeship as aforesaid [he] has not rented a house for £10 a year, or paid any parochial taxes, or done any act or thing, to the best of his knowledge, whereby to gain a settlement. Stephen Pewsey, his mark. Sworn, 1 Feb. 1739/40, before us, Peter Elers, Richard Farwell. Passed the parish of Richmond.

79. [n.p] Middlesex, to wit. William Young, gardener, aged about 60 years, born in Scotland, upon oath says that about 24 years ago he, this examinant, lived a servant hired by the year with one Mr Mayheau of Wandsworth in the county of Surrey, merchant, in the station of a gardener, with whom he continued and served two years, and received his full wages for the said time at the rate of £11 per annum, meat, drink, washing and lodging. And says that soon after he quitted the said service of Mr Mayheau's, he married his late wife (Jane) who is dead. And further says that since such the time of living a hired servant by the year as a aforesaid [he] has not rented a house for £10 a year, or paid any parochial taxes, or done any act or thing (to his knowledge) to gain a settlement. William Young. Sworn, 5 Feb. 1739/40, before us, Peter Elers, Thomas de Veil. Passed to Wandsworth.

80. [n.p.] Middlesex sessions. Anne Ross, the wife of Alexander Ross, deceased, aged about 67 years, born at Chelsea in the county of Middlesex, upon oath saith that about 38 years ago she was married to her said husband (Alexander Ross) at the chapel in the Fleet Prison. And saith that her said husband was an out pensioner of Chelsea College at the time she, this examinant, married him, and was so till he died. And this examinant further saith that her said late husband was a Scotsman, and was a soldier in the late wars in Flanders before he was admitted an out pensioner as aforesaid. And that she does not know he ever rented a house of £10 a year, or paid any parochial taxes, or done any act or thing (to the best of her knowledge) to gain a settlement since he left Scotland. The mark of Anne Ross. Sworn, 25 Feb. 1739/40, before me, Peter Elers.

81. [n.p] The examination of Honor Harris, single woman, taken voluntary upon oath before us, Peter Elers and Robert Mann esqs . . . Middlesex, to wit. Who saith that on 6 Feb. last she was delivered of a male bastard child in the dwelling house of John Gordon, a carpenter, in Chelsea, which is baptised and named John. And was unlawfully begotten on her body by one John Thompson, late of Chelsea aforesaid, who had carnal knowledge the first time in or about the month of May last in the dwelling house of the late Mr Wachter in Chelsea aforesaid, and several times after in the said house, where this examinant lived fellow servants with the said John Thompson. And this examinant further saith that the said John Thompson is the true and only father of the said child. And further saith not. Honor Harris. Sworn at Chelsea, 15 Mar. 1739/40, before us, Peter Elers, Robert Mann.

82. [n.p.] Middlesex, to wit. Charles Rider, gardener, aged about 40 years, born at Battersea in the county of Surrey, upon oath saith that about 27 years since he, this examinant, became a servant hired by the year to Robert Peek, a baker of Battersea aforesaid, with whom he continued and served one year and upwards, and received for the said time of his said master at the rate of £5 a year wages, meat, drink, washing and lodging. And saith that since he quitted the said service of Mr Peek [he] has not rented a house of £10 a year, or paid any parochial taxes, or done any act or thing (to the best of his knowledge) to gain a settlement. And further saith that about seventeen years ago he, this examinant, was married to Mary, his present wife, at the parish of Battersea aforesaid, by whom he hath three children now living; vizt, Charles, aged about 14 years, William, aged about 6 years, and Anne, aged about 4 years. Charles Rider. Sworn, 17 Mar. 1739/40, before us, Peter Elers, Robert Mann. [See **49**, **65**, **230**, **243**].

83. [n.p.] Middlesex, to wit. James Mackall of the parish of St Giles in the Fields in the county of Middlesex, leather clog maker, upon oath saith that Mary Mackall, an infant, aged about 6 months, the daughter of David Mackall by Sarah Mackall his late wife, was born in Plumtree Court in the parish of St Andrews Holborn Below the Bars, London. And saith that the said David Mackall, the father of the said child, before marriage, lived a servant hired by the year to one Mr Archer of the said parish of St Andrew Holborn Above the Bars for about the space of seven years. And also saith that the said David Mackall (who is the brother of this examinant) is gone to sea and left his said child unprovided for. James Mackall. Sworn, 4 July 1740, before us, Peter Elers, Thomas de Veil. Passed to St Andrew Holborn Above the Bars.

84. [n.p.] Middlesex, to wit. Mary White, widow, aged about 47 years, upon oath saith that about 25 years since she, this examinant, was married to her late husband (Thomas White, who has been dead about three years) at Bath in Somerset. By whom she hath had two children, one is living, being a daughter & married. And saith that her husband was bound apprentice by the parish officers of Lewis in Sussex to one William Danks of the parish of St John at Wapping in the said county of Middlesex, anchorsmith. With whom he continued and served ten years. And further saith that since the time her said husband served the said William Danks as aforesaid, he has not done any act or thing (to the best of this examinant's knowledge) to gain a settlement elsewhere. Mary White. Sworn, 18 Aug. 1740, before us, Peter Elers, Robert Mann. Passed to St John at Wapping.

85. [n.p] Middlesex, to wit. John Littlefoot, gardener, aged about 40 years, born at Willey in Shropshire, upon oath saith that about eleven years since this examinant left the service of one Mr [blank] Pace who keeps livery stables at the sign of the Green Man in Coleman Street, being in the parish of St Stephen Coleman Street, London. Where he continued and served for the space of about ten years in the station of a horse keeper, and received of his master for the said time his full wages, at the rate of £2 10s.

a year, meat, drink and lodging. And saith that about nine years ago he married Mary, his late wife, at the parish church of St George Hanover Square in the said county, by whom he hath two children living; vizt, John, aged about 8 years, and Anne, aged about 5 years. And also saith that since he quitted the service of the said Mr Pace [he] has not rented a house of £10 a year, or paid any parochial taxes, or done any act or thing (to the best of his knowledge) whereby to gain a settlement elsewhere. And this examinant further saith that being afflicted with the rheumatism in one of his hands [he] is not able to work to maintain and support his said family. John Littlefoot, his mark. Sworn, 22 Sept. 1740, Peter Elers, Thomas de Veil. Passed to the parish of St Stephen Coleman Street, London. [See **244**].

86. [n.p.] Middlesex, to wit. Richard Boshur, husbandman, aged about 53 years, born at Cholsey near Abingdon in Berkshire, upon oath saith that about 26 years ago he quitted the service of one Mrs Onslow who then lived in a house of Mr William Burchett's at Little Chelsea, being in the parish of Chelsea in the said county, with whom he continued and served in the station of a coachman for the space of two years. And [he] received his wages for the said time at the rate of £6 per annum, meat, drink, washing and lodging. And saith that about a quarter of a year after he quitted the said service he married Fruzan, his present wife, in the liberty of the Fleet, by whom he hath one daughter living named Jenny, aged about 16 years. And further saith that since the time of his quitting the said service of Mrs Onslow, [he] has not rented a house of £10 a year, or paid any parochial taxes, or done any other act or thing (to the best of his knowledge) to gain a settlement elsewhere. Richard Boshur [his mark]. Sworn, 29 Sept. 1740, before us, Peter Elers, James Cardonnel. A certificate granted the parish of Dorking [in] the county of Surrey.

87. [n.p.] Middlesex, to wit. Robert Richardson, fisherman, aged about 36 years, borne at Lambeth in the county of Surrey, upon oath saith that about seventeen years ago he, this examinant, was bound apprentice for seven years to one James Searing of Chelsea in the said county, fisherman (who was at the same time, as this examinant hath heard, a certificate man from the parish of Chiswick in the said county). With whom he continued and served his full term of apprenticeship. And saith that about six years ago he was married to Judith, his present wife, in the liberty of the Fleet, by whom he hath two children living; vizt, Robert, aged about 5 years, and James, an infant, aged about 15 months. And further saith that since the time of his birth he has not rented a house of £10 a year, or paid any parochial taxes, or done any act or thing (to the best of his knowledge) to gain a settlement. Robert Richmond, his mark. Sworn, 3 Nov. 1740, before us, Peter Elers, William Morice.

88. [n.p.] Middlesex, to wit. Mary Kimberly, single woman, aged about 40 years, born at Kensington in the said county, upon oath saith that she, this examinant, about seventeen years ago became a servant hired by the year to one Mr Francis Sawle, a woollen draper in the Strand (then in the parish of St Mary Savoy, and now the parish of St Mary Le Strand in the said county of Middlesex). With whom she continued and served for the space of seven years, and received her full wages for the said time; vizt, the first two years at £4 per annum, and the remainder of the time at the rate of £5 per annum, meat, drink, washing and lodging. And saith that since the time of quitting the said service of Mr Sawle [she] has not lived a year in service, or paid any parochial taxes, or done any act or thing (to the best of her, this examinant's, knowledge) to gain settlement elsewhere. Mary Kimberly, her mark. Sworn, 17 Nov. 1740, before us, Peter Elers, William Morice.

89. [n.p.] The voluntary examination of Mary Drew, single woman, taken upon oath before me, Peter Elers esq. . . . Middlesex, to wit. Who saith that she is now pregnant of a bastard child or children, which was unlawfully begotten on her body by one John Cord, gentleman, who is a housekeeper in Church Lane in Chelsea in the said county (where this examinant lived a hired servant). Who had carnal knowledge of her body the first time in the month of July last in the dwelling house of the said John Cord in Church Lane aforesaid, and several times after in the said house. And this examinant further saith that the said John Cord is the true and only father of the said child or children (when born). And further saith not. Mary Drew. Sworn at Chelsea, 12 Dec. 1740, before me, Peter Elers.

90. [n.p.] Middlesex, to wit. Joseph Northest, weaver, aged about 63 years, born at the Castle of Ballikilcaven in Queen's county in Ireland, upon oath saith that he, this examinant, was bound an apprentice to his father, William Northest, weaver, who then lived at a place called Dardistown about 24 miles from Dublin in Ireland, with whom he continued and served his full time. And that soon after he had served his apprenticeship he married Rebecca, his first wife, in Ireland, and that about 5 years after such his marriage he entered himself for a soldier and is now an in pensioner of Chelsea College. And this examinant also saith that his said father (as he hath heard and been informed) was born in the town of Stafford in Staffordshire and that he served his apprenticeship there. And this examinant also saith that about nine years since he married Catherine, his present wife, at the Fleet, by whom he hath two children living; vizt, John, aged about 4 years, and Edith, aged about 2 years. And that at the time he married his said last wife he was a hired servant to one Captain Trigeer, who then was a housekeeper in Chelsea where he lived upwards of a year and received £4 per annum wages. And this examinant further saith that since the time of serving his apprenticeship as aforesaid [he] has not rented a house of £10 per annum, or done any act or thing (to the best of his knowledge) to gain a settlement. Joseph Northest, his mark. Sworn, 29 Dec. 1740, before me, Peter Elers.

91. [n.p.] Middlesex, to wit. Mary Obrian, widow, aged about 40 years, upon oath saith that about eight years ago she, this examinant, was married at Ludgate Church, London, to her late husband, Thomas Obrian, by whom she hath had two children, both living; vizt, Jenny, aged near 7 years, and Elizabeth, aged about 4 years. And saith that her said late husband, about four years since, rented a house of £11 a year at Walham Green in the parish of Fulham in the county of Middlesex where he followed his trade of a smith and farrier for the space of five years and upwards, and paid all parochial taxes there. And also saith that since the time of his quitting the said house she, this examinant (nor her said late husband), has not rented a house of £10 per annum, or paid any parochial taxes, or done any act or thing (to the best of her knowledge) whereby to gain a settlement. Mary Obrian. Sworn, 29 Jan. 1740/1, before us, Peter Elers, Robert Mann. Passed to Fulham.

92. [n.p.] Middlesex, to wit. Mordecai Moulslow (by trade a tobacconist), aged about 41 years, born near Portsmouth in Hampshire, upon oath saith that about 24 years ago he, this examinant, was bound an apprentice to one Mr John Sparkes of the parish St Giles Crippegate, London, with whom he continued and served seven years. And saith that since the time of serving his apprenticeship as aforesaid, he has not rented a house of £10 per annum, or paid any parochial taxes, or done any act or thing (to the best of his knowledge) to gain a settlement. And this examinant also saith that about fourteen years ago he married Mary, his second wife (deceased), in the liberty of the Fleet, London, by whom he hath one child living named Henry, aged about 8 years. And further saith that about six years ago he married Anne, his present wife, in the liberty of the Fleet aforesaid. By whom he hath also two children; vizt, Jane, aged about 5 years, and Hammand, aged about 2 years. And saith that he being afflicted with sickness and almost blind is not capable to work to support his said family, who are also in a deplorable condition. Mordecai Moulslow. Sworn, 29 Jan. 1740/1, before us, Peter Elers, Robert Mann. Passed to St Giles Cripplegate, London.

93. [n.p.] Middlesex, to wit. John Drew, sawyer, aged about 59 years, born at Westerham in the county of Kent, upon oath saith that about 22 years ago he, this examinant, married Elizabeth, his last wife, by whom he hath one child living named Jane, aged about 10 years. And saith that about 37 years ago, which was before he married his first wife, he lived a servant hired by the year with William Hooker of the parish of Greenwich in the said county of Kent, esquire, in the station of groom. With whom he continued and served one whole year and upwards, and received of his said master his full wages for this said time at the rate of 50s. a year, meat, drink, washing and lodging. And saith that his said master kept another house in Boswell Court in the parish of St Clement Danes in the said county of Middlesex. But [he] was discharged by his said master at Greenwich aforesaid, where he, this examinant, had resided more than the last 40 days. And this examinant also saith that since he quitted the said service of Mr Hooker's, he has not lived a hired servant, or paid any parochial taxes, or done any act or thing (to the best of his knowledge) to gain a settlement. John Drew, his mark. Sworn, 10 Feb. 1740/1, before us, Peter Elers, Robert Mann. Passed to Greenwich in Kent.

94. [n.p.] Middlesex, to wit. Richard Boozes, labourer, aged about 40 years, born in the parish of Epping in the county of Essex, upon oath saith that he lived in the said parish of Epping for 20 years and upwards, and that from the time of his birth and quitting the said parish, he has not rented a house of £10 a year, or paid any parochial taxes, or done any act or thing (to the best of his knowledge) to gain a settlement. Richard Boozes. Sworn, 30 Jan. 1740/1, before us, Peter Elers, Robert Mann. Passed to Epping.

95. [n.p.] Middlesex, to wit. Mary Milliard, the widow of William Milliard, waterman, deceased, maketh oath that in and about the month of Sept. 1738 she, this examinant, and two children were removed by an order under the hands and seals of two of His Majesty's justices of the peace for the said county of Middlesex from the parish of Chelsea to the parish of Ealing in the said county as the place of their legal settlement. And saith that since the time of such her removal she has not rented a house of £10 per annum, or paid any parochial taxes, or done any act or thing (to the best of her knowledge) to gain a settlement elsewhere. And this examinant also saith that she hath one child by her said late husband now living, named Maria Milliard, aged about 1 year. Mary Milliard, her mark. Sworn, 16 Mar. 1740/1, before us, Peter Elers. [See **61**].

96. [n.p.] The voluntary examination of Mary Steward, single woman, taken upon oath before me, Peter Elers esq. . . . Middlesex sessions. Who saith that she is now pregnant of a bastard child or children which was unlawfully begotten on her body by one John Pink, gardener to the Right Honourable the Lady King, at Ockham Mill in the county of Surrey (where this examinant lived a hired servant). Who had carnal knowledge of her body the first time in the month of September last in the tool house in the garden belonging to the said Lady King at Ockham aforesaid, and several times after in other places. And this examinant further saith that the said John Pink is the true and only father of the said child or children (when borne). And further saith not. Mary Steward, her mark. Sworn at Chelsea, 17 Mar. 1740/1, before me, Peter Elers.

97. [n.p.] Middlesex, to wit. Anne Everson, widow, aged about 55 years, born at a place called West Felton in Shropshire, upon oath saith that about 37 years ago she, this examinant, was married to her late husband, Joseph Everson, gardener, deceased, at one of the parish churches in the town of Shrewsbury in Shropshire aforesaid (but cannot remember the name of the church). And saith that she hath heard that her said late husband served his apprenticeship to his uncle, Samuel Chapman, at a place called (as she, this examinant, says) Abby-Foregate in Shrewsbury aforesaid, but does not know neither the name of the parish Abby-Foregate is in. And also saith that since the time of her being married, he has not rented a house of £10 a year, or paid any parochial taxes, or done any act or thing whereby to gain a settlement. Only says that she hath lived in Chelsea as a inmate for upwards of 30 years. [Blank]. Sworn, [blank], before me, [blank].

98. [n.p.] Middlesex, to wit. Isaac Webb, by trade a basket maker, aged about 33 years, born at Chelsea in the said county of Middlesex, upon oath saith that on or about 9 July 1722 he, this examinant, was bound an apprentice to one Samuel Field of the parish of Kensington in the said county, basket maker, for the term of seven years, with whom he continued and served his full time of apprenticeship. And saith that about six years ago he, this examinant, was married to Mary, his present wife, at the parish church of St Martin in the Fields in the said county, by whom he hath two children living; vizt, John, aged about 5 years, and Elizabeth, an infant, aged about 7 weeks. And saith that since the time of serving his apprenticeship as aforesaid [he] has not rented a house of £10 a year, or paid any parochial taxes, or done any other act or thing (to the best of his, this examinant's, knowledge) whereby to gain a settlement elsewhere. And further saith that his said wife being now lunatic, [he] is not capable to support his said family without relief. Isaac Webb. Sworn, 28 May 1741, before us, Peter Elers, George Howard. Passed to Kensington.

99. [n.p.] Middlesex, to wit. Edward Crook of the parish of Harlington in the county of Middlesex aforesaid, husbandman, maketh oath that his brother-in-law, John Jennings, lately deceased, was a housekeeper in the parish of Dinton in the county of Buckinghamshire for about the space of 20 years, and was by trade a weaver and shopkeeper in the said town. And saith that since the said John Jennings lived a housekeeper at Dinton aforesaid he, this examinant, does not know that he ever rented a house of £10 a year, or paid any parochial taxes, or done any other act or thing (to the best of his knowledge) whereby to gain a settlement. And this examinant also saith that the said John Jennings has left two children by Sarah, his late wife; vizt, Mary Jennings, aged about 10 years, and Christopher Jennings, aged about 6 years. Both born in the said parish of Dinton in the county of Buckinghamshire. And further saith not. Edward Crook, his mark. Sworn, 9 June 1741, before us, Peter Elers, Robert Mann.

100. [n.p.] Middlesex, to wit. Sarah Gilbert, widow, aged about 30 years, born at Islington in the said county, upon oath saith that about eleven years since she, this examinant, was married to her late husband, William Gilbert, at the parish church of St George, Southwark. And that she hath four children by her said late husband living; vizt, William and Susannah (twins), aged about 10 years, Sarah, aged about 4 years, and John James Gilbert, an infant, aged about 5 months. And this examinant also saith that her said late husband was born (as she hath been informed) in the parish of Fulham in the said county and that the father of this examinant's husband was a housekeeper in the said parish of Fulham for many years and paid parochial taxes there. And further saith that her said late husband followed the business of brick making and sometimes a chairman, but does not know that he ever rented a house for £10 a year, or paid any parochial taxes, or done any other act or thing (to the best of her knowledge) to gain a settlement since the time of his birth. The mark of Sarah Gilbert. Sworn, 27 June 1741, before us, Peter Elers, Henry Vincent.

101. [n.p.] Middlesex, to wit. Anne Coxon, the wife of William Coxon, shoemaker, upon oath saith that about nineteen years ago she, this examinant, was married to her said husband at Northampton, by whom she hath two children living; vizt, Mary, aged about 17 years, now at service, and Richard, aged about 14 years, who is employed (this examinant says) below bridge at work. And says that it appears by an indenture bearing date 18 Jan. 1716/7, that her said husband was bound apprentice to one Francis Arthur of the parish of St Giles in the Fields in the said county of Middlesex, cordwainer, for the term of seven years. And that by an endorsement thereon, bearing the date on or about 9 Mar. 1720/1, the said Francis Arthur turned over the said William Coxon, his said apprentice, to his son, John Arthur, who lived in the said parish of St Giles in the Fields for the remainder of his term of apprenticeship. And this examinant further saith that her said husband is gone to sea. And she having been afflicted with illness and being very lame [she] is not capable to subsist without relief. The mark of Anne Coxon. Sworn, 24 Aug. 1741, before us, Peter Elers, Richard Farwell.

102. [n.p.] Middlesex, to wit. William Browne, aged about 28 years, born at Cirencester in Gloucestershire, upon oath saith that about fourteen years ago he, this examinant, was bound apprentice for seven years to one Mr John Varnon, who kept the Swan and Rumer Tavern in Fince Lane, in Cornhill. With whom he continued and served the space of four years, at which time his said master failed in his business and he was soon after turned over to one Mr Thomas Crawford, vintner, who then kept the Bear and Harrow Tavern in the Butcher Row in the parish of St Clement Danes in the said county of Middlesex, where he continued and served the remainder of the term of his apprenticeship (wanting about eight months). And saith that about the time he quitted the said Mr Crawford's service, he married Anne, his present wife, at the new church in Spitalfields, by whom he hath two children living; vizt, Thomas, aged about 5 years, and Anne, an infant, aged about 3 months. And this examinant saith that since the time of quitting the service of the said Mr Crawford, he has not rented a house of £10 a year, or paid any parochial taxes, or done any act or thing (to the best of his, this examinant's, knowledge) to gain a legal settlement. William Browne. Sworn, 17 Sept. 1741, before me, Peter Elers, Richard Farwell.

103. [n.p.] Middlesex, to wit. John Redbath, single man, aged about 34 years, born at a place called Tranent near Edinburgh in Scotland. And says that about fourteen years ago he was bound an apprentice for seven years to one William Hamsead, a barber and peruke maker in the town of Dalkeith in the shire of [blank, Midlothian] with whom he continued and served his full term of apprenticeship. And says that since the time of his serving his apprenticeship as aforesaid, he has not rented a house of £10 a year, or paid any parochial taxes, or done any act or thing (to the best of his, this examinant's, knowledge) whereby to gain a settlement. [Blank]. Sworn, [blank] Feb. 1741/2, before me, [blank].

104. [n.p.] Middlesex, to wit. Thomas Wythes, by trade a baker, aged 61 years, upon oath saith that about the year 1714 he, this examinant, became a servant hired by the year to Richard Lockwood esq., Turkey merchant. Who then lived on College Hill in the parish of St Michael Royal in the city of London, with whom he continued and served above the space of one year and a quarter of a year in the capacity of a brewer and baker. And [he] received of his said master his full wages for the said time, meat, drink, washing and lodging (at the rate of £6 a year). And saith that his said master at the time he, this examinant, lived with him had a country seat near Hatfield in Hertfordshire, where he was some part of the said time employed to brew and bake. But says that he was for the last two months of his said service at his master's London house on College Hill aforesaid, when he was discharged. And saith that about two years after he quitted the said service he married Elizabeth, his present wife, by whom he hath one son living, named Thomas, aged about 11 years. And also saith that since he, this examinant, quitted the said service of Mr Lockwood [he] has not lived a hired servant a year before marriage, or rented a house for £10 per annum, or paid any parochial taxes, or done any act or thing (to the best of his knowledge) to gain a legal settlement. Thomas Wythes. Sworn, 1 Mar. 1741/2, before us, Peter Elers, Robert Mann.

105. [n.p.] Middlesex, to wit. Thomas Patterson, aged about 72 years, born at Tangiers, upon oath saith that about the year 1684 he was bound an apprentice for seven years to one Mr William Hyde of Queens Head Alley in Newgate Street in the parish of Christ Church, London, house joiner, with whom he continued and served about the space of three years and half of his said apprenticeship. And then [he] voluntary entered himself a soldier and was abroad in part of King James' the Second reign, and in the late King William's wars and has continued in the army till he was admitted an in pensioner of Chelsea College, where he is now provided for. But says he is not capable of supporting or maintaining his wife, named Joan, aged about 80 years, to whom he was married in the liberty of [the] Fleet in the parish of St Brides, London, as appears by a certificate bearing date 5 Nov. 1732. And this examinant further saith that since the time of quitting his said master, Mr Hyde's service (to whom he was bound apprentice as aforesaid) [he] has not rented a house for £10 a year, or paid any parochial taxes, or done any other act or thing (to the best of his knowledge) to gain a settlement elsewhere. The mark of Thomas Patterson. Sworn, 12 March 1741/2, before us, Peter Elers, Robert Mann.

106. [n.p.] Middlesex, to wit. Frances Harris, aged about 64 years, the widow of Thomas Harris, brewer, deceased, upon oath saith that about three years and a half ago her said husband rented a house in a place called the Hop-Garden in the parish of St Martin in the Fields in the said county, for which he paid at the rate of £13 per annum rent, and held the same about the space of six months only. But [she] does not know that her said late husband paid any parochial taxes for the same. And saith, that her said late husband also rented a brew house in the said parish of St Martin in the Fields at the yearly rent of £11, which he held about a year and half till he died. And this examinant further saith that since she has been a widow she has not rented a house of £10 a year, or paid any parochial taxes, or done any act or thing (to the best of her, this examinant's, knowledge) whereby to gain a settlement. Frances Harris. Sworn, 23 Mar. 1741/2, before us, Peter Elers, Thomas de Veil.

107. [n.p.] Middlesex, to wit. Martha Guilder, alias Geldart, single woman, aged about 19 years, upon oath says that it appears by a certificate under the seal of the rulers of the Waterman's Company, bearing date 28 Nov. 1715, that Philip Guilder (the late father of this examinant) was bound apprentice to Mary Roe of the parish of Rotherhithe in the county of Surrey, widow, for 7 years from 22 Aug. 1712. And that on 29 May 1713 [he] was by order of the said rulers turned over to Thomas Avery to serve the remainder of his time unexpired. And that on 4 June 1714, the said Philip Guilder was again by an order of the said rulers, turned over to Alexander Crocker of the parish of Lambeth in the county of Surrey, waterman, to serve the residue of his time. And this examinant saith that her said late father, since the time of his serving the remainder of the term of his apprenticeship with Alexander Crocker of the parish of Lambeth as aforesaid, does not know that he ever did rent a house of £10 a year, or paid any parochial taxes, or done any act or thing (to the best of her knowledge) to gain a settlement. And this examinant further saith that she hath three brothers; vizt, Philip, Joseph, and George. Philip and Joseph are placed out apprentice by the parish of Lambeth. And. . . George, who is aged about 9 years is not provided for, he having been lately discharged by a gentleman, who is the brother of Mr Arrundell of Chelsea in the county of Middlesex aforesaid, for his misbehaviour, and who only kept him out of charity and compassion for some time, with an intention (if he had behaved well) to have made him a servant. And that the said George Guilder alias Geldart, is now lain chargeable to the said parish of Chelsea. Martha Geldart, her mark. Sworn, 12 Apr. 1742, before us, Peter Elers, George Abbott.

108. [n.p.] Middlesex, to wit. Mary Bradly, aged about 27 years, the wife of George Bradly, upon oath says that about eleven years ago she, this examinant, was married to her said husband at the parish church of St Clement Danes in the liberty of Westminster in the said county of Middlesex. By whom she has three children living; vizt, Mary, aged about 10 years, Lucy, aged about 7 years, and George, aged about 5 years. And says that her said husband (as she, this examinant, has been informed) was born in the royal palace at Kensington where his father and mother then resided as having a place at Court and being one of the King's band of music. And further says that she cannot give any particular account with regard to her said husband's settlement. [Blank]. Sworn, [blank] May 1742, before me, [blank]. [See **110**].

109. [n.p.] Middlesex, to wit. John Ford, aged about 36 years, soldier in Captain Criche [blank] Company of Foot commanded by the Honourable

Brigadier General Cornwallis, upon oath says that about 23 years ago he, this examinant was bound an apprentice for seven years to Mr Michael Jennings of Chelsea in the county of Middlesex, baker, with whom he continued and served six years and nine months of his time. And says that the reason he did not serve his full time out was because he absconded and stayed out all one night from his said master's service at Greenwich and that he would not receive him when he return[ed]. So that he was obliged to go to his friends in Hertfordshire where he stayed about a fortnight, at which time his said master delivered this examinant up his indenture, and by endorsement thereon promised him his full liberty of following his trade. And he would not molest or hinder him during the remainder of his apprenticeship (being then about ten weeks to come). And this examinant also says that soon after he had his indentures given him, he lived a journeyman by the week with one Mr Sandford, a baker at Wandsworth in the county of Surrey. Where he continued about the space of three months, and received of the said Mr Sandford 5s. a week wages, meat, drink and lodging. And says that since the time of serving his apprenticeship in manner aforesaid, he, this examinant, has not rented a house of £10 per annum, or done any act or thing (to the best of his knowledge) to gain a settlement. And further says that about twelve years ago, he married Isabell, his present wife, in the city of Edinburgh in Scotland, by whom he has two children living; vizt, James, aged 10 years, and John, aged about 7 years. John Ford. Sworn, 21 May 1742, before me, Peter Elers.

110. [n.p.] Middlesex sessions. George Bradly, aged about 37 years, upon oath saith that he was born in that part of the royal palace at Kensington which is in the parish of St Margaret, Westminster in the said county. And saith that the late Dr Richard Bradly, professor of botany, was this examinant's father, and that he rented a house of about £7 a year about 25 years ago at North End in the parish of Fulham in the county of Middlesex, about the space of seven years and paid all parochial taxes for the same. And that this examinant lived with his said father at the same time. And further saith that since he lived with his father at the time aforesaid [he] has not been an apprentice, or rented a house of £10 a year, or paid any parochial taxes, or done any act or thing (to the best of his knowledge) to gain a settlement. And saith that in the month of Feb. 1731 he, this examinant, was married to Mary, his present wife, at the parish church of St Clement Danes in the said county, by whom he has three children living; vizt, Mary, aged about 10 years, Lucy, aged about 7 years, and George, aged about 5 years. George Bradly. Sworn, 22 June 1742, before us, Peter Elers, Richard Farwell. [See **108**].

111. [n.p.] Middlesex, to wit. John Pritchett, a sawyer, aged about 54 years, upon oath says that he was born in the parish of Garway in Herefordshire. And that about 28 years since he, this examinant, lived a servant hired by the year to one Mr Murdock Broomer, a soap maker, who then lived in West Smithfield in the parish of St Sepulchres, London, with whom he continued and served the space of two years and upwards, and received his full wages of his said master for the said time at the rate of £8 per annum, meat, drink, washing and lodging. And says that about seventeen years ago he married Elizabeth, his present wife, in the liberty of the Fleet. And further says that since the time that he lived a hired servant by the year as aforesaid (which was before he married) [he] has not rented a house of £10 per annum, or done any act or thing (to the best of his knowledge) to gain a settlement elsewhere. The mark of John Pritchett. Sworn, 20 July 1742, before us, Peter Elers, Robert Mann.

112. [n.p.] Middlesex, to wit. William Dyos of Catherine Street in the Strand, painter, says upon oath that John Bell, a child aged about 2 years and a quarter, is the son of John Bell, brewer, deceased, by Sarah Bell, alias Morgan, who is also deceased. And that the said child was born in Blackfriars, which is in the parish of St Ann Blackfriars, London, where the said John Bell (the father) rented a house of about £20 per annum and lived and cohabited together with the said Sarah Bell as man and wife. And this examinant also says that he was a lodger in the said house at the time the said child was born and is godfather to it and was a near relation to the mother of the said child. But [he] cannot say that the said Sarah Bell, alias Morgan, was ever married to the said John Bell, though she went always by his name and was reputed to be his wife. William Dyos. Sworn, 31 July 1742, before us, Peter Elers, Robert Mann.

113. [n.p.] Middlesex, to wit. John Edlin, shoemaker, aged about 47 years, born at East Acton in the said county of Middlesex, upon oath says that in the year 1708 he, this examinant, was bound apprentice to one Richard Simmons, shoemaker in New Brentford in the parish of Hanwell in the said county for the term of seven years, with whom he continued and served his full time of apprenticeship. And says that since the time of serving his apprenticeship as aforesaid he has not rented a house of £10 a year, or paid any parochial taxes, or done any act or thing (to the best of his knowledge) whereby to gain a legal settlement. And further says that about fourteen years ago he, this examinant, married Betty, his present wife, at Bristol, by whom he hath two children living; vizt, Betty, aged 8 years, and Polchampton, aged about 4 years. John Edlin. Sworn, 16 Aug. 1742, before us, Peter Elers, George Abbott.

114. [n.p.] Middlesex, to wit. Hester Coronel, widow, upon oath says that she is a midwife, and that on or about the nineteenth day of this instant August last, was twelve month, she, this examinant, delivered one Mrs Mary Delacoste of a female child which is (as she has since heard) called or named Mary. And says that the said Mary Delacoste (the mother) is a foreigner and does not know that she ever gained a settlement in England. And that at the time when she, this examinant, delivered her of the said child, the said Mary Delacoste (the mother) lodged in the dwelling house of one Mr John Lecam, a jeweller, who lives in that part of the Strand which is in the parish of St Clement Danes in the said county of Middlesex. And further saith not. [Blank]. Sworn, 30 Aug. 1742, before us, [blank].

115. [n.p.] Middlesex, to wit. Augustine Eggburt, aged abut 22 years, the widow of Thomas Eggburt, gardener, lately deceased, upon oath says that about thirteen years ago she, this examinant, was married to her said late husband at the parish church of St George Hanover Square in the said county, by whom she hath six children living; vizt, Phillis, aged about 12 years, Sarah and Anne (twins), aged about 9 years, Casander, aged about 7 years, Thomas, aged about 4 years, and William, an infant, aged about a month. And this examinant says that her said husband before marriage lived with one Mr Wright of Earls Court in the parish of Kensington in the county aforesaid, merchant, about the space of three years as a hired servant by the year in the capacity of a gardener, and had meat, drink, washing and lodging, besides about £10 a year wages. And this examinant further says that since her said late husband lived with Mr Wright a hired servant before marriage as aforesaid, [he] has not rented a house of £10 a year, or done any act or thing, to the best of her knowledge, to gain a settlement. Augustine Eggburt. Sworn, 13 Sept. 1742, before us, Peter Elers, William Miller.

116. [n.p.] Middlesex, to wit. Sarah Cadles, aged about 25 years, the wife of James Cadles, a gardener (who is a soldier in the Second Regiment of Foot Guards, now in Flanders), upon oath says that on 21 Oct. 1739 she, this examinant, was married to her said late husband in the liberty of the Fleet, London, by whom she has one child living, named Elizabeth, aged about a year and three quarters. And says that at the time she was married to her said husband he was apprentice, bound for seven years, to one Thomas Arnold of the parish of St George Hanover Square in the said county, gardener. And that when she married him he wanted about a year and four months to serve of his apprenticeship; which he served his master out faithfully notwithstanding his marriage with this examinant. And this examinant further says that since her said husband served his apprenticeship as aforesaid, he has not rented a house of £10 per annum, or paid any parochial taxes; or done any act or thing (to the best of her knowledge) whereby to gain a settlement. Sarah Cadles, her mark. Sworn, 2 Nov. 1742, before us, Peter Elers, Henry Villiers.

117. [n.p.] The examination of Barbara Frampton, single woman, taken voluntary upon oath before me, Peter Elers esq. . . .Middlesex sessions. Who says that on 20 Oct. last she was delivered of a dead female bastard child in the workhouse at Chelsea. Which was unlawfully begotten on her body by one James Hoar who was servant to Lord Frederick Murray, then a lodger to Mr Greenhead, an apothecary in Mealman's Row at Chelsea in the said county, where the said James Hoar had carnal knowledge of her body the first time, which was on the fourteenth day of February last (being Valentine's day) and several times after in the said house. And that the said James Hoar was the true and only father of the said female child. And further saith not. The mark of Barbara Frampton. 16 Nov. 1742, before me, Peter Elers. [See **182**].

118. [n.p.] Middlesex sessions. Elenor Digsby, single woman, aged about 21 years, born at Chertsey in the county of Surrey, upon oath says that about three years ago she, this examinant, became a servant hired by the year to one Mr Shutes in Berry Street in the parish of St James in the liberty of Westminster in the said county, snuff maker. With whom she continued and served for the space of a whole year and upwards, and received her full wages of her said master for the said time (meat, drink, washing and lodging) at the rate of £3 10s. per annum. And says that she has not lived a year a hired servant in any place since, or done any other act (to the best of her knowledge) to gain a settlement elsewhere. The mark of Elenor Digsby. Sworn, 23 Nov. 1742, before us, Peter Elers, Robert Mann.

119. [n.p.] Middlesex sessions. The examination of Anne Eliker, single woman, taken voluntary upon oath before me [blank] esq. . . . Who says that she is now pregnant of a bastard child or children which was unlawfully begotten on her body by one Robert Barnes (who is now a journeyman to Mr John Chipperfield, a farmer in Chelsea in the said county). And says that the said John Barnes had carnal knowledge of her body the first time on Christmas day last in the dwelling house of Mr [blank] Hanks of Little Chelsea in the parish of Kensington in the said county, blacksmith and farrier, where this examinant and the said Robert Barnes at the time lived fellow servants, and several times after in the said house. And also says that the said Robert Barnes is the true and only father of the said child or children (when born). And further saith not. [Blank]. Sworn at Chelsea, [blank] Dec. 1742, before me, [blank]. [See **121**].

120. [n.p.] Middlesex sessions. Jane Moles, single woman, aged about 23 years, born at Gibraltar (where her father was a soldier), upon oath says that about fifteen years ago she, this examinant, was bound an apprentice at Gibraltar to one John Richardson for seven years, who soon after came to England with his family and this examinant. And [he] rented a house in Rochester Row in Tuttleffields, which is in the parish of St John the Evangelist, Westminster, which was at the time an alehouse known by the sign of the Sun and which the said Richardson kept (as this examinant believes) about the space of four years and paid about £18 per annum rent besides parochial taxes. And says that after the said Richardson quitted the said house he went to Guernsey and Jersey. And this examinant further says that since the time of her living with her said master (Richardson) while she was an apprentice in Rochester Row as aforesaid, she has not been a hired servant in any place by the year, or done any act or thing, to the best of her knowledge, to gain a settlement. The mark of Jane Moles. Sworn, 27 Jan. 1742/3, before us, Robert Mann, Thomas de Veil.

121. [n.p.] The examination of Anne Eliker, single woman, taken voluntary upon oath before us, Peter Elers and Robert Mann esqs . . . Middlesex sessions. Who says that on 12 Dec. last she was delivered of male bastard child in the workhouse belonging to the parish of Chelsea in the said county, which is baptised and named Clement. And was unlawfully begotten on her body by one Robert Barnes now or lately a journeyman to Mr Chipperfield, a farrier at Chelsea aforesaid, who had carnal knowledge of her body the first time on Christmas day last, was twelve month, in the dwelling house of one Mr Hanks at Little Chelsea in the parish of Kensington in the said county, where this examinant and the said Barnes lived as fellow servants. And at several times after in the said house. And this examinant says that the said Robert Barnes is the true and only father of the said male bastard child. And further says not. The mark of Anne Eliker. Sworn at Chelsea, 19 Jan. 1742/3, before us, Robert Mann, Peter Elers. [See **119**].

122. [n.p.] Middlesex sessions. Mary Ossiter, widow, aged about 28 years, born at Fulham in the county of Middlesex, upon oath saith that about six years ago she, this examinant, became a servant hired by the year to one Catherine Thomas, widow, who keeps a public house near Chelsea College known by the sign of the Coach and Horses. With whom she continued and served five years and received of her said mistress £4 per annum wages, meat, drink, washing and lodging. And says that since the time of her quitting the said service (which was at Christmas last, was twelve month) she has not been a hired servant by the year or done any act or thing, to the best of her knowledge, to gain a settlement. [Blank]. Sworn, 27 Jan. 1742/3, before me, [blank].

123. [n.p.] Middlesex, to wit. Elizabeth Freeman, single woman, aged about 18 years, upon oath says that she was born in the parish of Fulham in the said county of Middlesex where her late father, David Freeman, lived, who was a farmer and rented near £100 a year in land and paid all parochial taxes in the said parish of Fulham. And this examinant says that she has not lived a year in service, but has lived most of her time with her mother since her said late father died. And also says that she has not done any act or thing (to the best of her knowledge) to gain a settlement since she lived with her parents. The mark of Elizabeth Freeman. Sworn, 7 Apr. 1743, before us, Peter Elers, Robert Mann.

124. [n.p.] Middlesex, to wit. Bartholomew Vinet, aged about 32 years, by trade a weaver but now a seafaring man, upon oath says that he was bound apprentice for seven years as appears by his indenture dated 14 Nov. 1726, to one James Grimall (by the name of James Grimall, weaver of London) who was then a housekeeper in Fleet Street in the hamlet of Bethnall Green, which is in the parish of St Dunstan at Stepney, in the county of Middlesex. With whom he continued and served the space of about two years of his said time. And then he absented himself from his said master's service about the space of one year, part of which time he lived with one Mr Cowley, an apothecary near Cripplegate, as a hired servant at the rate of £3 a year wages, where he continued about three months. And afterwards [he] returned again to his said master (Mr Grimall) and continued about eight months, and then quitted his said master's service again and went to work as a journeyman in different places, sometimes by the week and at other times worked by the piece for the remainder of his apprenticeship.

During which time he lived in lodgings and dieted and maintained himself. And also says that since the time of his being an apprentice in manner as aforesaid, he has not rented a house of £10 a year, or paid any parochial taxes, or done any act or thing (to the best of his knowledge) whereby to gain a settlement. And further says that about nine years ago he, this examinant, was married in the liberty of the Fleet to Dorothy, his present wife, by whom he has two children living; vizt, Margaret, aged about 8 years, and George, aged about 6 years. The mark of Bartholomew Vinet. Sworn, 31 Mar. 1743, before us, Peter Elers, Robert Mann.

125. [n.p.] The voluntary examination of Anne Scafe, single woman, taken before me, Peter Elers esq. . . . Middlesex sessions. Who says that she is pregnant of a bastard child or children, which was unlawfully begotten on her body by one Benjamin Durant, a gardener, who had carnal knowledge of her body the first time about eight months ago in the dwelling house of Mrs Perriman in Chelsea in the said county (where this examinant and the said Benjamin Durant lives fellow servants). And several times after in the same house. And says that the said Benjamin Durant is the true and only father of the said bastard child or children (when born). And further says not. The mark of Anne Scafe. Sworn at Chelsea, 22 May 1743, before me, [blank]. [See **126**].

126. [n.p.] Middlesex sessions. Anne Scafe, single woman, aged about 27 years, born at Islington in the county of Middlesex, upon oath says that about three years ago she, this examinant, lived a hired servant with one Mr Henry Borer of Vauxhall, innholder (which is in the parish of Lambeth in the county of Surrey). With whom she continued and served fourteen months, and received her full wages for the said time of her said master at the rate of £3 per annum, meat, drink, washing and lodging. And says that since she lived with the said Mr Borer as aforesaid, [she] has not lived a year in any service, or done any act or thing, to the best of her knowledge, to gain a settlement elsewhere. [Blank]. Sworn, [blank] May 1743, before us, [blank]. [See **125**].

127. [n.p.] Middlesex. Elizabeth Hutchinson, single woman, aged about 23 years, born in Ireland, upon oath saith that about six years ago she, this examinant, was a hired servant by the year to one Mr [blank] Irbey, a cheesemonger, who then lived near the church in the parish of St Giles in the Fields in the said county of Middlesex. With whom she continued and served for the space of two years and upwards, and received her full wages of her said master for the said time at the rate of £5 a year, meat, drink, washing and lodging. And saith that since she left the said service [she] has not lived a year in any other place or done any act or thing (to the best of her knowledge) to gain a settlement. And also saith that her father is a soldier lately come from America and now receives his pay from the agent belonging to Chelsea College, and that [she] having a bad sore leg is not able to work to support and maintain herself without relief. The mark of Elizabeth Hutchinson. Sworn, 17 Oct. 1743, before us, Peter Elers, William Morice.

128. [n.p.] Middlesex. Christopher Cam, coachman, aged about 50 years, born at a place called Congresbury in Somerset, upon oath says that about sixteen years ago he, this examinant, lived a servant hired by the year with Edward Southwell esq., in Spring Garden, which is in the parish of St Martin in the Fields in the said county of Middlesex where he continued and served for the space of two years as postillion and coachman, and received his full wages of his said master for the said time at the rate of £7 per annum, meat, drink, washing and lodging. And says that about half a year after he quitted the said service, he married Anne, his present wife, in the liberty of the Fleet, by whom he has had one child, since dead. And also says that since he quitted the said Mr Southwell's service [he] has not rented a house of £10 a year, or paid any parochial taxes, or done any act or thing (to the best of his knowledge) whereby to gain a settlement. The mark of Christopher Cam. Sworn, 19 Jan. 1743/4, before us, Peter Elers, Richard Farwell.

129. [n.p.] Middlesex. Hannah Lowry, single woman, aged about 32 years (the daughter of John Lowry by Margaret his wife), upon oath says that she was born near Chelsea in that part of the parish which was then St Martin in the Fields but now St George Hanover Square in the county of Middlesex aforesaid. In which said parish this examinant's father rented a house and paid parochial taxes. And says that since the time of her birth she has not lived a servant hired by the year in any place, or done any act or thing (to the best of her knowledge) to gain a settlement elsewhere. Hannah Lowry, her mark. Sworn, 17 Apr. 1744, before us, Peter Elers, Thomas de Veil.

130. [n.p.] The examination of Margaret Dean, widow, taken voluntary upon oath before me, Peter Elers esq. . . . . Middlesex. Who saith that on 18 Apr. last, was twelve month, she, this examinant, was delivered of a male bastard child in a little cottage or tenement in Whiteharte Alley in the parish of Chelsea in the county aforesaid (who is baptised and named John). And was unlawfully begotten on her body by one John Hoskins of Strand-on-the-Green in the said county, fisherman, who had carnal knowledge of her body at [the cottage] several times, and in particular on 3 Aug. last, was twelve month, and several times after in the said cottage or tenement. And this examinant saith that the said John Hoskins is the true father of the said child. And further saith not. Margaret Dean. Sworn at Chelsea, 5 May 1744, before me, Peter Elers.

131. [n.p.] The examination of Anne Oliphant, widow, taken voluntary upon oath before me, Peter Elers esq. . . . . Middlesex. Who saith that on 21 Apr. last she, this examinant, was delivered of a female bastard child in the then dwelling house of one Turnor Desborough in the parish of Chelsea in the said county (who is baptised and named Mary). And was unlaw-fully begot on her body by one Francis Willoughby, who is an out pensioner of Chelsea College and late of Colonel Douglas's Regiment of Marines. And that the said Francis Willoughby had carnal knowledge of her body the first time in or about the month of July last in the said dwelling house of the said Turnor Desborough and several times after in the said house. And this examinant saith that the said Francis Willoughby is the true father of the said child. And further saith not. The mark of Anne Oliphant. Sworn at Chelsea, 18 June 1744, before me, Peter Elers.

132. [n.p.] Middlesex. William Prouting, by trade a shoemaker, aged about 70 years, born at a place called Boxgrove near Chichester in Sussex upon oath says that about 48 years ago he, this examinant, was bound an apprentice for seven years to one William Howgett, shoemaker, who at that time lived at the Point in Portsmouth in Hampshire (which is in the parish of [blank]). With whom he continued and served about the space of two years only of his said time and then entered himself a soldier in the army and is now an in pensioner of Chelsea College. And says that about 30 years ago he married Elizabeth, his first wife, at the parish church of St Margaret, Westminster, by whom he believes he has a daughter living and married. And also says that about the year 1725 he married Margaret, his second wife, deceased, at Port Royal in South Carolina, by whom he has one child living with him, named Susanna, aged about 9 years. And further says that since the time of living with his said master William Howgett as an apprentice, he has not rented a house of £10 a year, or paid any parochial taxes, or done any act or thing (to the best of his knowledge) whereby to gain a settlement elsewhere. [Blank]. Sworn, [blank].

133. [n.p.] Middlesex. Margaret Rogers, single woman, aged about 28 years, born in Chelsea in the said county, upon oath says that about five or six years ago she lived with the late Lady Catherine Jones at Chelsea aforesaid at several times in the space of six years (but not as a hired servant). And says that about three years ago she, this examinant, lived a hired servant by the year with the then Right Honourable Sir Robert Walpole (now Lord Orford) in the station of laundry maid, and afterwards upper house maid. Where she continued for the space of two years and received her full wages for the said time at the rate of £6 per annum when laundry maid, and £7 per annum when house maid, meat, drink, washing and lodging. And says that at the time she was discharged the said Sir Robert Walpole's service, she lived at his Chelsea house and had resided there for above three months before. And further says that since she quitted the service of Sir Robert Walpole's [she] has not been a hired servant by the year, or done any act or thing (to the best of her knowledge) whereby to gain a settlement elsewhere. [Blank]. Sworn, [blank], before me, [blank].

134. [n.p.] The voluntary examination of Elizabeth Dawson, single woman, taken upon oath before me, Peter Elers esq. . . . . Middlesex. Who says that she is pregnant of a bastard child or children which was unlawfully begotten on her body by one Thomas Bowes, footman to [blank] Dorrell of Richmond in the county of Surrey, esq. Who had carnal knowledge of her body at one John Wood's at Richmond aforesaid, gardener (where this examinant lodged and passed for the wife of the said Thomas Bowes). And several times after in the said house and other places. And this examinant also says that the said Thomas Bowes is the true father of the bastard child or children (when born). And further says not. Elizabeth Dawson. Sworn at Chelsea, 31 July 1744, before me, Peter Elers. [See **138**].

135. [n.p.] Middlesex. John Bishop, waterman, aged about 62 years, born at Chelsea in Middlesex, upon oath says that in the year 1699 he, this examinant, was bound an apprentice for seven years to one John Davis, waterman, who then kept a house in Chelsea known by the sign of the Three Cranes. With whom he continued and served about the space of one year and half of his said time, and afterwards went to sea and continued in the navy a sailor for thirteen years successively in Queen Ann's wars. And says that since the time of his said apprenticeship he has not rented a house of £10 a year, or paid any parochial taxes, or done any act or thing (to the best of his knowledge) to gain a settlement. And also says that in April last he was married to Deborah, his present wife, who is of the age of 52 years, at Chatham aforesaid. The mark of John Bishop. Sworn, 2 Nov. 1744, before me, Peter Elers.

136. [n.p.] Middlesex. Mary Whitehead, aged about 38 years, the widow of Daniel Whitehead, shoemaker, deceased, upon oath says that about eleven years ago she, this examinant, lived a servant hired by the year with one Mrs Rider in the parish of Chelsea in the county of Middlesex. With whom she continued and served for the space of fourteen months and upwards and received her full wages for the said time at the rate of £5 a year, meat, drink, washing and lodging. And says that she entered upon the said service in May 1733 and was married in the liberty of the Fleet in March following to her said late husband (who was an Irishman). And [she] continued in her said service notwithstanding her marriage for the said time. And further says that since her marriage as aforesaid neither this examinant or her said late husband did not rent a house of £10 per annum, or paid any parochial taxes, or done any other act or thing (to the best of her knowledge) to gain a settlement since she lived with Mrs Rider as aforesaid. The mark of Mary Whitehead. Sworn, 10 Oct. 1744, before me, Peter Elers.

137. [n.p.] The examination of Jane Phillips, single woman, taken before me, Peter Elers esq. . . . Middlesex. Who saith that on 15 Aug. last she, this examinant, was delivered of a female bastard child (baptised and named Mary) in the house of one [blank] Maine in the parish of Chelsea in the county of Middlesex aforesaid. And was unlawfully begotten on her body by one Samuel Price (by trade a carpenter). And says that the said Samuel Price had carnal knowledge of her body the first time about fifteen months since at one Mr Edward's at the Black Horse at Kensington in the said county, and several times after in other places. And says that the said Samuel Price is the true and only father of the said female bastard child. And further saith not. The mark of Jane Phillips. Sworn before me at Chelsea, 6 Nov. 1744, Peter Elers.

138. [n.p.] Middlesex. Elizabeth Dawson, single woman, aged about 29 years, upon oath says that in the month of February last, was twelve month, she, this examinant, became a servant hired by the year to one Mrs Hally Candy of the hamlet of Kew in the parish of Richmond in the county of Surrey, widow. With whom she continued and served until 29 Mar. last (being a year and upwards), and received her full wages for the said time of her said mistress at the rate of £6 per annum, meat, drink, washing and lodging. And says that since she quitted the service of the said Mrs Hally Candy [she] has not rented a house of £10 a year, or paid any parochial taxes, or done any act or thing (to the best of her knowledge) to gain a settlement. And says that she has a child living named Christiana, aged about 10 months, which is a bastard and was born in the hamlet of Kew aforesaid. Elizabeth Dawson. Sworn, 14 Nov., 1744, before us, Peter Elers, Henry Villiers. Passed to Kew. Kew appealed [against] . . . the order, but it was confirmed in January sessions, 1744/5. [See **134**].

139. [n.p.] Middlesex. Thomas Morless, waterman, aged about 32 years, upon oath says that about twelve years ago he, this examinant, became a servant hired by the year to Mr John Medley of Battersea in the county of Surrey, ferryman, deceased. With whom he continued and served for the space of one year and upwards and received his full wages for the said time at the rate of £8 a year, meat, drink, washing and lodging. And says that after he received his said wages he continued with his said master for the further term of about one year and half, and had meat, drink, washing and lodging. And also says that in the year when the hard frost was (in 1739) he married Susanna, his present wife, in the liberty of the Fleet, London, by whom he hath a child living named Thomas, aged about 18 months. And further says that since he lived servant with the said Mr Medley [he] has not rented a house of £10 per annum, or paid any parochial taxes, or done any act or thing (to the best of his knowledge) to gain a settlement. The mark of Thomas Morless. Sworn this 26 Nov. 1744, before us, Peter Elers, Henry Villiers. Passed to Battersea.

140. [n.p.] Middlesex. James Morgan, by trade a sawyer, upon oath says that he was born in the parish of St John the Evangelist in the town of Brecon in the county of Brecknock in South Wales. And says that since the time of his birth as aforesaid he, this examinant, has not rented a house of £10 a year, or paid any parochial taxes, or done any act or thing (to the best of his knowledge) whereby to gain a settlement. And also says that about fourteen years ago this examinant was married to Elizabeth Morgan, his present wife, at the parish church of St David's in Brecon aforesaid, by whom he hath one child living named James, aged about 3 years. The mark of James Morgan. Sworn at Chelsea, 10 Dec. 1744, before me, Peter Elers. Ordered to bring a certificate.

141. [n.p.] Middlesex. Martha Vandan, aged about 36 years, the widow of Charles Vandan, deceased, upon oath says that she was married to her said late husband at the parish church of St Ann Blackfriars, London, on 22

44

Aug. 1733. By whom she hath had four children, who are all living; vizt, Anne, aged about 10 years, Sarah, aged about 8 years, James, aged about 6 years, and Elizabeth, aged about 2 years. And says that her said late husband belonged to the army when she was married to him and was a trumpeter in Sir James Chamberlaine's Troop of Horse Guards (blue) when he died, which was in Hanau in High-Germany by an accident he received from his horse at the late battle of Dettingen. And this examinant says that her said late husband was born and baptised in the parish of St James in Westminster in the said county of Middlesex (as appears by a certificate from the register book of the said parish). And also says that from the time she was married to her said late husband he never rented a house of £10 a year, or paid any parochial taxes, or done any act or thing (to the best of her, this examinant's knowledge) whereby to gain a settlement. Martha Vandan. Sworn, 10 Jan. 1744/5, before us, Peter Elers, Henry Villiers. Passed to St James, Westminster.

142. [n.p.] Middlesex. Easter Graham, widow, aged about 75 years, born at Thame in Oxfordshire, upon oath saith that about 37 years ago she was married to her first husband (Abraham Hazard) at the parish church of Ealing in the county of Middlesex, who was an out pensioner of Chelsea College, and that he never did rent a house of £10 a year, or paid any parochial taxes, or done any act (to her knowledge) to gain a settlement. And this examinant also says that in the year 1732 she was married to her last husband (Thomas Graham) in the liberty of the Fleet, London, and that he was a Scotsman and an in pensioner of Chelsea College. And says that she does not know that he ever rented a house of £10 a year, or paid any parochial taxes, or done any act or thing since he came from Scotland to gain a settlement. And this examinant also says that before she was married to her said first husband (some short time) she lived a servant hired by the year to Charles Batemen esq. at his seat called Castle Bear in the parish of Ealing in the said county of Middlesex, with whom she continued and served for one year and a quarter and received her full wages for her said time at the rate of £3 a year, meat, drink, washing and lodging. And further says that since the time of last living with Mr Bateman as aforesaid [she] has not done any act, to the best of her knowledge, to gain a settlement. Easter Graham, her mark. Sworn, 10 Jan. 1744/5, before us, Peter Elers, Henry Villiers. Passed to the parish of Ealing.

143. [n.p.] Middlesex. Phillarista Keen, aged about nineteen years, the wife of George Keen, shoemaker, upon oath says that about two years and a quarter ago she, this examinant, was married to her said husband in the liberty of the Fleet, London, and that he hath lately absconded and left her big with child unprovided for. And says that she hath frequently heard her said husband say that he was born in Earls Court in the parish of St Martin in the Fields in the county of Middlesex, and was bound out apprentice by the said parish to one John Lewin, shoemaker, who then lived in Red Cross Court in Long Acre in the parish of St Martin in the Fields aforesaid. And also says that her said husband since his marriage had not rented a house of £10 a year, or paid any parish taxes; or done any act (to the best of her knowledge) to gain a settlement. The mark of Phillarista Keen. Sworn, 22 Jan. 1744/5, before us, Peter Elers, Henry Villiers. Passed to the parish of St Martin in the Fields. St Martins appealed to the order and she was again removed to St Giles in the Fields.

144. [n.p.] Middlesex. Sarah Brown, widow, aged about 60 years, born at Crookham in Hampshire, upon oath says that about fourteen years since she, this examinant, was married to her late husband, Denis Brown, deceased, in the liberty of the Fleet, London. And says that he was born in Ireland and does not know that he ever gained a settlement in England. And also says that before she was married to her said late husband this examinant lived a servant hired by the year to one Mr Thomas Walton of the Neat Houses, gardener, which is in the parish of St George Hanover Square in the said county of Middlesex, with whom she continued and served two years and upwards and received her full wages for the said time at the rate of £4 a year, meat, drink, washing and lodging. The mark of Sarah Brown. Sworn, 22 Jan. 1744/5, before us, Peter Elers, Henry Villiers. Passed to St George Hanover Square.

145. [n.p.] Middlesex. Elizabeth Wilkinson, aged about 65 years, the widow of Richard Wilkinson, deceased, upon oath says that about 37 years ago she, this examinant, was married to her said late husband in Gray's Inn Chapel (who died about seven years after). And says that she cannot give any account of any settlement that her said husband ever gained either before or after marriage. And further says that about 23 years ago she, this examinant, became a servant hired by the year to one Crew Offley esq., who at that time lived in St James Place, which is in the parish of St James in the liberty of Westminster in the county of Middlesex, where she continued and served about the space of ten years (as nurse), and received her full wages for the said time (meat, drink, washing and lodging) at the rate of £20 per annum. Elizabeth Wilkinson. Sworn, 22 Jan. 1744/5, before us, Peter Elers, Henry Villiers. Passed to St James, Westminster.

146. [n.p.] The voluntary examination of Elizabeth Inwood, single woman, taken before me, Peter Elers esq. . . . (upon oath). Who saith that a week before Christmas day last, was twelve month, she, this examinant, was delivered of a female bastard child in a little cottage in Chelsea Park in Middlesex inhabited by one Thomas Pim (who is baptised and named Elizabeth). And was unlawfully begotten on her body by one Francis Newton [blank] who lives at Wandsworth in the county of Surrey, who had carnal knowledge of her body the first time in the month of March last, was twelve month, in an open field near Battersea in Surrey aforesaid and once in the room where this examinant lodged at Thomas Pim's aforesaid. And several times in the open fields. And says that the said Francis Newton is the true father of the said female bastard child. And further says not. The mark of Elizabeth Inwood. Sworn, 22 Jan. 1744/5, before me, Peter Elers. [See **198**].

147. [n.p.] The voluntary examination of Susan Street, single woman, taken upon oath before me, Peter Elers esq. . . . Middlesex. Who saith that she is now pregnant of a bastard child or children which was unlawfully begotten on her body by one John Sprawley now at Wandsworth in the county of Surrey, shoemaker. Who had carnal knowledge of her body the first [time] about the latter end of July last in this examinant's mother's house at Wandsworth aforesaid, and several times after in the said house and other places. And this examinant saith that the said John Sprawley is the true father of the said bastard child or children (when born). And further saith not. The mark of Susan Street. Sworn at Chelsea, [blank] Feb. 1744/5, before me, Peter Elers. [See **157**].

148. [n.p.] Middlesex. Frances Capel, single woman, aged about 47 years, born in Chelsea College, upon oath says that (to the best of her knowledge) about Michaelmas 1740 she became a servant hired by the year to Thomas Chester esq., Member of Parliament at his seat at Knowles, which is in the parish of Almondsbury in the county of Gloucester with whom she continued and served a year and six weeks (except two weeks that she was away on account of sickness). But [she] received her full wages for the said time at the rate of £10 per annum, meat, drink, washing and lodging. And says that since the time of her living with the said Thomas Chester esq. she has not lived a year in any place as a hired servant, or done any act or thing (to the best of her knowledge) to gain a legal settlement. [Blank]. Sworn at Chelsea, [blank] Feb. 1744/45, before me, [blank].

149. [n.p.] The voluntary examination of Mary Snaggs, single woman, taken before me, Peter Elers esq. . . . Middlesex. Who says that on 8 Jan. last she, this examinant, was delivered of a male bastard child (baptised and named William) in the dwelling house of Mr Stephen Fisher in Chelsea in the said county of Middlesex. And was unlawfully begotten on her body by one Mr Joseph Collett of the parish of St Clement Danes in the said county of Middlesex, who had carnal knowledge of her body the first time in the month of April last at a bagnio in Spring Garden near Charing Cross. And several times after in the said bagnio and other places. And this examinant says that the said Joseph Collett is the true father of the said male bastard child. And further says not. Mary Snaggs. Sworn at Chelsea, 11 Feb. 1744/5, before me, Peter Elers.

150. [n.p.] Middlesex, to wit. The examination of James Clarke taken on oath 19 Mar. 1744. This examinant, aged about 59 years, on his oath saith that in the year 1707 he was hired by the year to one Francis Clarke, a farmer, who then lived at Nottinghill in the parish of Kensington in the said county of Middlesex. With whom he continued and served for two years and upwards, and received his full wages for the said time of his said master at the rate of £7 per annum, meat, drink, washing and lodging. And saith that from the time of his living with Mr Clarke as aforesaid he has not been a hired servant a year in any place, or rented a house of £10 a year, or done any other act or thing (to the best of his knowledge) to gain

47

a settlement. And this examinant further saith that in the year 1717 he was married to Elizabeth, his wife, in the liberty of the Fleet by whom he has a daughter named Anne, aged about 24 years (if living). James Clarke. Sworn the day and year above written, Peter Elers, Henry Withers. Passed to Kensington.

151. [n.p.] The voluntary examination of Catherine Watson, single woman, taken before me, Peter Elers esq. . . . Middlesex. The examinant, on her oath, saith that on Monday last, being the first of this instant April, she was delivered of a male bastard child in the apartment in Chelsea in the said county of Middlesex, belonging to her father (which is baptised and named Alexander). And was unlawfully begotten on her body by Mr Alexander Reid of Chelsea aforesaid, surgeon, who had carnal knowledge of her body on a Sunday in the month of August last, in the said apartment of her father's (where she now lies in). And this examinant saith that the said Alexander Reid is the true father of the said male bastard child. And further saith not. The mark of Catherine Watson. Sworn at Chelsea, 10 Apr. 1745, before me, Peter Elers.

152. [n.p.] The voluntary examination of Anne Snelson, single woman, taken before me, Peter Elers esq. . . . Middlesex. The examinant on her oath saith that she is pregnant of a bastard child or children which was unlawfully begotten on her body by one George Dolly, a blacksmith now living with Mr [blank] Galland, blacksmith, near Grosvenor Square, who had carnal knowledge of her body the first time in the month of November last in the house of Mr Richard Haywood in the parish of Chelsea in the county of Middlesex aforesaid, and several times after in the said house and other places. And this examinant further saith that the said George Dolly is the true father of the said bastard child or children (when born). And further saith not. Ann Snelson. Sworn at Chelsea, 16 May 1745, before me, Peter Elers.

153. [n.p.] Middlesex. Isabella James, single woman, aged about 22 years, born at Kingston upon Thames in the county of Surrey, upon oath saith that her late father, Thomas James, deceased, was bound an apprentice for seven years to one John Wilkinson of the parish of St Martin in the Fields in the county of Middlesex, cordwainer (as appears by his indenture of apprenticeship bearing the date of 10 Mar. 1713). And saith that her said father, to the best of her knowledge, never rented a house of £10 a year, or did any act or thing to gain a settlement since the time of serving his apprenticeship as aforesaid. And this examinant further saith that from the time of her living with her said father she has not been a hired servant a year in any place, or done any act or thing, whereby to gain a legal settlement. The mark of Isabella James. Sworn, 13 May 1745, before us, Peter Elers, Henry Villiers. Passed to St Martin in the Fields.

154. [n.p.] The examination of Anne Smith, the wife of Leonard Smith, taken upon oath 11 June 1745. Middlesex, to wit. This examinant on her

48

oath saith that Mary Smith, single woman, aged about 21 years lived with her about eight or nine years ago in the parish of St Paul Covent Garden in the liberty of Westminster and county of Middlesex, a servant hired by the year for the space of two years and upwards. And received of this examinant her full wages for the said time at the rate of £3 for the first year and £4 for the second year (to the best of her knowledge). And this examinant verily believes that the said Mary Smith has not been a hired servant a year in any other place since she left her service as aforesaid, but has followed some business in Covent Garden Market which this examinant turned over to her. The mark of Anne Smith. Taken and sworn the day and year above written, before Henry Villiers, Peter Elers esqs . . . Removed to the parish of St Paul Covent Garden.

155. [n.p.] Middlesex. Elizabeth Gardner, single woman, aged about 22 years, upon oath says that near a year since she, this examinant, quitted the service of Mrs Norton at Cecil Street Coffee House in the Strand in the parish of St Martin in the Fields in the county of Middlesex. With whom she lived a servant hired by the year for the space of three years, and received her full wages for the said time at the rate of £3 per annum, meat, drink, washing and lodging. And says that since the time of quitting the said service of Mrs Norton's, she has not rented a house of £10 per annum, or done any act or thing (to the best of [her] knowledge) to gain a settlement. Elizabeth Gardner. Sworn, 29 June 1745, before us, Peter Elers, Peregrine Furye. Removed to St Martin in the Fields.

156. [n.p.] Middlesex. Edward Holland, aged about 71 years, born at Prestbury in the county of Cheshire, upon oath says that when he was about the age of 30 years, he entered himself a soldier in the First troop of Horse Guards and continued in the army till about twelve years since he was discharged. And that about four years ago he was admitted an in pensioner of Chelsea College, where he now belongs. And this examinant says that upwards of twenty years ago he rented a public house upon lease (known by the sign of the Red Lyon) in King Street in the parish of St Ann, Westminster, in the said county of Middlesex, for the space of five years at the yearly rent of £14, and paid all parochial taxes for the same. And says that since the time of renting the said house, he has not rented a house of £10 a year, or paid any parochial taxes, or done any act or thing (to his knowledge) to gain a settlement. And this examinant also says that about 50 years since he was married to Christiana, his present wife, and that he hath a daughter by his said wife (named Elizabeth Holland), aged about 27 years, who is not capable of service or maintaining herself, she being afflicted with convulsions and at intervals out of her reason. And this examinant further says that he having no other dependence than the said College, is not able to support his said wife and daughter. [Blank]. Sworn, [blank] 1745, before us, [blank]. Removed to the parish of St Ann, Westminster.

157. [n.p.] The examination of Susan Street, single woman, taken upon oath before us, Peregrine Furye and Peter Elers esqs . . . Middlesex. Who saith that on 14 May last she, this examinant, was delivered of a female bastard child (baptised and named Mary Sprawley) in the workhouse in the parish of Chelsea in the said county of Middlesex. And was unlawfully begotten on her body by one John Sprawley of Wandsworth in the county of Surrey, shoemaker, who had carnal knowledge of her body the first time about the latter end of July last, was twelve month, in the examinant's mother's house at Wandsworth aforesaid, and several times after in the said house and other places. And this examinant saith that the said John Sprawley is the true father of the said female bastard child. And further saith not. The mark of Susan Street. Sworn at Chelsea, 8 July 1745, before us, Peter Elers, Peregrine Furye. [See **147**].

158. [n.p.] The examination of Margaret Lumbey, single woman, taken upon oath before us, Peregrine Furye and Peter Elers, esqs . . . Middlesex. Who says that on 4 Sept. 1742 she, this examinant, was delivered of a female bastard child (baptised and named Anne Johnson, alias Lumbey) in the dwelling house of Mr Moody in Pipemaker's Alley in Bedford Bury, which is in the parish of St Martin in the Fields in the county of Middlesex. And was unlawfully begotten on her body by one Daniel Brown now of Chelsea in the said county of Middlesex, lighterman. And that the said Daniel Brown is the true father of the said female bastard child. And further says not. Margaret Lumbey. Sworn, 16 July 1745, before us, Peter Elers, Peregrine Furye.

159. [n.p.] Middlesex. Sarah Robinson, single woman, aged about 25 years, born at Southampton in Hampshire, upon oath says that about three years ago she, this examinant, lived a servant hired by the year with one Mr Edward Jones, a Plasterer, in Sandwich Court in Devonshire Street, which is in the parish of St Botolph without Bishopsgate, London, with whom she continued and served a year and five months, and received her full wages of her said master (Edward Jones) for the said time, meat, drink, washing and lodging, at the rate of £4 a year. And says that since the time of her quitting the said service of Mr Jones she, this examinant, has not lived a hired servant a year in any place, or rented a house of £10 per annum, or done any act or thing, to the best of her knowledge, to gain a settlement. Sarah Robinson. Sworn, 7 Oct. 1745, before us, Peter Elers, William Morice.

160. [n.p.] The voluntary examination of Mary Morrison, single woman, taken before me, Peter Elers esq. . . . . Middlesex. This examinant on her oath says that she is now pregnant of a bastard child or children, which was unlawfully begotten on her body by one William Radford (late a soldier in Lord Beauclerk's Regiment of Foot, but now admitted an out pensioner of the Royal Hospital in the parish of Chelsea). Who had carnal knowledge of her body the first time at a house at Brussels in Flanders, about eight months since, and several times after in other places. And this examinant further says that the said William Radford is the true father of the said bastard child or children (when born). And further says not. The mark of Mary Morrison. Sworn at Chelsea, 22 Oct. 1745, before me, Peter Elers.

161. [n.p.] Middlesex. Jane Scott, single woman, aged about 22 years, born at Stortford in Hertfordshire, upon oath says that about six years ago she, this examinant, became a servant hired by the year to one Captain Hogan at Chelsea in the said county of Middlesex, with whom she continued and served for the space of two years and received her full wages for the said time at the rate of 50s. for the first year, and £3 for the last year. And that soon after she quitted the said service this examinant was hired to one Joseph Batts of Chelsea aforesaid, where she also continued about two years and received her full wages of her said master for the said time, at the rate of £3, meat, drink, washing and lodging. And says that since she quitted the said Mr Batt's service [she] has not lived a year in any place, or done any act, to the best of her knowledge, to gain a settlement. The mark of Jane Scott. Sworn at Chelsea, 27 Dec. 1745, before me, Peter Elers. [See **162, 169**].

162. [n.p.] The voluntary examination of Jane Scott, single woman, taken before me, Peter Elers esq. . . . . Middlesex. This examinant on her oath says that she is pregnant of a bastard child or children, which was unlawfully begotten on her body by one George Adlam, who lives with one Mr Giles, a potter at Chelsea in the said county, and who had carnal knowledge of this examinant's body the first time on or about 28 Mar. last in the dwelling house of Robert Hopperton (where this examinant lived a hired servant), and several times after in the said house and other places. And this examinant says that the said George Adlam is the true father of the said bastard child or children (when born). And further saith not. The mark of Jane Scott. Sworn at Chelsea, 27 Dec. 1745, before me, Peter Elers. [See **161, 169**].

163. [n.p.] Middlesex. James Townsend, constable of the parish of Chelsea in the county of Middlesex, came this 2 Jan. 1745/6 before me, one of His Majesty's justices of the peace for the said county, and made oath that he, this deponent, did this day apprehend Alice Furnivall with two small children wandering and begging and committing the act of vagrancy in the said parish of Chelsea. James Townsend, constable.

The examination of Alice Furnivall taken upon oath the said 2 Jan. 1745/6. Who saith that her husband, Ralph Furnivall, was late a soldier of Beauclerk's Regiment of Foot and is now absconded and left this deponent without any subsistence. And says, that she was married to her said husband about five years ago at Chester in the county of Cheshire, by whom she hath two children now living, vizt, Ralph, aged about 4 years, and Mary, an infant aged about 6 months. And this deponent further says that her said husband was born at Sandbach in the county of Cheshire aforesaid, and served his apprenticeship there for the term of seven years to a shoemaker. And also says that her said husband since the time of his apprenticeship as aforesaid has not rented a house of £10 a year, or paid any parochial taxes, or done any act or thing (to her knowledge) to gain a legal settlement. The mark of Alice Furnivall. Sworn at Chelsea before me, Peter Elers.

164. [n.p.] Middlesex. Edward Preston, watchmaker, upon oath says that his late brother, Samuel Preston, deceased, about the year 1707 was bound an apprentice for seven years to his father, Samuel Preston, carpenter, deceased, who at that time lived in Green Arbour Court, in the parish of St Sepulchres, London. And with whom he continued and served about five years of his apprenticeship, and from that time was a soldier in the late Queen Ann's wars, and was ordered over to Ireland, where he continued about the space of thirteen years. And this deponent says that his said brother since the time of his serving his apprenticeship as aforesaid has never rented a house of £10 a year, or paid any parochial taxes, or done any act or thing (to the best of his knowledge) to gain a legal settlement. Edward Preston. Sworn at Chelsea, 5 Jan. 1745/6, before me, Peter Elers.

165. [n.p.] Middlesex. Catherine Preston, widow, aged about 60 years, upon oath says that she was married soon after the great eclipse of the sun (which was in the year 1715) to Samuel Preston, carpenter, deceased, at the parish Church of St Brides in Dublin. And this examinant says that she is well informed by Edward Preston, her said late husband's brother, that her said late husband was bound an apprentice to his father, Samuel Preston, carpenter, deceased, who then lived in Green Arbour Court in the parish of St Sepulchres, London, and served about five years of his apprenticeship. And then he was entered a soldier in the late Queen Ann's wars and was ordered to Ireland. And [he] continued there for about thirteen years. And this examinant says that since the time of her husband serving his apprenticeship as aforesaid, he did not rent a house of £10 a year, or done any act or thing (to her knowledge) to gain a settlement. The mark of Catherine Preston. Sworn, 9 Jan. 1745/6, before me, Peter Elers, Richard Farwell. Sent to St Sepulchres, London.

166. [n.p.] Middlesex. James Pope, by trade a baker, aged about 68 years, born at Hempstead in Hertfordshire, upon oath says that he was married to Mary, his present wife (who is of the age of about 53 years), in May last in the liberty of the Fleet, London. And that in the years 1692–3 he, this examinant, was bound apprentice to one James Ward, a baker, who then lived in German Street in the parish of St James Westminster in the said county of Middlesex, where he continued and served his full apprenticeship for the term of seven years, meat, drink, washing and lodging. And says that his said master (James Ward) died when he had served about three years of his time. And that his widow afterwards married one Thomas Brown. And this examinant further says that since the time of his serving his apprenticeship as aforesaid [he] has not rented a house of £10 a year, or paid any taxes, or done any other act or thing, to the best of his knowledge, to gain a settlement. And also says that his wife being lame, is not capable to help herself. And this examinant being but an in pensioner in Chelsea College is not able to support his said wife. Signed by James Pope. Sworn, 11 Mar. 1745/6, before us, Peter Elers, Edward Impey. Mary Pope sent to St James.

167. [n.p.] Middlesex. Elizabeth Roson, widow, aged about 30 years, upon oath says that last New Years Day, was twelve month, she, this examinant, was married to her late husband, William Roson, shoemaker, deceased, in the liberty of the Fleet, London. By whom she hath one child living, named James who is of the age of about 15 months. And says that she never heard or can give an account of her said late husband's settlement, he being only a journeyman shoemaker at the time she married him. And as to her own settlement, before her marriage she says as follows, that about seven years ago she lived a servant hired by the year with one Mr Guerin in Henrietta Street in the parish of St Pauls Covent Garden in the county of Middlesex, with whom she continued and served two years as cook, and received her full wages of her said master at the rate of £5 a year, meat, drink, washing and lodging. And further says that she has not been a yearly hired servant or housekeeper since she quitted the said Mr Guerin's. Elizabeth Roson, her mark. Sworn, 12 Mar. 1745/6, before us, Peter Elers, J. Bromfield. Sent to St Paul Covent Garden.

168. [n.p.] William Rose, shoemaker, aged about 37 years, born in the parish of St Giles in the Fields in the county of Middlesex, upon oath says that about the year 1722 he, this examinant, was bound an apprentice for seven years to one Mr Jonas LeBatt, shoemaker, who at that time lodged in Lloyd's Court in the parish of St Giles in the Fields aforesaid, with whom he continued and served his full term of his apprenticeship. And says that his said master lived the last year of his apprenticeship in Lloyd's Court aforesaid. And also says that since the time of serving his apprenticeship as aforesaid he, this examinant, has not rented a house of £10 a year, or paid any parochial taxes, or done any act or thing whereby to gain a settlement (to the best of his knowledge). William Rose. Sworn, 20 Mar. 1745/6, before us, Peter Elers.

169. [n.p.] The examination of Jane Scott, single woman, taken upon oath before us, [blank] . . . Middlesex. Who saith that on 14 Feb. last she, this examinant, was delivered of a female bastard child (baptised and named Jane) in the workhouse in the parish of Chelsea in the said county of Middlesex. And was unlawfully begotten on her body by one George Adlam, who at that time lived with one Mr Giles, a potter in Chelsea aforesaid, who had carnal knowledge of her body the first time on or about 28 Mar. last, in the dwelling house of Robert Hopperton at Chelsea (where this examinant lived a servant), and several times after in the said house and other places. And this examinant says that the said George Adlam is the true father of the said female bastard child. And further says not. [Blank]. Sworn at Chelsea, [blank], before us, [blank]. [See **161**, **162**].

170. [n.p.] The voluntary examination of Mary Hughes, single woman, taken before me, Peter Elers esq. . . . Middlesex. This examinant on her oath says that she is pregnant of a bastard child or children which was unlawfully begotten on her body by one James Clayton, a chairman, who lodges at the sign of the Marlborough Head in Great Marlborough Street. Who had carnal knowledge of her body the first time at a house known by the sign of the Bunch of Grapes in a lane [Hartshorne Lane] almost opposite the Star Inn in the Strand near Hungerford Market, on or about 14 or 15 Aug. last, and at no other time. And this examinant says that the said James Clayton is the true father of the said bastard child or children (when born). And further saith not. Mary Hughes. Sworn at Chelsea, 12 Apr. 1746, before me, Peter Elers. [See **178**].

171. [n.p.] Middlesex. Thomas Fairbrother, shoemaker, upon oath says that in the year 1723 he, this examinant, was bound an apprentice for seven years to his uncle John Fairbrother, shoemaker, who at that time lived in White Harte Yard in Brook's Market in the parish of St Andrews Holborn above the Bars in the county of Middlesex. With whom he continued and served his full term of apprenticeship. And says that for the last two years of his time his said master lived in Spread Eagle Court in Gray's Inn Lane, which is in the said parish of St Andrews Holborn above the Bars. And says that his said master paid parochial taxes in the said parish of St Andrews Holborn. And this examinant further says that since the time of serving his said apprenticeship [he] has not rented a house of £10 a year, or paid any parochial taxes, or done any act or thing (to the best of his knowledge) to gain a legal settlement. And also says that he was married about twelve years since to Mary, his present wife, aged about 27 years, in the liberty of the Fleet, London, but has not any children by her living. Thomas Fairbrother. Sworn, 2 June 1746, before us, Peter Elers, Thomas DeVeil.

172. [n.p.] Middlesex. James Brown, shoemaker, aged about 57 years, upon oath says that he was born in Hungerford Market in the parish of St Martin in the Fields in the county of Middlesex. And that he was bound apprentice for seven years to one William Honnor of the parish [of] Lambeth in the county of Surrey, shoemaker, with whom he continued and served about three years of his said time, and was then turned over to one Mr Killway, a shoemaker who lived in Cloth Fair in the parish of St Bartholomew [blank], London, where he continued about half a year. And was again turned over to one Jacob Webb, shoemaker, who lived at Charing Cross in the said parish of St Martin in the Fields, where he continued and served the remainder and full term of his apprenticeship. And says that since the serving his apprenticeship as aforesaid he has not paid any parochial taxes, or done any act or thing, to his knowledge, to gain a settlement. James Brown. Sworn, 22 July 1746, before us, Peter Elers, Henry Villiers.

173. [n.p.] Middlesex. George Alexander, aged about 70 years, an in pensioner of Chelsea Hospital, upon oath says that he, this examinant, by indenture bearing date 12 July 1734 bound his son David Alexander (who is about 25 years of age) to one William Darlington of the parish of St Giles in the Fields in the said county, barber surgeon, for the term of seven years. With whom he continued and served till 18 October 1737 when the said David Alexander was again bound an apprentice for four years (as appears by the said respective recited indentures) to one John Nisson of the parish of St Paul Covent Garden in the said county, peruke maker, with him he continued and served the said term of four years (wanting about twelve days or there[abouts]). And this examinant also says that his said son David Alexander since the time of his serving his apprentice[ship] in manner as aforesaid has not lived a year a hired servant in any place, or rented a house of £10 a year, or done any act or thing (to his knowledge) to gain a settlement. And further says that his said son being lame and at present not in his reason is not capable to support and maintain himself without relief. George Alexander. Sworn, 4 Aug. 1746, before us, Peter Elers, Henry Villiers.

174. [n.p.] Middlesex. Thomas Coules, carpenter, aged about 51 years, upon oath says that he was born at Binstead in Hampshire and that about 30 years ago he was bound apprentice for seven years to one Henry Hammond of the parish of Alton in Hampshire aforesaid, carpenter. With whom he continued and served about five years and half of his said time and was then turned over to one John Watts of the parish or town of Farnham in the county of Surrey, carpenter. With whom he served the remainder and full term of his said apprenticeship. And this examinant says that since the time of serving his term of apprenticeship as aforesaid he has not rented a house of £10 a year, or paid any parochial taxes, or done any act (to his knowledge) to gain a settlement. And also says that he has four children living by Mary his late wife; vizt, Elizabeth, aged about 22 years, Allieueser, aged about 19 years, Thomas, aged about 13 years, and James, aged about 10 years. The mark of Thomas Coules. Sworn at Chelsea, 13 Sept. 1746, before me, Peter Elers.

175. [n.p.] Middlesex. William Stapleton, husbandman, aged about 60 years, born in the parish of St Anns in the liberty of Westminster in the county of Middlesex, upon oath says that about 30 years ago he, this examinant, became a servant hired by the year to Mr George Burr of Chelsea, gardener, with whom he continued and served about the space of three years and received his full wages for the said time at the rate of £5 per annum, meat, drink, washing and lodging. And says that since he lived with Mr Burr as aforesaid he, this examinant, has not lived a hired servant a year or rented a house of £10 per annum, or paid any parochial taxes, or done any act (to his knowledge) to gain a settlement. The mark of William Stapleton. Sworn this, 11 Oct. 1746, before me, Peter Elers.

176. [n.p.] Middlesex, to wit. The voluntary examination of Martha Kemp, widow, taken upon oath before us, King Gould and Peter Elers, esqs . . . Who saith that on Sunday 9 Nov. last past she, this examinant, was delivered of a male bastard child in the dwelling House of Mrs Jane Dawson in Lordship Yard in Chelsea in the county of Middlesex (which is baptised and named John). And was unlawfully begotten on her body by one Mr John Hamilton a dealer in Scotch linen, now living at one Mr Youngs, a Broker, in High Holborn. Who had carnal knowledge of her body the first time the day after Michaelmas day last, was twelve month, in the room where the said John Hamilton then lodged at Mrs [blank] Ogelby's in Cecil Court in St Martin's Lane and where this examinant lived a hired servant, and had carnal knowledge several times after in the said house. and this examinant further saith that the said John Hamilton is the true father of the said child. And further saith not. The mark of Martha Kemp. Sworn at Chelsea, 9 Jan. 1746/7, before us, Peter Elers, King Gould.

177. [n.p.] Middlesex. Anne Sprew, aged about 45 years, the wife of Thomas Sprew, mariner, upon oath says that about 27 years ago she, this examinant, was married to her said husband in the liberty of the Fleet, London, by whom she has a daughter named Mary, a single woman aged about 24 years, who has always lived with this examinant ever since she was born. And says that her said husband, before her marriage with him served his apprenticeship to one Thomas Clark, a green grocer, who than lived in Eagle and Child Yard near the church in the parish of St Giles in the Field in the said county of Middlesex. And also says that her husband from the time of her said marriage has not rented a house of £10 a year, or paid any parochial taxes, or done any act or thing (to the best of her knowledge) to gain a settlement. And further says that her said husband, about 22 years since, went to sea and that she has not seen him since. The mark of Anne Sprew. Sworn, 20 Feb. 1746/7, before us, Thomas Burdus, Peter Elers.

178. [n.p.] Middlesex. The voluntary examination of Mary Hughes, single woman, taken upon oath before us, Thomas Burdus and Peter Elers, esqs . . . Who saith that 7 May last past she, this examinant, was delivered of a female bastard child (baptised and named Frances) in the dwelling house of one Mr Harris in a place called Jew's Row in the parish of Chelsea in the said county of Middlesex. And was unlawfully begotten on her body by one James Clayton, a chairman, who then lodged at the sign of the Marlborough Head in Great Marlborough Street. Who had carnal knowledge of her body at a house then known by the sign of the Bunch of Grapes in Hartshorne Lane in the parish of St Martin in the Fields in the said county on or about 14 Aug. last, was twelve month, and at no other time. And this examinant saith that the said James Clayton is the true father of the said child. And further saith not. Mary Hughes. Sworn, 28 Feb. 1746/7, before us, Thomas Burdus, Peter Elers. [See **170**].

179. [n.p.] Middlesex. William Swaine, gardener, upon oath saith that Jane Allcock, spinster, aged about 40 years, lived a servant hired by the year with Mrs Sarah Horton in that part of the parish of St George Hanover Square in the said county of Middlesex next Chelsea. With whom she continued and served a year and half, and received her full wages for the said time, meat, drink, washing and lodging. And this examinant says that the said Jane Allcock left the service of the said Mrs Horton about three weeks ago, and has not gained a settlement since. And further says that the said Jane Allcock is not capable to provide for herself, she being a lunatic. [Blank]. Sworn, [blank] June 1747, before us, [blank].

180. [n.p.] Middlesex. Elizabeth Brittain (the wife of Richard Brittain, an out pensioner of Chelsea Hospital, and late of the late Colonel Anthony Lowther's Regiment of Marines), upon oath saith that her husband and family lodges at one Mrs Harris's in Jew's Row in the parish of Chelsea. And that she had a child (named Dinah) [that] died there last Saturday. And says that her said husband being but an out pensioner of the said hospital is in very mean and poor circumstances and not able to pay the charges of the burial of the child, which obliges her to apply to the parish officers for relief. And further saith that she has two children living by her said husband; vizt, Elizabeth, aged about 3 years and Susanna, an infant aged 11 weeks. And that she is so much distressed that she has pawned most of her cloths for the present support of her family, her husband having taken up his pension money of the said Mrs Harris, where he now lodges to Christmas next. Elizabeth Brittain, her mark. Sworn at Chelsea, before me, Peter Elers.

181. b [n.p.] Middlesex. Elizabeth Rumney, aged about 28 years, the wife of Valentine Rumney, upon oath says that in June 1740 she, this examinant, was married to her said husband in the liberty of the Fleet, London, by whom she has a son living, named Valentine, who is aged about 4 years. And this examinant says that her said husband before her marriage with him lived a servant hired by the year with one Councillor White about ten years ago in Took's Court, which is in the parish of St Andrews Holborn above the Bars in the county of Middlesex, with whom he continued and served upwards of seven years. And this examinant has heard and believes her said husband received his full wages for the said time of his said master at the rate of £6 per annum, meat, drink, washing and lodging. And this examinant further says that her said husband since his living with Councillor White aforesaid has not rented a house of £10 a year or done any act or thing (to the best of her knowledge) to gain a settlement. And also says that her husband (as she is informed) is gone to Ireland, and being with child and near her time, [she] is not capable to support herself without relief. Elizabeth Rumney. Sworn, 7 Sept. 1747, before us, Peter Elers, Thomas Burdus. Passed to the parish of St Andrews Holborn above the Bars.

182. [n.p.] Middlesex. Barbara Frampton, single woman, aged about 30 years, upon oath says that she lived a servant hired by the year with Mr Robert Arther who keeps White's Chocolate House in the parish of St James in the liberty of Westminster in the county of Middlesex, with whom she continued and served upwards of a year and received £5 a year wages of her said master, meat, drink, washing and lodging. And says that since she, this examinant, quitted the said service of Mr Arther (which was about two years ago), [she] has not lived a year in service, or done any act or thing (to the best of her knowledge) to gain a settlement. Barbara Frampton. Sworn, 15 Dec. 1747, before us, Peter Elers, Thomas Burdus. Passed to St James Westminster. [See **117**].

183. [n.p.] Middlesex. Mary Groom, aged about 38 years (the wife of Thomas Groom), upon oath says that she, this examinant, was married about eleven years since to her said husband at the parish church of St Mary Le Strand in the liberty of Westminster in the county of Middlesex. By whom this examinant has five children living; vizt, Elizabeth, aged about 9 years, Mary, aged 7 years, William, aged about 5 years, Thomas, aged near 3 years, and Jonas, an infant, aged a year and upwards. And says that her said husband's last place of service before her marriage was with the late Mr Kingsmil Eyre, secretary of Chelsea Hospital, with whom he lived a hired servant a year and upwards, and received his full wages of his said master for the said time at the rate of £8 8s. a year, meat, drink, washing and lodging. And this examinant also says that her said husband since living a servant with the late Mr Eyre as aforesaid has not rented a house of £10 a year, or paid any parochial taxes, or done any act or thing (to the best of her knowledge) to gain a legal settlement. And further says that her said husband, being dangerously ill of a pleurisy, is not capable of providing for his said family without relief from the parish. [Blank].

184. [n.p.] Middlesex. Anne Jordan, aged about 48 years, the widow of the late William Jordan, tailor, deceased, upon oath says that about sixteen years ago she, this examinant, was married to her said late husband at the parish church of Chelsea in the county of Middlesex, by whom this examinant has three children living; vizt, Anne, aged about 15 years (who is now in service), Alexander, aged about 13 years, and George, who is of the age of 11 years and upwards. And this examinant says that from the year 1734 to 1737 her said late husband rented a house in Swallow Street which is in the parish of St James, Westminster, where they paid £26 a year rent and parochial taxes, as appears by the overseers of the poor's receipts of the said parish. And says that after they quitted the said house her said late husband rented a house in Princess Street in the parish of St Ann, Westminster at the yearly rent of £16, where they continued about three years and half, and paid parochial taxes for the same. And says that when they quitted the last mentioned house her said late husband rented a house in Little Marlborough Street at the yearly rent of £18 (which is in the parish of St James, Westminster, aforesaid) and continued in the said last mentioned house for the space of three years and upwards, but was excused paying any parochial taxes. And this examinant further says that since her said late husband quitted the said house in Little Marlborough Street as aforesaid her said late husband has not rented a house of £10 a year, or paid any parochial taxes, or done any act or thing (to the best of her knowledge) whereby to gain a legal settlement. And this examinant also says that her said late husband, having been dead about three months, [she] is not capable of providing for herself and children with out some relief of the parish. The mark of Anne Jordan. Sworn, 8 Feb. 1747/8, before us, Peter Elers, Luke Robinson. Passed to St James, Westminster.

185. [n.p.] Middlesex. Sarah Curtis, aged about 53 years, the widow of Edward Curtis, bricklayer, deceased, upon oath says that she, this examinant was married to her said late husband about 25 years ago in the liberty of the Fleet, London. By whom she had four children, one of which is living, named Mary, aged about 18 years (who is provided for). And this examinant says that her said husband was bound an apprentice to one Mr Kilcott of the parish of Kensington in the county of Middlesex, bricklayer, with whom he served his full term of apprenticeship. And this examinant also says that her said late husband since the time of his serving his said apprenticeship has not rented a house of £10 a year, or done any act, to her knowledge, to gain a settlement. The mark of Sarah Curtis. Sworn, 9 Feb. 1747/8, before us, Peter Elers, Luke Robinson. Passed to Kensington.

186. [n.p.] Middlesex. Martha Winter, aged about 33 years, the wife of Richard Winter, distiller, upon oath says that about fifteen years ago she was married to her said husband at the parish church of St Katherine near the Tower, London, by whom she had five children (all dead). And says that her said husband being reduced but to mean and low circumstances was forced to enter himself as a marine and has been abroad about eight years. And further says that the last house her said husband lived in before he absconded and left this examinant was in Carnaby Street in the parish of St James, Westminster in the said county of Middlesex, at the yearly rent of £20, where he continued about two years and paid parochial taxes for the same. The mark of Martha Winter. Sworn, 19 February 1747/8, before us, Peter Elers, Thomas Burdus. Passed to St James, Westminster.

187. [n.p.] Middlesex. Mary Lunn, aged about 40 years, the wife of Daniel Lunn, wine cooper, upon oath says that she, this examinant, about seven years ago was married to her said husband at the parish church of Lambeth in the county of Surrey, by whom she hath had three children, one of which is living, named Mary, an infant who is of the age of 14 months. And says that her said husband was bound an apprentice to one Mr Bodicoate of Cruched Friars in the parish of St Katherine Coleman, London, wine cooper, with whom he continued and served his full term of apprentice-ship. And says that her said husband since the time of serving Mr Bodicoate as aforesaid has not rented a house of £10 a year, or paid any parochial taxes, or done any act or thing (to the best of her knowledge) to gain a legal settlement. And further says that her said husband being gone for Barbados she, this examinant, is not capable to provide for herself and child without relief. And [she] is big with child and near her time. Mary Lunn. Sworn, 7 Mar. 1747/8, before us, Peter Elers, Luke Robinson. Passed to St Katherine Coleman.

188. [n.p.] Middlesex. Melon Thompson, widow, aged about 76 years, upon oath says that about 60 years ago she was married to her first husband, John Banfield, at the church at Stepney in the county of Middlesex, who was a foreigner and came over with King William and died in about fifteen months after she was married to him. And says that after her said first husband died she, this examinant, rented a house for three years in Red Lyon Street in the parish of St Mary at Whitechapel in the said county of Middlesex, and paid £10 a year rent for the same and all parochial taxes. And also says that about ten years ago she was married to one James Thompson, who was an in pensioner of Chelsea Hospital and had been always a soldier from the time he was capable of serving in the army. And says that he was a Scotsman and never rented a house of £10 a year, or paid any parochial taxes, or done any act or thing, to the best of her knowledge, to gain a settlement. Melon Thompson, her mark. Sworn, 26 Apr. 1748, before us, Peter Elers, J. Poulson. Passed to St Mary Whitechapel.

189. [n.p.] Middlesex. Rebecca Clements, single woman, aged about 21 years, upon oath says that she, this examinant, about three years ago lived a servant hired by the year with Mr Andrew Banton, parish clerk of Chelsea in the county of Middlesex, with whom she continued and served for the space of two years and received her full wages of the said Mr Banton at the rate of 50s. per annum, meat, drink, washing and lodging. And says that since the time of living with Mr Banton as aforesaid she, this examinant, has not been a hired servant a year in any place, or paid any parochial taxes, or done any act or thing, to the best of her knowledge, to gain a settlement. Rebecca Clement, her mark. Sworn, 29 Apr. 1748, before me, Peter Elers. Passed from Wandsworth in Surrey. [See **190**].

190. [n.p.] Middlesex. The voluntary examination of Rebecca Clements, single woman, taken upon oath before me, Peter Elers esq. . . . This examinant on her oath says that she is pregnant of a bastard child or children which was or were unlawfully begotten on her body by one Mr John Coustos, a jeweller, who now lodges at a house in Tibals Row near Red Lyon Square, London. And says that he had carnal knowledge of her body the first time about two years ago at the Angel Inn behind St Clements Church, London, and several times after at the said inn. And particularly about eight months ago at a house known by the sign of the Cheshire Cheese near the creek adjoining to Chelsea in the said county of Middlesex. And this examinant further says that the said John Coustos is the true father of the said child or children (when born). And further saith not. The mark of Rebecca Clements. Sworn, 29 Apr. 1748, before me, Peter Elers. [See **189**].

191. [n.p.] Middlesex. The voluntary examination of Elizabeth Edwards, widow, taken upon oath before us Luke Robinson and Peter Elers, esqs . . . Who says that on 11 Apr. last past she, this examinant, was delivered of a male bastard child in the workhouse of the parish of Chelsea in the said county of Middlesex (which is baptised and named Thomas). And was unlawfully begotten on her body by one Richard Jones of Chelsea, waterman, who had carnal knowledge of her body the first time at the dwelling house of the said Richard Jones at Chelsea aforesaid about three years ago. At which time this examinant nursed his wife in her lying-in. And this examinant says frequently afterwards in the said house and other places, and particularly at an apartment of her sister Mary's in Chelsea Park, until she proved with child by him, and several times after. And this examinant also says that the said Richard Jones is the true father of the said child. And further says not. The mark of Elizabeth Edwards. Sworn, 21 May 1748, before us, Peter Elers, Luke Robinson.

192. [n.p.] Middlesex. Mary Poole, single woman, aged about 46 years, born at Weston in Staffordshire, upon oath says that about 25 years ago she, this examinant, lived a servant hired by the year with one James Lesley late of Chelsea, gardener, with whom she continued and served two years and received of her said master her full wages [for] the said time, at the rate of £4 a year, meat, drink, washing and lodging. And says that since she left the said service of Mr Lesley she, this examinant, has not lived a whole year in any service, or done any act or thing, to the best of her knowledge, to gain a settlement. The mark of Mary Poole. Sworn, 21 May 1748, before us, Peter Elers.

193. [n.p.] Middlesex. Mary Mascall (widow of Charles Mascall, deceased), aged about 60 years, born in the parish of St Margaret, Westminster, upon oath says that about fifteen years ago she, this examinant, was married to her said late husband at the parish church of St Margaret, Westminster aforesaid. Says that her said late husband was an Irishman (as she always counted) and a captain in Chelsea Hospital. And [he] never rented a house of £10 a year, or paid any parochial taxes, or done any act or thing (to her knowledge) to gain a settlement since he came from Ireland. And this examinant says that her father (whose name was Edward Mascall) was a baker and lived in his own house in Millbank, which was then in the said parish of St Margaret, Westminster, with whom this examinant lived till she was 30 years of age. And says that the last place she lived in before she was married to her said husband was with one Mr Lock, a carpenter, in Channel Row in the parish of St Margaret, Westminster, aforesaid, and with whom she continued and served a year and upwards, and received her full wages at the rate of £6 a year, meat, drink, washing and lodging. Mary Mascall. Sworn, 2 Sept. 1748, before us, Peter Elers, J. Poulson. Passed to St Margaret, Westminster. St Margaret, Westminster, appealed and upon trial her settlement was found to be at Gillingham in Dorsetshire. Vide the examination of William Mascall two leaves further. [See **196, 315**].

194. [n.p.] Middlesex. Elizabeth Shurkett, widow, aged about 30 years, upon oath says that about six years and half ago she, this examinant, lived a hired servant a year and upwards with one Mr John Hanover of Tuttle Fields in the parish of St Margaret in the liberty of Westminster in the county of Middlesex, cow keeper, and received her full wages of her said master for the said time at the rate of £3 a year, meat, drink, washing and lodging. And says, that about a half a year after she quitted the said service of Mr Hanover's she was married to her late husband, Christopher Shurkett, in the liberty of the Fleet, London, by whom she has two children living; vizt, Joseph, aged about 4 years, and Mary, about 2 years. And says that her said husband was an in pensioner of Chelsea Hospital and an Irishman, and never gained a settlement (to this examinant's knowledge) since he came from Ireland, by renting a house, or paying parochial taxes. And this examinant further says that she having had a hurt in her back is not able to work to maintain herself and two children. The mark of Elizabeth Shurkett. Sworn, 2 Sept. 1748, before us, Peter Elers, J. Poulson.

195. [n.p.] Middlesex. John Chappel, aged about 65 years, born in Old White Lyon Street near the Seven Dials in the parish of St Giles in the Fields in the county of Middlesex, where his father (as he was informed) was a lodger, and that his father was only a labourer and worked for bricklayers and never was a housekeeper, as he ever heard. And this examinant says that in the year 1718 he was married to Margaret, his present wife, near Aberdeen in Scotland. And says that since the time of his birth as aforesaid he has not rented a house of £10 a year, or paid any parochial taxes, or done any act or thing, to his knowledge, to gain a settlement. And further says that he being but an in pensioner of Chelsea Hospital is in low circumstances and not capable of supporting his said wife without relief. John Chappel. Sworn, 2 Sept. 1748, before us, Peter Elers, J. Poulson. [See **266**].

196. [n.p.] Middlesex. William Mascall of Falmouth in the county of Cornwall, gentleman, upon oath says that his late uncle, Charles Mascall, was born at a place called Gillingham in Dorsetshire (as he has been credibly informed and verily believes). And says that from the time of such his birth he never knew or heard that his said uncle ever rented a house of £10 a year or paid any parochial taxes, or done any act or thing (to the best of this examinant's knowledge) to gain a settlement. But says that his said uncle was a trooper in the late Queen Ann's wars, and was afterwards an in pensioner of Chelsea Hospital, and was a captain there at the time of his death, which was about six month since. William Mascall. Sworn, 13 Oct. 1748, before us, Peter Elers, Francis Hale. [See **193, 315**].

197. [n.p.] Middlesex. John Kimberly, basket maker, aged about 30 years, born at Eaton in Buckinghamshire, upon oath says that about seventeen years ago he, this examinant, was bound apprentice by a charitable gift belonging to Eton College to one John Pearless esq., of the parish of St George in the borough of Southwark in the county of Surrey, basket maker, for the term of seven years. With whom he continued and served his full term of apprenticeship and was made free of the Haberdashers' Company (of which his said master was a liveryman). And says that since which time of serving his apprenticeship as aforesaid he, this examinant, has not rented a house of £10 a year, or paid any parochial taxes, or done

62

any act or thing (to the best of his knowledge) to gain a settlement. John Kimberly. Sworn, 3 Feb. 1748/9, before us, Peter Elers, Henry Fielding. Passed to St George in the borough [of Southwark].

198. [n.p.] Middlesex. Elizabeth Inwood, single woman, aged about 40 years, upon oath says that about nine years ago she, this examinant, lived a servant hired by the year with Mr John Savage, vintner at the sign of Pontac, in Abchurch Lane in the parish of [St Mary] Abchurch in the city of London, with whom she continued and served in the station of a housemaid for the space of one whole year. And [she] received her full wages for the said time, which was £5 10s., meat, drink, washing and lodging. And further says that since the time of her quitting the said service of Mr Savage [she] has not rented a house of £10 a year, or paid any parochial taxes, or done any act, to the best of her knowledge, to gain a settlement. Elizabeth Inwood, her mark. Sworn, 10 Feb. 1748/9, before us, Peter Elers, Henry Fielding. Passed to the parish of St Mary Abchurch. [See **146**].

199. [n.p.] Middlesex. William Sexton, labourer, aged about 25 years, upon oath says that he was born (as he has been informed and verily believes) in the parish of Teddington in the county of Middlesex and that he was baptised and registered in the said parish. And says that since the time of his birth he, this examinant, has not rented a house of £10 a year, or been bound an apprentice, or been a yearly servant, or done any act or thing, to the best of his knowledge, to gain a settlement. And also says that having a wound in his back which is in danger of a mortification [he] is not able to work to maintain himself, and therefore cannot subsist without relief. William Sexton, his mark. Sworn, 10 Feb. 1748/9, before us, Peter Elers, Henry Fielding. Passed to Teddington.

200. [n.p.] Middlesex. Rebecca Guilford, single woman, aged about 28 years, born at Chelsea in Middlesex, upon oath says that about nine years ago she, this examinant, lived a hired servant with one Mr Charles Palmer in King Street in the parish of St James, Westminster, in the county of Middlesex aforesaid, with whom she continued and served a whole year and upwards, and received her full wages for the said time at the rate of 40s. per annum, meat, drink, washing and lodging. And say that since the time of her living with Mr Palmer as aforesaid, she, this examinant, has not rented a house of £10 a year, or paid any parochial taxes, or done any act, or lived a year in service, to gain a settlement. Rebecca Guilford, her mark. Sworn, 17 Feb. 1748/9, before us, Peter Elers, Luke Robinson. Passed to St James, Westminster.

201. [n.p.] Middlesex. The voluntary examination of Martha Howard, single woman, taken upon oath before me Peter Elers esq. . . . Who says that on Candlemas Day, being 2 Feb. last, she, this examinant, was delivered of a female bastard child in an apartment of one William Downing, gardener, in the stable yard behind Sir Hans Sloane's dwelling house in the parish of Chelsea in the said county of Middlesex (which was baptised and named Sarah). And was unlawfully begotten on her body by one Augustine Cooper of Richmond Park in the parish of Mortlake in the county of Surrey, husbandman, who had carnal knowledge of her body the first time in Richmond Park aforesaid, in or about the month of April last, and several times after in the said park and other places. And this examinant also says that the said Augustine Cooper is the true father of the said child. And further says not. The mark of Martha Howard. Sworn, 21st Mar. 1748/9, before me, Peter Elers.

202. [n.p.] Middlesex. Margery Iliffe, widow, aged about 49 years, upon oath says that about nine years ago she, this examinant, was married to her late husband (William Iliffe) in the liberty of the Fleet London, who was at the time she married him an in pensioner of Chelsea Hospital. And says that her said late husband in his lifetime often declared and informed this examinant that he was born at Nether Kibworth in Leicestershire, and that he served his apprenticeship to the business or trade of a woolcomber in the said town of Nether Kibworth. And says that her said late husband also informed and told her that after he had served his apprenticeship as aforesaid that he entered himself a soldier in the army, in which station he continued till he died at a place called Upton Castle near the garrison of Shurny. And this examinant further says that she does not know or ever heard that her said late husband ever rented a house of £10 a year, or paid any parochial taxes, or done any act or thing (to her knowledge) to gain a settlement, since he served his apprenticeship as aforesaid. The mark of Margery Iliffe. Sworn, 12 Mar. 1748/9, before us, Peter Elers, Henry Fielding. Passed to Kebworth in Leicestershire.

203. [n.p.] Middlesex. Elizabeth Holland, single woman, aged about 32 years, the lawful daughter of Edward Holland, deceased, by Christiana Holland his wife, also deceased, upon oath says that her said late father (as she has been credibly informed and of her own knowledge has some remembrance) rented a house upwards of 20 years ago in King's Street in the parish of St Ann in the liberty of Westminster in the county of Middlesex, known by the sign of the Red Lion, which was a public house, for and about the term of five years and at the yearly rent of £14, and paid all parochial taxes for the same. And says that some years after her said late father quitted the said house he was admitted an in pensioner of Chelsea Hospital, where he continued till he died (which is about a month since). And this examinant further says that her said late father, after he left the said house in St Ann parish, did not rent a house of ten pounds a year, or paid any parochial taxes, or done any act or thing (to her knowledge) to gain a legal settlement. The mark of Elizabeth Holland. Sworn, 4 Apr. 1749, before us, Thomas Ellys, Peter Elers. Passed to St Ann.

204. [n.p.] Middlesex. Susanna Jones, aged upwards of 30 years, the widow of Thomas Jones, deceased, upon oath says that in April 1743 she was married to her said late husband in the liberty of the Fleet, London, and in the presence of her kinswoman, one Frances Allen, who keeps a public house at Kensington gravel pits. And says that her said late husband was bound an apprentice in the year 1739 (as appears by his indenture) to one John Partridge of Kensington in the county of Middlesex, peruke maker, for the term of seven years, with whom he continued and served out almost all his apprenticeship, when his master gave him up his indentures. After which, her said late husband entered himself a soldier in the marine service and went to Newfoundland where he died (as this examinant has since been informed). And this examinant says that her said late husband had not done any act (to her knowledge) to gain a settlement since he served his apprenticeship aforesaid. And this examinant also says that she has a child living (named Mary), aged about 18 months, born in the dwelling house of one Mr George Walker at Kensington Gore in the parish of Kensington aforesaid, which was unlawfully begotten on her body by one Benjamin Smith, a gardener. But this examinant further says and declares that she was never married to the said Benjamin Smith, though they lived and cohabited together as man and wife. Susanna Jones, her mark. Sworn, 4 Apr. 1749, before us, Thomas Ellys, Peter Elers. Passed to Kensington.

205. [n.p.] Middlesex. Alice Mason, aged about near 40 years, the wife of Dennis Mason, gardener, upon oath says that she, this examinant, about seven years ago was married to her said husband at the parish church of Kensington in the county of Middlesex, by whom she hath four children living; vizt, Dennis, aged near 6 years, John, aged 4 years and upwards, Hester, aged about 3 years, and Elizabeth, an infant aged about 3 months. And this examinant says that her said husband (before marriage) lived as a servant hired by the year with one Mr Richard Newton at Little Chelsea in the parish of Kensington aforesaid in the station of a gardener, where he continued and served a whole year and upwards. And says that he received of his said master his full wages for the said time at the rate of ten pounds per annum, meat, drink, washing and lodging. And this examinant also says that her said husband after he quitted Mr Newton's service has not rented a house of £10 a year, or paid any parochial taxes, or done any act (to her knowledge) to gain a legal settlement. And this examinant further says that her said husband, being absconded and gone from her, and taken with him one of her children only (named John), [she] is not capable of supporting the other three children without some relief. Alice Mason, her mark. Sworn, 4 April 1749, before us, Thomas Ellys, Peter Elers. Passed to Kensington; vizt, Alice Mason and three of her children, Dennis, Hester and Elizabeth. John, the father took away.

206. [n.p.] Middlesex. Elizabeth Wells, widow, aged about 27 years, upon oath says that about eleven years ago she was married to her first husband, John Dennison, at the Roman Catholic Chapel in Lincoln Inn Fields, London, by whom she has a child living (named Sarah), who is 5 years of age and upward, and was born in the parish of Chelsea in the county of Middlesex. And this examinant says that her said first husband was a peruke maker by trade and an Irishman. And [she] does not know that he ever rented a house of £10 a year, or paid any parochial taxes, or done any act or thing (to her knowledge) to gain a settlement. And this examinant also says that the last place that she lived in as a hired servant before her said marriage with her first husband was with one Mr Cornelius who then kept the Rose Tavern at Temple Bar in the parish of St Clement Danes in the said county. With whom she continued and served one year and upward and received her full wages of her said master at the rate of £5 a year, meat, drink, washing and lodging. And this examinant further says that about four years ago she was married to her second husband (William Wells, deceased) who was a parishioner in Chelsea aforesaid. And says that she is not capable of supporting her said child without some relief. Elizabeth Wells, her mark. Sworn, 29 May 1749, before us, Peter Elers, Thomas Ellys. Passed to St Clement Danes.

207. [n.p.] Middlesex. Hannah Elliett, aged about 18 years, the wife of George Elliet, upon oath says that on 31 May last, was twelve month, she, this examinant, was married to her said husband in the liberty of the Fleet, London, by whom she has a child living (named Mary), an infant aged near 3 months. And says that her said husband is by trade or employment a tailor, and that he learnt it of his uncle at Drogheda in Ireland without serving an apprenticeship. And says that her said husband has been a soldier and is now an out pensioner of Chelsea Hospital, and does not know that he ever rented a house of £10 a year, or done any act, to her knowledge, to gain a settlement. And this examinant says that as to herself, she has not lived a year in any service before her marriage, but says that her late father (Edward Penny) served his apprenticeship with one Mr Hugh Hopkins, a lighterman, then of the parish of St Olave, but now the parish of St John in the borough of Southwark in the county of Surrey, with whom he continued and served the full term of his apprenticeship (as this examinant has been informed by her mother now living). And that her said late father from the time he served his apprenticeship, had never rented a house of £10 a year, or paid any parish taxes, or done any act (to her knowledge), to gain a subsequent settlement. And this examinant further says that her said husband being absconded and left her, [she] is not capable of providing for her said child without relief. Hannah Elliet, her mark. Sworn, 6 June 1749, before us, Peter Elers, Henry Fielding. Passed to St John in Southwark.

208. [n.p.] Middlesex. John Oridge, aged about 52 years, born at Pentrich in the county of Derby, upon oath says that about 40 years ago he, this examinant, was bound an apprentice to one William Wakefield of Arnold in the county Nottingham, carpenter, for the term of seven years. With whom he continued and served upwards of five years only of his apprenticeship, and then entered himself a soldier in a marching regiment of foot, and continued in the army about 27 years. And upon his discharge was admitted an out pensioner of Chelsea Hospital (where he now belongs). And says that since the time of serving part of his apprenticeship he, this examinant, has not rented a house of £10 a year, or paid any parochial taxes, or done any act (to the best of his knowledge) to gain a settlement. And says that about ten years ago he, this examinant, was married at Dublin to Elizabeth, his present wife, by whom he has two children living; vizt, Stephen, aged near 7 years, and Catherine, aged near 3 years. And further says that his said wife being absconded and gone away from him, and having no other subsistence than the said out pension, and not able to support his said children. The mark of John Oridge. Sworn the 12 June 1749, before us, Peter Elers.

209. [n.p.] Middlesex. Elizabeth Mason, widow, aged near 63 years, upon oath says that about 27 years ago she was married to her late husband, Daniel Mason, at the parish church of Whitby in Worcestershire, by whom she has a daughter living, named Mary Mason, a single woman, aged near 25 years. And says that about five years ago her said daughter lived a servant hired by the year with one Mr Lowe, a dancing master in Great James which is in the parish of St Andrews Holborn above the Bars in the county of Middlesex. With whom she continued and served a whole year and upwards, and received her full wages of her said master at the rate of £3 10s. a year, meat, drink, washing and lodging. And this examinant also says that her said daughter has not lived [a] year in any other service since she quitted that of the said Mr Lowe, or done any other act to gain a settlement. But says that her said daughter being now afflicted with lunacy, and the said examinant herself in very mean and low circumstances, [she] is not capable of providing, or taking care of her in order for a cure without relief. Elizabeth Mason. Sworn, 1 July 1749, before us, Peter Elers, John Gascoyne. Passed to St Andrew Holborn above the Bars.

210. [n.p.] Middlesex. The voluntary examination of Dorothea Fielding, widow, taken upon oath before us, Peter Elers and Thomas Ellys, esqs . . . Who says that on 31 Dec. last she, this examinant, was delivered of a female bastard child in the house belonging to one Mr Hoddy in that part of Little Chelsea which is in the parish of Great Chelsea in the county of Middlesex aforesaid (which child is baptised and named Mary). And was unlawfully begotten on her body by one Mr Richard Vincent the elder, a musician living at the Turks head and Cock in Bedford Street in the parish of St Paul Covent Garden in the said county. Who had carnal knowledge of her body the first time in the dwelling house of Mrs Thorogood in Panton Square near Leicester Fields, and several times after in the said house and other places. And this examinant also says that the said Richard Vincent is the true father of the said child. And further saith not. Dorothea Fielding. Sworn, 27 June 1749, before us, Peter Elers, Thomas Ellys.

211. [n.p.] Middlesex. Francis Dolley, husbandman, aged 63 years and upwards, born at a place called Bramley within four miles of Basingstoke in Hampshire, upon oath says that upwards of 40 years ago he, this examinant, lived servant hired by the year with Mr John Chase of the parish of Hartley (where Lord Stowell's seat is) near Basingstoke aforesaid, yeoman. With whom he continued and served three years and received his

full wages for the said time at the rate of £5 10s. a year, meat, drink, washing and lodging. And says that since the time of his living with the said Mr Chase as aforesaid [he] has not been a servant a year in any place, or rented a house of £10 a year, or done any act (to his knowledge) to gain a legal settlement. The mark of Francis Dolly, Sworn, 8 Sept. 1749, before us, Philip Dyos, Thomas Berry. Passed to Hartley.

212. [n.p.] Middlesex, to wit. John King, apothecary, aged about 67 years, upon oath says that he was born at Mecklenburg in Germany. Says that he has lived in and near London upwards of 22 years and followed his said business as a journeyman apothecary most part of the time. And says that the first place where he lived after he came to England was, a hired servant by the year (about twenty years since), with one Mr Anthony Dalbis, an apothecary, who then lived in Great Suffolk Street in the parish of St Martin in the Fields in the county of Middlesex. With whom he continued and served the space of two years and upwards, and received of his said master (Mr Dalbis) for the first year, £10, and for the remainder of the said time at the rate of £12 wages, meat, drink, washing and lodging. And this examinant further says that he has not lived a year in any other service since he left that of the said Mr Dalbis, or done any act or thing (to the best of his knowledge) to gain a legal settlement elsewhere. John King. Sworn, 17 Jan. 1749/50, before us, William Withers, George Errington. Passed to St Martin in the Fields.

213. [n.p.] Middlesex. Anne Fretter, widow of John Fretter, aged about 59 years, upon oath says that 38 years ago she, this examinant, was married to her said late husband at the parish church of St Benet Paul's Wharf, London, by whom she had two children, both dead. Says that she lived with her said husband about ten years. And says that her said husband, some time after her marriage, rented half a shop and part of the house in the alley behind the then Three Tunn Tavern in Newgate Street in the parish of St Faith under St Paul's, London, where they continued a year and upwards, and paid at the rate of £10 pounds a year rent. And says that her said husband, some time after he quitted the said shop and business of selling worsted, he went to sea and never after rented a house of £10 a year, or had done any act (to her knowledge) to gain a legal settlement. And this examinant says that the said parish of St Faith under St Paul's took care and provided for one of her children for some time after her said husband left her. Anne Fretter, her mark. Sworn, 17 Jan. 1749/50, before us, William Withers, George Errington. Passed to St Faith's parish.

214. [n.p.] Middlesex. John Bryne, aged about 74 years, born at Lee in Devonshire, upon oath says that he, this examinant, about 60 years ago was bound an apprentice to one John Hall, a carpenter in Tuttle Street in the parish of St Margaret, Westminster, in the county of Middlesex, for the term of seven years. With whom he continued and served about five years of his time. After which he says that he entered himself in the army, where he continued until the peace which was made in King William's time.

And this examinant {He has as a wife named Elizabeth aged about 54 years and four children, but the children are all provided for.} also says that since the time of serving part of his apprenticeship as aforesaid, he has not rented a house of £10 a year, or paid any parochial taxes, or done any act or thing (to his knowledge) to gain a legal settlement. John Bryne. Sworn, 17 Jan. 1749/50, before us, William Withers, George Errington. Passed to St Margaret, Westminster.

CHELSEA SETTLEMENT AND BASTARDY EXAMINATIONS, 1750–1766

215. [fol.1–12. A contemporary names index incorporated into the original book structure, and organised around individual letter tags. This index is largely accurate and complete.]

216. [fol.13–4. A contemporary names index organised in a grid pattern. Very incomplete.]

217. [p.1] Middlesex. Elizabeth Fox, widow, aged 77 years, upon oath says that 37 years ago she, this examinant, was married in the liberty of the Fleet, London, to Thomas Fox her late husband, deceased. And says that he was at the time she married him a foot soldier in the Second Regiment of Guards, and that he continued in the army till he was admitted an in pensioner of Chelsea Hospital, where he died last Shrove Tuesday. And this examinant says that her said late husband never rented a house of £10 a year, or paid any parochial taxes, or done any act or thing (to the best of her knowledge) to gain a settlement. But says that she has heard and been informed he was born in Northamptonshire. As to the parish she does not know or can give any account. And this examinant further says that as to her own settlement, she lived a servant hired by the year (before marriage) with one Mr Samuel Hiles, victualler, who then kept the sign of the Duke of Marlborough, opposite the end of Holloway Lane in Shoreditch in the county of Middlesex. With whom she continued and served nine years, and received her full wages of her said master for the said time at 50s. per annum, meat, drink, washing and lodging. The mark of Elizabeth Fox. Sworn before us, 7 May 1750, Henry Fielding, George Errington. Passed to St Leonard Shoreditch.

218. [p.2] Middlesex. Charles Lukey, labourer, aged about 32 years, born in Bow Street, alias Thieving Lane in the parish of St Margaret in the city of Westminster and county of Middlesex, upon oath says that his father (John Lukey) served his apprenticeship with one Mr Rose a joiner who lived in the said parish of St Margaret (as he had often been told and informed by his said father). And says he, this examinant, from the time of his birth has not lived a hired servant a whole year in any place, or paid any parochial taxes, or done any act (to his knowledge) to gain a legal settlement. And this examinant also says that he was married to Mary, his present wife, about twelve years since in the liberty of the Fleet, London, by whom he has two children living; vizt, Charles, aged about 10 years, and Frances, aged near 3 years. And says that he having a swelled foot which is in great danger of mortification [he] is not able to work to support his said family. The mark of Charles Lukey. Sworn before us, 28 May 1750, Thomas Rea, Henry Fielding. Passed to St Margaret, Westminster.

219. [p.3] Middlesex. Thomas Todd, by trade a brazier, aged near 47 years, born at a place called Diss in the county of Norfolk, upon oath says that about seventeen years ago he, this examinant, was bound an apprentice to Joseph Watson late of Chelsea in Middlesex, brazier, for the term of seven years. With whom he continued and served four years only of his apprenticeship, and after that time he went about to different places and did jobbing work. And this examinant also says that since the time of his leaving Mr Watson's service he has not rented a house of £10 a year, or paid any parochial taxes, or done any act or thing (to the best of his knowledge) to gain a legal settlement. The mark of Thomas Todd. Sworn, 9 Aug. 1750, before me, Peter Elers.

220. [p.4] Middlesex. Mary Reynolds, widow, aged about 50 years, born in the parish of St Ann, Westminster, upon oath says that she hath had two husbands. Both of them were soldiers in the army, but cannot give any account of either of their settlements. [She] says that after her last husband died (Melsha Reynolds) she, this examinant, (not having any children) lived a servant hired by the year with one Anthony Hanks in the parish of St Martin in the Fields, victualler, who at that time kept the sign of King Charles' Head at Charing Cross, where she continued and served about four years at the rate of £4 a year wages, and of which she received upwards of two years of her said master, meat, drink, washing and lodging. And says that after she quitted the said service of Mr Hanks, which is about a year since, she has not paid any parochial taxes, or done any other act, to her knowledge, to gain a settlement. The mark of Mary Reynolds. Sworn before us, 27 Aug. 1750, Peter Elers, Henry Fielding. Passed to St Martin in the Fields.

221. [p.5] Middlesex. Elizabeth Kemish, the wife of Edward Kemish, aged about 49 years, upon oath says that on 6 Oct. 1739 she, this examinant, (as appears by a certificate) was married to her said husband in the liberty of the Fleet, London, by whom she has two children living; vizt, Edward, aged about 6 years, and William, aged upwards of 4 years. And says that her said husband, before her marriage, lived a hired servant by the year with one Mr Thomas Thorogood of New Brentford in the parish of Hanwell in the county of Middlesex, tripe man. With whom he continued and served three years. And says that her said husband had £9 a year wages of his said master, meat, drink, washing and lodging. And this examinant says that she lived fellow servant with her said husband in the same place a year before her marriage. And also says that her said husband from the time of his living with Mr Thorogood as aforesaid has not paid any parish taxes, or done any act, to her knowledge, to gain a settlement. And says that her husband being absconded and left her, [she] is not able to provide for herself and two children. The mark of Elizabeth Kemish. Sworn before us, 4 Sept. 1750. Peter Elers, Richard Chamberlayne. Passed to Hanwell.

222. [p.6] Middlesex. Mary Dimond, widow of Peter Dimond, aged about 50 years; and Sarah Ward otherwise Sarah Dancer, aged about 30 years (the daughter of Mary Dimond, by Nathaniel Dancer, her first husband), severally maketh oath. And first, the said Mary Dimond, says that she was married to her said first husband (Nathaniel Dancer) at the Fleet Chapel, and that her said husband before marriage was bound an apprentice to one Mr Best, a wheelwright at Walham Green in the parish of Fulham in the county of Middlesex. And says that her said first husband since the time he served his apprenticeship as aforesaid, had not rented a house of £10 a year, or paid any parish taxes, or done any other act, to her knowledge, to gain a settlement. And the said Sarah Ward, otherwise Sarah Dancer, as to herself, says that on 21 Jan. 1745/6 she was married to one John Ward in the liberty of the Fleet, who was at that time a soldier in the foot guards, but is now absconded and gone from her, so that she cannot give any account as to his settlement. And says that as to herself, she never lived a year in any service. And further says that she has been informed that her said husband, at the time he married her, had another wife who is now living in some part of Wiltshire, where this examinant imagines he is gone. Mary Dimond, her mark. Sarah Ward, her mark. Sworn before us, 12 Sept. 1750, Peter Elers, Boulton Mainwaring. Sarah Ward, otherwise Sarah Dancer, passed to Fulham.

223. [p.7] Middlesex. Thomas Mercer, waterman, aged about 27 years, born at Chelsea in the county of Middlesex, upon oath says that about thirteen years ago he, this examinant, was bound apprentice at Waterman's Hall to one James Hull, waterman, who lived at Wandsworth in the county of Surrey. With whom he continued and served one year of his apprenticeship, and afterwards went to sea for the remainder six years of his time. And says that he never rented a house of £10 a year, or paid any parochial taxes, or done any act, to his knowledge, to gain a settlement since the time of his apprenticeship as aforesaid. And further says that about four years ago this examinant was married to Elizabeth his wife in the liberty of the Fleet, by whom he has one child, named William, aged near 2 years. Thomas Mercer. Sworn before us, 8 Sept. 1750, Peter Elers, Richard Chamberlayne. Passed to Wandsworth.

224. [p.8] Middlesex. Elizabeth Bussell, single woman, aged about 26 years, maketh oath that she has lived with Mr Firmin of the parish of St Clement Danes, button seller, as a hired servant about three years and half, at the rate of £4 a year wages (of which this examinant says she has received about £6 in part). Says that she was at Mr Firmin's house at Chelsea from August last, was twelve month, until she was taken into Chelsea workhouse on 16 June last. And this examinant voluntarily says that on the Sunday night the riot happened in the Strand (which was on 14 Apr. last) her young master (Mr Samuel Firmin) then took an opportunity, as there was only an errand boy besides themselves in the house, to lock him out of the room where they were, and forcibly lay with her, this examinant, which was effected by his taking a penknife out of his pocket and threatening to kill her if she refused. With which she was so much terrified and weak by struggling, [she] was obliged to comply against her will. And this examinant also says that the said Samuel Firmin several times afterwards lay with her by frightening her with his drawn penknife and beating and bruising her frequently. And one time in particular he beat her so much about the eyes, which were so bad, she was obliged [p.9] to apply to one Mrs Dean, an oculist, for a cure. And this examinant further says that she believes she had a miscarriage by her young master, as Mr Stammers (Mrs Firmin's father) very well knows. For she says that Mr Stammers often persuaded and prevailed on her to drink warm ale in which she had great reason to believe he had put something extraordinary, for it always soon after made her sleep very much. And says that Mr Stammers himself has used her very ill, and often attempted to get into her room when she was in bed to lay with her. And this examinant says that in her conscience she really believes that the illness and unhappy disorder she has lately been under in the said workhouse was occasioned wholly by the base and unkind treatment both of young Mr Samuel Firmin and the said Mr Stammers. Elizabeth Bussell. Sworn, 13 Oct. 1750, before me, Peter Elers.

225. [p.10] Middlesex. The voluntary examination of Elizabeth Edmunds, the wife of John Edmunds, an out pensioner of Chelsea Hospital, taken upon oath before me Peter Elers, esq. . . . Who saith that about ten years ago she was married to the said John Edmunds in the liberty of the Fleet, London, by whom she hath one child living named Matthew, aged about 9 years. Says that when the said child was but three weeks old her said husband left this examinant and entered himself a marine in the army, and was beyond sea till last May. And says that after the said Edmunds was gone from her about three years she, this examinant, was several times informed and told that he died abroad and that he was so put down upon the list, and that the newspapers likewise mentioned that the Winchester Man of War (which was the ship he was aboard of) was cast away. And this examinant says that some time after this information she was again married at the Fleet aforesaid to one James Lindsay an in pensioner of Chelsea Hospital, and [with] him [p.11] she has two children living; vizt, Elizabeth, aged near 5 years, and John, an infant aged about 15 months, both born in the parish of Chelsea in the county of Middlesex aforesaid. And this examinant further says that the said James Lindsay is the real true and only father of the said last mentioned two children, and that John Edmunds her said first husband has been from this examinant and beyond the sea for about nine years till May last as aforesaid. And this examinant further saith not. Elizabeth Edmunds, her mark. Sworn at Chelsea before me, 17 Dec. 1750, Peter Elers. [See **226**].

226. Middlesex, to wit. This examinant, Elizabeth Edmunds above mentioned, aged about 45 years, on her voluntary oath further says that she has now living by the said James Lindsay three other children born on her body in the parish of Chelsea in the county of Middlesex; vizt, James, aged about 16 years, Margaret, aged about 13 years, Ann, aged about 10 years. And that the said James Lindsay is the real and true father of the aforesaid children and no man else, and that she has not been married to any man since. Elizabeth Edmunds, her mark. Sworn before me, . . . 24 Jan. 1769, Paul Vaillant. [See **225**].

227. [p.12] Middlesex. Ephraim Hillary, mariner, aged about 30 years, born at a place called Evershot in Devonshire [Dorset], upon oath says that he, this examinant, was brought up and lived with his father, Ephraim Hillary, till he attained the age of 13 years, and then he went to sea, where he afterwards made several voyages. And when he returned from thence, he lived with his father again (so that he did not gain any settlement but from his father's). Says that upwards of six years ago he was married at Mayfair Chapel to Mary, his wife, by whom he has three children living; to wit, Ephraim, aged about 4 years, Elizabeth, aged near 3 years, and Sarah, an infant, aged almost 4 months. And this examinant says that when he lived with his father about eight years ago, that his father rented a house and some land in the parish of Fulham in the county of Middlesex of above £10 a year rent of one Mr Anderson and Mr Shreeve. And this examinant further says that since the time of his marriage and living with his father as aforesaid, he has not rented a house of £10 a year, or otherways done any act, to his knowledge, to gain a legal settlement. Ephraim Hillary. Sworn, 26 Dec. 1750, before us, Peter Elers, John Powell. Passed to Fulham. [See **231**].

228. [p.13] Middlesex. Elizabeth Jones, widow, aged about 66 years, maketh oath and saith that on 16 Apr. 1745 she was married (as appears by a certificate) to her late husband, Edward Jones, deceased, in that part of the parish of St Brides, which is in the liberty of the Fleet, London. Says that her said husband at the time she married him was an in pensioner of Chelsea Hospital, where he continued till the time he died, which is almost two years ago. And this examinant says that she hath often heard her said husband declare in his lifetime that he was born in the parish of St Giles in the Field in the county of Middlesex, and that he never rented a house, or paid any parish taxes, or done any other act, to her knowledge, since the time of his birth to gain a legal settlement. And this examinant further says that she is well informed that it does appear by her late husband's affidavit filed in the secretary's office in Chelsea Hospital, upon his admittance there, that he was born in the said parish of St Giles in the Fields. And that it does likewise appear by an entry made in the register book of the said parish of St Giles, that he was born there in Oct. 1706. Elizabeth Jones, her mark. Sworn, 7 Jan. 1750/1, before us, Peter Elers, Henry Fielding. Passed to St Giles.

229. [p.14] Middlesex. The voluntary examination of Amey Nixon, single woman, taken 12 Jan., before me, Peter Elers esq. . . . Who upon oath saith that she is now pregnant of a bastard child or children which was, or were, unlawfully begotten on her body by one John Cuthbert, footman to Andrew Hopegood esq. at Hadley near Barnet in the said county of Middlesex. Who had carnal knowledge of her body the first time in the beginning of the month of April last in the dwelling house of Mrs Denham in South-hampton Street near Covent Garden, London (where this examinant and the said John Cuthbert lived at the same time fellow servants). And says that the said John Cuthbert had carnal knowledge of her body several times after in the said house, and that the said John Cuthbert is the true and only father of the said child or children she now goeth with. And further says not. Amey Nixon. Sworn at Chelsea, the day and year above written, before me, Peter Elers.

230. [p.15] Middlesex. Catherine Rider, widow, aged 40 years, upon oath says that about eighteen years ago she, this examinant was married to her late husband, Emanuel Rider, deceased, at the parish church at Limehouse in the county of Middlesex. By whom she has two children living; vizt, Charles, aged about 14 years (who is not capable of any employment he being out of his senses), and Nicholas, aged near 12 years. And this examinant says that her said late husband often declared and informed this examinant in his life time that he lived as a covenant servant by the year before he married with one Mr Miller near Horsely Down Stairs, in the parish of St John Southwark, in the county of Surrey, boat builder. And with whom he said that he continued and served between two and three years, and that he received at the rate of £20 a year wages of his said master, meat, drink, washing and lodging. And this examinant also says that her said late husband after marriage never rented a house of £10 a year, or paid any parochial taxes, or otherwise done any act (to her knowledge) to gain a legal settlement. But says that she being left a widow, and in very mean and low circumstances, is not able to provide for and support her said two children without some relief. Catherine Rider. Sworn, 10 May 1751, before us, Peter Elers, Henry Fielding. [See **49, 65, 82, 243**].

231. [p.16] Middlesex. Ephraim Hillary, yeoman, aged about 65 years, maketh oath and saith that in the year 1742 (before his son Ephraim's marriage in December in the same year) he, this examinant rented of one Mr Andrews a house and some land in the parish of Fulham in the county of Middlesex at the yearly rent of £9 10s., as appears by the said Mr Andrews' receipts. And this examinant says that in the said year 1742 he also rented other land in the said parish of Fulham of one Isaac Stevens at the yearly rent of £1 10s., which rent he paid Stevens as appears by his receipt. And this examinant further says that in the said year 1742 he likewise rented some pasture land in Town Mead in the said parish of Fulham, of one [blank] Burton, a widow, at the yearly rent of £3 15s., which last mentioned rent he paid to the said [blank] Burton for that year. And further saith not. Ephraim Hillary. Sworn, 13 May 1751, before us, Peter Elers, Henry Fielding. [See **227**].

232. [p.17] Middlesex. William Cooke, aged about 75 years, an in pensioner of Chelsea Hospital, born at Grimoldby in Lincolnshire, upon oath says that upwards of 50 years ago he, this examinant, lived a servant hired by the year with one Joseph Eldon, a farmer who lived at Little Carlton in the county of Lincoln (the farm was called and known by the name of Little Carleton Uphall). And says that he continued and served his said master a whole year, and received his full wages for the said time, at the rate of £3 a year, meat, drink, washing and lodging. And this examinant says that soon after he quitted the service of the said Joseph Eldon, he entered himself a soldier in the army, where he continued till he was admitted a pensioner of Chelsea Hospital, . . . where he now belongs as aforesaid. And further says that in the month of Apr. 1743 he, this examinant, was married to Jane, his present wife, in the liberty of the Fleet, London, who is of the age of 75 years or thereabouts. And says that he is not able to maintain her without relief. The mark of William Cook. Sworn, 22 June 1751, before us, Peter Elers.

233. [p.18] Middlesex. Sarah Jenkins, widow, aged near 70 years, born in the parish of St Sidwell in the county of Exon [Exeter], upon oath says that about 25 years ago she, this examinant, was married to Jacob Jenkins, her late husband, at the parish church of St Sidwell aforesaid. And that her said late husband was a soldier when she married him, and that he continued in the army till he was admitted an in pensioner of Chelsea Hospital, where he died about three years ago. And this examinant says that she has been told by her husband that he was born in Wales, but in what part or where his settlement was she declares she does not know, or can give any particular account. And as to her own settlement before marriage, she says that she was brought up and lived with her father (Thomas Cole) till she was married to her said late husband. And that her said father was a weaver by trade and served his apprenticeship in the parish of Crediton, near Exeter in the county of Exon aforesaid. And says that she cannot give any further account either of her father's or her own settlement. The mark of Sarah Jenkins. Sworn, 9 July 1751, before me, Peter Elers.

234. [p.19] Middlesex. Susannah Harvey otherwise Watson, aged 50 years, upon oath says that she, this examinant, upwards of eight years ago was married to one George Harvey, a footman at Mayfair Chapel, . . . by whom she has one child living, named John Daniell Harvey, aged about 7 years, who was born in the dwelling house of one Mr Newman, a hatter in Carnaby Market in the parish of St James, Westminster, in the county of Middlesex. And this examinant says that about a year and half after she was married to the said George Harvey, she was informed that he had another wife living in the country, who soon after came to this examinant, took her goods, and turned her out of doors. And says that soon after that transaction the said George Harvey left this examinant and went to Flanders with General Otway, and has not been heard of since. And also says that the last place she lived in upwards of a year was with Governor Worsley in Golden Square in the parish of St James aforesaid. Says that she lived with the said Governor in the station of a cook upwards of two years, and received £10 a year wages. The mark of Susannah Harvey. Sworn, 27 July 1751, before us, Peter Elers, Henry Fielding. Passed to St James, Westminster.

235. [p. 20] Middlesex. Elizabeth Houseman, single woman, aged about 27 years, upon oath says that about 18 months ago she lived a servant hired by the year with Mr Henry Lewer the elder at Little Chelsea in the parish of Great Chelsea in the county of Middlesex, butcher. With whom she continued and served eleven years, and received all her wages due of her said master, meat, drink, washing and lodging. And this examinant says that after she quitted the said service of Mr Lewer's, she was hired to Mr William Burchett of Little Chelsea aforesaid, yeoman, and lived [a] servant there upwards of a year and received her full wages of the said Mr Burchett at the rate of £5, also meat, drink and lodging. And says that since she quitted the said service of Mr Burchett about eleven months since, [she] has not done any act, to her knowledge to gain a settlement. [Blank]. Sworn, [blank] July 1751, before me, [blank]. [See **236**].

236. [p.21] Middlesex. The voluntary examination of Elizabeth Houseman, single woman, taken upon oath before me, Peter Elers esq. . . . Who saith that she is pregnant of a bastard child or children which was or were unlawfully begotten on her body by one William Groves, husbandman, who is now a lodger at one Mr [blank] Davis', a stocking weaver at Little Chelsea. Who had carnal knowledge of her body the first time in the month of August last in a garret of the dwelling house of the said Mr Davis, and several times after in the said garret, where this examinant and the said William Groves lodged together for about four months. And this examinant says that the said William Groves is the true father of the said child or children she now goeth with. And further says not. The mark of Elizabeth Houseman. Sworn at Chelsea, 27 July 1751, before me, Peter Elers. [See **235**].

237. [p.22] Middlesex. Jane Suckley, widow, aged about 63 years, born in Wales, upon oath says that 30 years ago she, this examinant, was married to her late husband, Robert Suckley, in the liberty of the Fleet, London. And that her said husband at the time she married him was a brewer's servant and never rented a house of £10 a year, or paid any parochial taxes, or otherwise done any act, to her knowledge, to gain a settlement. And this examinant says that her said late husband was a Cheshire man, but does not know where he was born or the parish he belonged to. And this examinant says as to her own settlement she lived a servant hired by the year (about five years before she was married) with one Mr Hartoe, a dyer who lived in New Prison Walk in the parish of St James Clerkenwell in the county of Middlesex. With whom she continued and served one year and seven months, and received her full wages of her said master for the said time at the rate of £5 a year, meat, drink, washing and lodging. And says that after she quitted the said service [she] has not done any act, to her knowledge, to gain a settlement. The mark of Jane Suckley. Sworn, 8 Aug. 1751, before me, Peter Elers, Richard Chamberlayne. Passed to St James Clerkenwell.

238. [p.23] Middlesex. John Tallent, labourer, aged about 27 years, born in the parish of St Martin in the Fields in the county of Middlesex, upon oath says that his father, Humphry Tallent, was by trade a mason and rented a house and yard in the parish of St Martin in the Fields aforesaid. And this examinant says that he lived with his said father till he died about eight years ago. And since his death, says that he has not lived a servant hired by the year in any place, or been bound an apprentice, or otherwise done any act, to his knowledge, to gain a settlement. But says he has been rambling about the country and chiefly drove gardeners' carts, who frequently gave him victuals, by which he subsisted. The mark of John Tallent. Sworn, 17 Aug. 1751, before us, Peter Elers, Richard Chamberlayne. Passed to St Martin in the Fields.

239. [p. 24] Middlesex. Edward Main, an in pensioner of Chelsea Hospital, aged upwards of 70 years, upon oath says that he lived and cohabited with one Elenor Strong, widow, deceased, for several years in the parish of Chelsea in the county of Middlesex, and has had a child by her who is now living, named Ann Main, aged about 17 years. And who being an idiot and not in her senses is not capable of working to support and maintain herself. And this examinant further says, though he lived and cohabited in manner as aforesaid he declares that he was never married to the said Elenor Strong, and that the said Anne Main is a bastard and was born in the said parish of Chelsea. The mark of Edward Main. Sworn, 24 Aug. 1751, before me, Peter Elers.

240. [p.25] Middlesex. Joseph Beach, aged about 77 years, who is an in pensioner of Chelsea Hospital, upon oath says that he has cohabited and lived with one Susannah Shutter, otherwise Seeney, for about ten years. By whom he has two sons living; vizt, Joseph Beach, aged about 9 years, and Benjamin Beach, aged near 7 years. And this examinant positively declares and says that he never was married to the said Susannah Shutter, otherwise Seeney (though they cohabited together). But says that his said two boys are bastards and were born in the parish of Chelsea in the county of Middlesex. The mark of Joseph Beach. Sworn, 24 Aug. 1751, before me, Peter Elers.

241. [p.26] Middlesex. Thomas Spelman, labourer, aged about 65 years, upon oath says that about 20 years ago he was married at Cripplegate Church, London, to Mary, his present wife, who is of the age of about 50 years. And says that before the time of his said marriage he, this examinant, lived a servant hired by the year with one Captain Richard Newton of Little Chelsea in the parish of Kensington in the county of Middlesex. With whom he continued and served eight years and upwards, and received his full wages of his said master for the said time at the rate of [blank] a year, meat, drink, washing and lodging. And also says that after he quitted the said service of Captain Newton's he has not rented a house of £10 a year, or paid any parochial taxes, or done any act (to his knowledge) to gain a settlement. [Blank]. Sworn, [blank] Nov. 1751, before us, [blank]. Vide page 38. [See **253**].

242. [p.27] Middlesex. Anne Piper otherwise Anne Clarke, spinster, aged 18 years or thereabouts, upon oath says that at the age of about 13 years she was bound an apprentice by the parish officers of Chelsea to one Mary Perry, a milk woman in Charles Street in the parish of St Margaret, Westminster, in the county of Middlesex, until she should attain the age of 21 years or day of marriage {indenture bears the date 26 Aug. 1746}. And says that she continued and served her said mistress until she died, which was about a year after she this examinant was bound. And that afterwards she continued with her said mistress's two daughters at the same place where her mistress lived in Charles Street, Westminster, for about eighteen weeks, but having been (she says) ill used by their milk carrier she absconded and came from them and lived with her grandmother at Chelsea till she died about nine months ago. And this examinant further says that since the time of her living with her said mistress (Mary Perry) as aforesaid, [she] has not lived a servant in any place, or otherwise done any act (to her knowledge) to gain a settlement. The mark of Anne Piper. Sworn, 7 Dec. 1751, before us, Peter Elers, Henry Fielding. Passed to St Margaret, Westminster.

243. [p.28] Middlesex. William Rider of Chelsea, shoemaker, maketh oath and saith that about 34 years ago his late brother, Emanuel Rider, was bound an apprentice for seven years to one Richard Kenton of the parish of Battersea in the county of Surrey, boat builder. And says that he continued and served his said master the full term of his apprenticeship. And that his said late brother, since his apprenticeship as aforesaid, did not rent any house of £10 a year, or otherwise do any act or thing (to his knowledge) to gain a settlement. William Rider. Sworn, 7 Dec. 1751, before us, Peter Elers, Henry Fielding. Passed to Battersea. [See **49**, **65**, **82**, **230**].

244. [p.29] Middlesex. Anne Littlefoot, single woman, aged about 16 years, daughter of John Littlefoot by Mary his wife (both deceased), upon oath says that she is informed and it does appear by the examination upon oath of her said late father, that in the month of Sept. 1740 she, this examinant, was with her said late father and brother, also deceased, removed by a pass warrant or order from the parish of Chelsea in Middlesex to the parish of St Stephen Coleman Street, London, as the place of their last legal settlement, by which said parish they were received and did not appeal to the said order. And this examinant says that she has not lived a hired servant by the year, or otherwise done any act (to her knowledge) to gain a settlement since she lived with her said late father, John Littlefoot. The mark of Anne Littlefoot. Sworn, 13th Dec. 1751, before us, Peter Elers. Passed to St Stephen Coleman Street. [See **85**].

245. [p.30] Middlesex. Edward Austin, labourer, aged about 25 years, upon oath says that upwards of six years ago he, this examinant, was married to Elizabeth his wife in the liberty of the Fleet, London, by whom he has three children living; vizt, Benjamin, aged about 5 years, John, aged about 2 years, and Jane, an Infant, aged about 4 months. And this examinant says that his late father, William Austin (who was a carpenter by trade), about thirteen years ago rented a house in Chick Lane in the parish of St Sepulchres, London. As to the rent which his father paid for the said house, he does not know, but says that he paid parochial taxes for the said house (and that his father soon after died), and did not rent any house after that in Chick Lane aforesaid. And this examinant further says that since the time of living with his father he has not rented a house of £10 a year, or paid any parochial taxes, or done any act (to his knowledge) to gain a settlement. Edward Austin. Sworn, 13 Dec. 1751, before us, Peter Elers, Henry Fielding. Passed to St Sepulchres parish. [See **337**].

246. [p.31] Middlesex. Joseph Bedford, aged 67 years, upon oath says that at the age of about 15 years he, this examinant, was bound an apprentice to one Mr Stephen Bingham of the parish of Digbeth in the town of Birmingham in the county of Warwick, file cutter, for the term of seven years. And says that he served his said master five years only of his said apprenticeship and then entered himself a soldier in the army, in which station he continued until he was admitted an in pensioner of Chelsea Hospital, where he now belongs. And this examinant says that since the time of being an apprentice as aforesaid he has not rented a house of £10 a year, or paid any parochial taxes, or otherwise done any act (to his knowledge) to gain a settlement. And further says that about nineteen years ago he was married in Edinburgh Castle to Margaret, his present wife (who is about 45 years of age). By whom he has two daughters living; to wit, Mary, aged 17 years (who is ill of a fever), and Hannah, aged about 12 years. And says that he is not able to maintain his said family without relief. Joseph Bedford. Sworn, 23 Dec. 1751, before me, Peter Elers, Samuel Bever. Vide page 39. [See **254**].

247. [p.32] Middlesex. The voluntary examination of Elizabeth White, single woman, taken [blank] Jan. 1752 before me, Peter Elers esq. . . . . Who upon oath saith she is now pregnant of a bastard child or children which was or were unlawfully begotten on her body by one William Brown, servant to William Heiat, a baker in Chelsea in the said county of Middlesex, who had carnal knowledge of her body the first time in the beginning of the month of April last in the dwelling house of the said William Heiat at Chelsea in the county aforesaid, where this examinant and the said William Brown lived at the same time as fellow servants. And says the said William Brown had carnal knowledge of her several times after, and the said William Brown is the true and only father of the said child or children she now goeth with. And further says not. [Blank]. Sworn at Chelsea the day and year above written, before me, [blank].

248. [p.33] Middlesex. The voluntary examination of Anne Hunt, single woman, taken before us, Peter Elers and Samuel Bever, esqs . . . Who upon oath says that on 29 Dec. last she, this examinant, was delivered [of] a female bastard child in the dwelling house of one Mrs Reid in the parish of Chelsea in the county of Middlesex aforesaid (which is baptised and named Elizabeth). And was unlawfully begotten on her body by one John Kensy who was an apprentice at that time with one Mr Conquest Jones, an ironmonger in Piccadilly. And says that the said John Kensy had carnal knowledge of her body the first time in the dwelling house of the said Conquest Jones (where the examinant lived as a servant). And at several times after in the said house. And this examinant says that the said John Kensy is the true father of the said child. And further says not. The mark of Anne Hunt. Sworn at Chelsea, 9 Mar. 1752, before us, Peter Elers, Samuel Bever.

249. [p.34] Middlesex. Susanna Prouton, single woman, aged about 17 years, daughter of William Prouton, late an in pensioner of Chelsea Hospital, deceased, upon oath says that she, this examinant, lived in the family of the late Captain Stuart, adjutant of Chelsea Hospital, for upwards of five years till he died, but not as a hired servant for wages, only for her diet, washing, lodging and clothes. And this examinant says that soon after she came away from the said Captain Stuart's, she lived a servant hired by the year with Mr John Gray, victualler at the Coach and Horses in Chelsea, where she continued and served a year and upwards, and received her full wages of her said master for the said time at the rate of 30s. per annum, meat, drink, washing and lodging. And says that since she quitted the service of the said Mrs Gray's (which was about two months since) she has not done any act, to her knowledge, to gain a settlement. The mark of Susanna Prouton. Sworn at Chelsea, 20 Mar. 1752, before me, Peter Elers. [See **250**].

250. [p.35] Middlesex, to wit. The voluntary examination of Susanna Prouton, single woman, taken 20 Mar. 1752, before me Peter Elers esq. . . . Who saith upon oath that she is now pregnant of a bastard child or children which was or were unlawfully begotten on her body by one Thomas Price, otherwise Fly, a labouring man who lodges at the house of John Gray, victualler at the Coach and Horses in Chelsea (where this examinant lived a servant). And had carnal knowledge of her body the first time in or about the month of October last in the bed room where this examinant lay in her said master's house, and at several times after in the said room. And this examinant says that the said Thomas Price, otherwise Fly, is the true father of the said child or children with which she is pregnant. And further says not. The mark of Susanna Prouton. Sworn at Chelsea, 20 Mar. 1752, before me, Peter Elers. [See **249**].

251. [p.36] Middlesex. Thomas Darby, maltman, aged about 42 years, upon oath says that his late brother-in-law, Richard West, maltman, deceased, was the son of Thomas West late of South Weston under the Hills in the county of Oxford, tailor, also deceased. And says the said Thomas West (the father) served his apprenticeship (as this examinant often has heard him say and declare in his lifetime) to one Mr Rackley, a tailor at a place called Kingston in the parish of Aston in the said county of Oxford. And that the said Thomas West afterwards never did any act, to his knowledge, to gain a settlement. And this examinant further says that as to Richard West, the said son, he never did rent a house of £10 a year, or paid any parochial taxes, or other ways done any act, to his knowledge, to gain a settlement since the time of living with his father, Thomas West. Thomas Darby. Sworn, 14 Apr. 1752, before us, Peter Elers. [See **252**].

252. [p.37] Middlesex. Ann West, aged about 26 years, the widow of Richard West, maltman, deceased, upon oath says that she, this examinant, was married to her said late husband at the parish church of St Benet Paul's Wharf, London, by whom she has three children living; to wit, Elizabeth, aged about 6 years, Anne, aged upwards of 3 years, and Jane, aged about 2 years. And this examinant says that her said husband (as she has been often informed by him) never rented a house of £10 a year, or been an apprentice, or otherwise done any act to gain a legal settlement since the time of living with his father, Thomas West, who served his apprenticeship as this examinant has been likewise informed at Kingston in the parish of Aston Rowant in the county of Oxford. The mark of Ann West. Sworn, 14 Apr. 1752, before us, Peter Elers, Henry Fielding. Passed to the parish of Aston Rowant. [See **251**].

253. [p.38] Middlesex. Thomas Spelman, labourer, aged 65 years, upon oath says that 20 years ago he was married to Mary his wife (who is of the age of 51 years or thereabouts) at the parish church of St Giles Cripplegate, London. And says that before the time of his said marriage he, this examinant, lived a servant hired by the year with one Captain Newton at Little Chelsea in the parish of Kensington in the county of Middlesex, with whom he continued and served eight years and upwards in the station of a gardener and coachman. And received of his said master his full wages for the said time at the rate of £7 10s. a year, meat, drink, washing and lodging. And this examinant also says that from the time of his leaving the said Captain Newton's service as aforesaid, he has not rent[ed] a house of £10 a year, or paid any parochial taxes, or otherwise done any act (to his knowledge) to gain a settlement. Thomas Spelman. Sworn, 30 May 1752, before us, Peter Elers, Henry Fielding. Passed [to] Kensington. [See **241**].

254. [p.39] Middlesex. Joseph Bedford, aged 67 years, upon oath says that when he was the age of about 15 years he was bound an apprentice to one Mr Stephen Bingham of Digbath Street, in the parish of St Martin, Birmingham, in the county of Warwick, file-cutter, for the term of seven years. With whom he continued and served five years of his said apprenticeship, and then entered himself a soldier in the army, in which station he continued until he was admitted an in pensioner of the Royal Hospital at Chelsea, where he now belongs. And this examinant says that since the time of living with the said Mr Stephen Bingham as an apprentice as aforesaid, he has not rented a house of £10 a year, or paid any parochial taxes, or otherwise done any act (to his knowledge) to gain a settlement. And further says that about nineteen years ago he, this examinant, was married in Edinburgh Castle to Margaret his present wife (who is about 45 years of age). By whom he has two daughters; to wit, Mary, aged 17 years, who is in service, [and] Hannah, of the age of 12 years, or thereabouts. And says that he is not in circumstances able to support and maintain his said family without relief. Joseph Bedford. Sworn, 5 June 1752, before us, Peter Elers, Henry Fielding. Margaret, the wife, and Hannah, the youngest daughter, were passed to Birmingham. [See **246**].

255. [p.40] Middlesex. Anne Boswell, widow aged 57 years, upon oath saith that about 24 years ago she, this examinant, was married to her second husband, John Boswell, gardener, deceased, in the liberty of the Fleet, London. By whom she has a son, aged about 21 years, now an apprentice. And saith that her said late husband (John Boswell) in his lifetime often declared and informed this examinant (and she believes it to be true) that before she was married to him he rented a house and garden ground in the parish of St Andrew in the town of Pershore in the county of Worcester for several years, and that he paid all taxes and served several parochial offices there. And this examinant further saith that she lived with her said husband at Pershore about thirteen years, and that since the time of his death, which was about eight years ago, she, this examinant, has not rented a house of £10 a year, or otherwise done any act, to her knowledge, to gain a settlement. The mark of Anne Boswell. Sworn, 12 Oct. 1752, before us, Peter Elers, Henry Fielding. Passed to St Andrew at Pershore.

256. [p.41] Middlesex. William Hawker, necklace maker, aged about 45 years, born in the parish of St Andrew Holborn in the county of Middlesex, upon oath says that when he was of the age of 14 years was bound out an apprentice by the parish officers of the said parish to [blank]. And on the same day he, this examinant, was turned over by his master (whose names he cannot recollect) to his son-in-law, one Patt Hammond, necklace maker. Who lived in the liberty of Saffron Hill in the parish of St Andrew Holborn in the county of Middlesex aforesaid, with whom he continued and served near five years of his apprenticeship. But his said master (Patt Hammond) having frequently beat and abused him, he absconded and left his said service. After which this Examinant says he got his living honestly by jobbing about in different places for near 20 years till he entered himself a soldier in the army, where he continued to 28 Aug. 1749, when he was discharged (as appears by his officer's certificate). And this examinant says that since the time of leaving his said master's service as aforesaid, this examinant has not rented a house of £10 a year, or paid any parochial taxes, or otherwise done any act (to his knowledge) to gain a settlement. The mark of William Hawker. Sworn, 27 Feb. 1753, before us, John Powell, Henry Fielding. Passed to the parish of St Andrew Holborn. [See **435**].

257. [p.42] Middlesex. Joseph Everad, gardener, aged near 48 years, born in the parish of Fulham in the county of Middlesex, upon oath says that about fourteen years since he, this examinant, rented a house with some land in the parish of Fulham aforesaid for eleven years and paid £10 a year rent for the same and all parochial taxes. And says that since the time of his renting the said house and land at Fulham aforesaid, he, this examinant, has not rented a house elsewhere, or paid any parochial taxes, or otherwise done any act, to his knowledge, to gain a settlement. And says that he has two sons living, the eldest named Thomas, aged about 21 years (by Mary, his first wife) who, being an idiot and lame with the palsy, is not able to work to maintain himself, [and] the other, named John, a child aged about 4 years by Sarah, his present wife. And says he is in such low and mean circumstances that he is not able to support his said family without some relief. Joseph Everad. Sworn, 6 Mar. 1753, before us, Henry Fielding, Thomas Lediard. Passed to Fulham.

258. [p.43] Middlesex. Gwin Goodyere, aged about 66 years, upon oath says that when he was of the age of 14 years he, this examinant, was bound an apprentice to one Mr Henry Shepard of the parish of St Lawrence Jewry in the city of London, vintner, for the term of seven years. With whom he continued and served his full time of apprenticeship. And says that afterwards he lived in several different places as a drawer, in and about London five years (but not in any one place more than four months at a time). After which he entered himself a soldier in the army where he continued till lately he was admitted an out pensioner of Chelsea Hospital. And further says that though he is entitled to receive his pay of the out pension money (when it becomes due to him or to his agent) he is not at present able to subsist without some relief. The mark of Gwin Goodyere. Sworn, 21 May 1753, before us, Thomas Lediard, Francis Bedwell. Passed to St Lawrence Jewry.

259. [p.44] Middlesex. Creswell Brown, labourer, aged about 30 years, born in Herefordshire, upon oath says that about eight years since he, this examinant, lived a servant hired by the year with one Mr Humphry Lewis of Carnaby Market in the parish of St James, Westminster, in the county of Middlesex, cheesemonger. With whom he continued and served a year and a quarter and received of his said master his full wages for the said time at the rate of £3 10s. a year, meat, drink, washing and lodging. And says that after he quitted the said service of Mr Lewis he got his living by jobbing work in several places but not as a hired servant by the year. After which he entered himself a soldier in the army. And [he] has not rented a house of £10 a year, or paid any parochial taxes, or otherwise done any act (to his knowledge) to gain a legal settlement. And further says that upwards of a year ago he, this examinant, was married to Catherine, his wife, in the liberty of the Fleet, London, by whom he has two children (twins), aged almost 2 months, named William and Joseph. And this examinant says he is not able by his labour to support his said family without some relief, and is now chargeable to the parish of Chelsea. The mark of Creswell Brown. Sworn, 12 July 1753, before us, Samuel Bever, Thomas Lediard. Passed to the parish of St James.

260. [p45] Middlesex. Thomas Boxall, by trade a whitesmith, aged about 21 years, born at Petworth in the county of Sussex, upon oath says that about a year ago he went away and left the service of his father, William Boxall, clock maker and whitesmith, with whom he lived the four preceding years and learnt his said trade of a whitesmith, but not as an apprentice. And says that his father during the said four years he lived with him found him in all necessary apparel, meat, drink, washing and lodging. And says that his said father followed the said trades of a clock maker and whitesmith in the parish of Chelsea in the county of Middlesex several years, and is now a parishioner there, having paid parochial taxes. And this examinant says that since he left his father's service as aforesaid, he has not rented a house of £10 a year, or paid any parochial taxes, or otherwise done any act, to his knowledge, to gain a settlement. And this examinant also says that about a year ago he was married to Elizabeth, his wife, in the liberty of the Fleet, London. And says that the parish officers of Petworth aforesaid (where he has been employed as a journeyman for some short time) will not let him continue there without bringing a certificate to indemnify their parish. {Memorandum: Thomas Boxall and Elizabeth his wife had a certificate from Chelsea to indemnify the parish of Petworth. } [See **261**, **352**, **452**].

261. A woman being come from Chatham with a permit pass pretending to be the wife of Thomas Boxall this 9 Jan. 1761, and says that her maiden name was Elizabeth Langford of the parish of Fulham, with one male child of 7 weeks old. Says that her husband aforesaid keeps another woman and therefore cannot keep her, and she now is chargeable to the parish of Chelsea. [See **260**, **452**].

262. [p.46] Middlesex. Jane Turner, widow, aged near 40 years, upon oath saith that about 20 years ago she was married to William Turner, her late husband, at a private house in the parish of St Paul Covent Garden in the liberty of Westminster. By whom she has a daughter living, named Elizabeth, aged 18 years, who is in service. And says that her said late husband was bound an apprentice to one William Billingham, white smith, who at that time lived in Butcherall Lane in the parish of Christ Church in the city of London. With whom he continued and served six years of his apprenticeship and then went to sea where he was blown-up on board his Majesty's ship the Tilbury Man of War. And this Examinant says as to her part she has never rented a house of £10 a year, or paid any parochial taxes, or otherwise done any act, to her knowledge, to gain a settlement since that of her said late husband's. And further says that she being in a very bad state of health is not capable to support herself without some relief. The mark of Jane Turner. Sworn, 2 Oct. 1753, before us, Philip Dyos, Francis Bedwell. Passed to Christ Church.

263. [p.47] Middlesex. Frances Cooke, single woman, aged near 26 years, upon oath saith that she, this examinant, about seven years ago quitted the service of Sir Humphry Moleneaux, who at that time lived in St James Place which is in the parish of St James in the liberty of Westminster in the county of Middlesex, where she lived as a hired servant by the year and continued in the said service near nine years. And [she] received her full wages for the last three years of the said time at the rate of £4 10s. a year, meat, drink, washing and lodging. And this examinant says that since her living in Sir Humphry Moleneaux's service as aforesaid, she has not been a hired servant a year in any other place, or otherwise done any act, to her knowledge, to gain a settlement. Frances Cook. Sworn, 17 Oct. 1753, before us, Francis Bedwell, Thomas Lediard. Passed to St James in the liberty of Westminster.

264. [p.48] Middlesex. Jonathan Ludler, labourer aged 33 years, born at Ardington in the county of Berkshire, upon oath saith that he, this examinant, lived a servant hired by the year with one Mr Nathaniel Cooper, a farmer in the parish of Mitcham, in the county of Surrey. With whom he continued and served one whole year and received of his said master his full wages for the said time (which was £7), meat, drink, washing and lodging. And says that he afterwards worked by the week with his said master (Mr Cooper) for near two years. And says that since he quitted the said service he has not lived a whole year as a hired servant in any place, or paid any parochial taxes, or done any act, to his knowledge, to gain a settlement. And this examinant further saith that about two years ago he was married to Elizabeth, his present wife, in the liberty of the Fleet, London, who at this time is big with child and near her time of reckoning. And says that he being in a very ill state of health is not able to work to maintain himself and wife without relief. Jonathan Ludler, his mark. Sworn, 24 Oct. 1753. Passed to Mitcham in the county of Surrey.

265. [p.49] Middlesex. Jane Webber, widow, aged near 60 years, upon oath saith that about three years ago she, this examinant, lived a servant hired by the year with Colonel Cossly, lieutenant governor of the Royal Hospital at Chelsea, in the station of a cook. Where she continued and served a year and half and received her full wages for the said time at the rate of £8 a year, meat, drink, washing and lodging. And this examinant says that since she quitted the said service of Colonel Cossly's, [she] has not been a hired servant a year in any place, or done any act, to her knowledge, to gain a settlement. Jane Webber. Sworn, 24 Oct. 1753, before us, Benjamin Cox.

266. [p.50] Middlesex. Margaret Chappel, widow, aged about 70 years, upon oath saith that she, this examinant, about five years ago was passed from the parish of Chelsea in the county of Middlesex to the parish of St

Giles in the Fields in the said county as the place of her last legal settlement. And says that she was received at that time by one of the parish officers of St Giles, and was sent by him to their workhouse, where she was kept and maintained for about ten months. Which pass warrant or order was grounded upon the affidavit of her late husband (John Chappel) that he was born in the said parish of St Giles in the Fields and never did any act afterwards to gain settlement, he having been a soldier for many years in the army and was admitted afterwards an in pensioner of Chelsea Hospital, where he continued till the time he died about five years since and upwards. And this examinant as to her own part saith that since the time of her being passed to the said parish of St Giles in the Fields and maintained in the workhouse there for ten months as aforesaid, she has not been married or done any other act, to her knowledge, to gain a settlement. The mark of Margaret Chappel. Sworn, 30 Oct. 1753, before us, Thomas Lediard, Benjamin Cox. Passed to St Giles parish and passed before to the parish of St Giles in the fields, 2 Sept. 1748. Vide old examination book. [See **195**].

267. [p.51] Middlesex. Jane Hunter, aged about 49 years, the widow of James Hunter, late an in pensioner of Chelsea Hospital, deceased, upon oath saith that about eight years ago she, this examinant, was married to her said late husband in the liberty of the Fleet, London, who was a Scotsman. But as to the particular place where he was born, or of his settlement, this examinant says she never heard him mention or declare, nor can [she] give any account thereof. And this examinant saith that about 22 years ago she was married to her first husband (John Ebsworth) in the Fleet aforesaid, by whom she has a daughter (named Mary) who was bound out apprentice by the parish officers of Croydon in the county of Surrey, and is now married and provided for. And this examinant also saith that she hath often heard her first husband declare (and she verily believes it to be true) that he was bound and served his apprenticeship to a barber and peruke maker in the parish of Croydon aforesaid. And says that when she had two children by her said husband (John Ebsworth) they lived as inmates in the parish of Fulham in Middlesex. At which time the parish officers of Fulham had a certificate from the parish of Croydon, to indemnify them from all charges and expenses on account of this examinant and family residing in their parish. And this examinant further saith that her first husband (John Ebsworth) since the time of serving his apprenticeship at Croydon aforesaid, she never heard nor does she believe he ever rented a house of £10 a year, or paid any parochial taxes, [or] otherwise done any act (to her knowledge) to gain a settlement. The mark of Jane Hunter. Sworn, 12 Nov. 1753, before us, Benjamin Cox, Francis Bedwell. Passed to the parish of Croydon.

268. [p.52] Middlesex. Elizabeth Moor, widow, aged about 40 years, born at Chelsea in Middlesex, upon oath saith that in the year 1738 she, this examinant, was married to William Moor, her late husband, in the liberty of the Fleet, London. And says that her said late husband was by trade a blacksmith, and that she hath often heard him say and declare to her, and this examinant verily believes it to be true, that he served his apprenticeship, or the greater part of it, with one Mr [blank] Twiford in the upper ground in the parish of Christ Church in the county of Surrey, blacksmith. And this examinant further saith that she doth not know, nor does believe, that her said husband ever rented a house of £10 a year, or paid any parochial taxes, or otherwise done any act (to her knowledge) to gain a legal settlement since serving his apprenticeship with Mr Twiford as aforesaid. The mark of Elizabeth Moor. Sworn, 30 November 1753, before us, Thomas Lediard, Benjamin Cox. Passed to Christ Church.

269. [p.53] Middlesex. Mary Andrews, aged about 34 years, the wife of James Andrews, basket maker, upon oath saith that about 8 years ago she, this examinant was married to her said husband in the liberty of the Fleet, London. By whom she has two children living; vizt, Thomas, aged near 4 years, and Mary, 2 years and upwards. And says that her said husband often told her, and she believes it to be true (she having the custody of his indentures), that he was bound to and served his apprenticeship with one Mr John Lovell, a basket maker in the parish of Wantage in the county of Berkshire for seven years. And says that her said husband, since the time of serving his apprenticeship as aforesaid, has not rented a house of £10 a year, or paid any parochial taxes or otherwise done any act (to her knowledge) to gain a legal settlement. And says that her husband having absconded and left her and she being ill, [she] is not capable of working to support her family. And this examinant farther says that she has a daughter named Elizabeth Carpenter, aged near 15 years, who was born about seven years before this examinant was married, at some village or place upon the road in Oxfordshire as she was going to Cirencester in order to lie-in at her father's house there. But the name of the place where she was delivered, this examinant declares she does not know or can remember. And this examinant also further says that as to her own settlement before her marriage (and at the time she was delivered of her said daughter Elizabeth) [it] was in the parish of Kensington in the county of Middlesex by living near four years a hired servant with one Mr Henry Linford, a farmer in the said parish of Kensington, of whom she received £4 pounds a year wages, meat, drink and lodging. The mark of Mary Andrews. Sworn, 10 Dec., before us, King Gould, Samuel Wegg. Mary Andrews and her two children; vizt, Thomas and Mary, were passed to Wantage.

270. [p.54] Middlesex. Jeffery Hunt, Midshipman, aged about 29 years, upon oath says that his father, Jeffery Hunt, peruke maker, often informed this examinant, and he believes it to be true, that his said father above 29 years ago rented a house of £40 a year, or thereabouts, for several years and paid all parochial taxes in the parish of St Peter and St Paul in the town or city of Bath in the county of Somerset (where this examinant was born). And that his father since the time of his quitting and leaving the said house had not rented any other house of £10 a year, or done any act to his, this examinant's knowledge, to gain a settlement elsewhere. And this examinant as to his own part, says he has not rented a house any where of £10 a year, or paid any parochial taxes, or otherwise done any act, to his knowledge, to gain a legal settlement since the time of his birth in the parish of St Peter and St Paul in the town of Bath aforesaid. Save and except this examinant being bound an apprentice about 13 years ago to one Mr Andrew Haws, captain of a man of war, who is since deceased. But says he did not serve his master one day, he going to sea without him. And as to the place of settlement of the said late captain, he declares he does not know or can give any account relating to it. And the examinant further says that about four years ago he was married to Betty Hunt, his present wife, at the parish church of Norton St Philip in the said county of Somerset, by whom he has two children; to wit, William, aged near 3 years, and Anne, an infant, aged almost 10 months. Says that his said wife is dangerously ill and he being at present out of employment, is not able to support his said family. Jeffery Hunt. Sworn, 28 Jan. 1754, before us, Benjamin Cox, Bartholomew Hammond. Passed the two children to the parish of St Peter and St Paul at Bath. N.B. The mother died upon the road going down.

271. [p.55] Middlesex. Charles Taylor, labourer, aged upwards of 27 years, upon oath says that he, this examinant, about 13 years ago was bound apprentice for seven years to Mr David Lee, distiller, who at that time lived in Old Pye Street in the parish of St John the Evangelist in the liberty of Westminster and county of Middlesex. With whom he continued and served his time except the last three months, which his master voluntarily forgave him and delivered him up his indentures. And this examinant says that since the time of his leaving his said master's service as aforesaid, he has not rented a house of £10 a year, or paid any parochial taxes, or otherwise done any act or thing, to his knowledge, to gain a settlement. Charles Taylor. Sworn, 13 Feb. 1754, before us, Benjamin Cox, Henry Fielding. Passed to the parish of St John the Evangelist.

272. [p.56] Middlesex. Rebecca Lord, widow, aged about 43 years, upon oath says that about three years ago she was married in the liberty of the Fleet, London, to John Lord, her late husband. And says that he served his apprenticeship (before her marriage with him) to his father for seven years in the parish of St James, Garlickhithe, London, where his father at that time lived a housekeeper and paid parish taxes (as this examinant's late husband frequently informed her, and by showing her his indentures and his freedom, which he took up). And this examinant says that her said late husband since the time of his serving apprenticeship with his father as aforesaid, had not rented a house of £10 a year, or paid any parochial taxes, or otherwise done any act, to her knowledge, to gain a settlement. Rebecca Lord, her mark. Sworn, 13 Feb. 1754, before us, Bejamin Cox, Henry Fielding. Passed to the parish of St James, Garlickhithe.

273. [p.57] Middlesex. William Pugh, out pensioner of Chelsea Hospital, aged 60 years, upon oath says that he, this examinant, about 30 years ago lived a servant hired by the year with the Reverend Doctor Mansar in [Holy] Trinity parish in the city of London. With whom he continued and served one year and three quarters in the station of footman and received his full wages of his said master for the said time at the rate of £5 pounds a year, meat, drink, washing and lodging. And this examinant says that about three months after he parted from his said place he was married to Mary, his first wife (who lived with him as fellow servant in the said place). And says that about two years after such his marriage, he entered himself a soldier in the army and is now an out pensioner as aforesaid. And [he] has not rented a house of £10 a year, or paid any parochial taxes, or otherwise done any act or thing, to his knowledge, to gain a settlement since the time of living a hired servant in the parish of [Holy] Trinity as aforesaid. And this examinant further says that on the month of June last he was married to Mary, his present wife, in the liberty of the Fleet, London. And he being ill of a consumptive disorder is not capable to support himself or wife. William Pugh. Sworn, 21 Feb. 1754, before us, Bejamin Cox, Francis Bedwell. Passed to [Holy] Trinity parish.

274. [p.58] Middlesex. John Goldhawk, basket maker, aged 45, upon oath says that he was born in the parish of Egham in the county of Surrey, where his father, Joseph Goldhawk, was an inhabitant and parishioner. And says that since the time of such his birth he, this examinant, has not been bound an apprentice, or rented a house of £10 a year, or paid any parochial taxes, or otherwise done any act (to his knowledge) to gain a legal settlement. And this examinant also says that about seventeen years ago he was married to Anne, his late wife, in the liberty of the Fleet, London, by whom he has four children living; to wit, John, aged 15 (who is now an apprentice), Joseph, aged 12, Thomas, aged 8, and Mary, aged 7 years. And says that at present he is not able by his labour to support and maintain Joseph, Thomas, and Mary aforesaid, without some assistance and relief. John Goldhawk. Sworn, 6 Apr. 1754, before us, Thomas Lediard, Benjamin Cox. Joseph, Thomas, and Mary were passed to Egham.

275. [p.59] Middlesex. William Muggeridge, aged about 32 years, born at Chislehurst in the county of Kent, upon oath saith that he was bound out an apprentice by his father to one John Branness of the parish of Crayford in the county of Kent, baker, for the term of seven years. With whom he continued and served his full time of his apprenticeship and had meat, drink, washing and lodging. And says that since the time of serving his apprenticeship as aforesaid he, this examinant, has not been a hired servant a year in any place, or otherwise done any act or thing, to his knowledge, to gain a settlement elsewhere. William Muggeridge. Sworn, 15 June 1754, before us, Benjamin Cox, Thomas Lediard. Passed to Crayford.

276. [p.60] Middlesex. John Rea, aged upwards of 77 years, born near Carlisle, upon oath says that when he was 17 years of age he was pressed for a foot soldier in the army. In which station he continued till he was admitted an out pensioner of Chelsea Hospital, and is now an in pensioner there. Says that about 50 years ago he, this examinant, was married at the chapel near the Blue Coat Hospital in Westminster to Mary, his wife, who is also 77 years of age. And says that at the time there was a camp in Hyde Park. In the late King George I's time he rented a house in Lloyd's Court in the parish of St Giles in the Fields in the county of Middlesex where he continued near four years and paid £15 a year rent, and all parochial taxes for the same. And says that since the time of his quitting the said house he, this examinant, has not rented any other house, or done any act, to his knowledge, to gain a settlement. And further says that he being ancient and infirm, and no other dependence but the said Hospital, is not able to support his said wife without relief. The mark of John Rea. Sworn, 15 Oct. 1754, before us, Thomas Lediard, Benjamin Cox. Mary the wife passed to St Giles parish.

277. [p.61] Middlesex and Westminster, to wit. The voluntary examination of Sarah Powell, single woman, taken 15 Oct. 1754, before Thomas Lediard esq. . . . Who upon oath saith that she is pregnant of a bastard child or children which was or were unlawfully begotten on her body by one James Silvester of the parish of Chelsea in the county of Middlesex aforesaid (with whom this examinant lived as a hired servant). [She] saith that the said James Silvester in the month of June last, about two o'clock in the morning (being just after her mistress was gone to market) came to this examinant's bedside in his dwelling house and waked her out of her sleep, and did take the advantage of getting to her in bed. And then [he] had carnal knowledge of her body the first time, and twice afterwards in the said dwelling house. And this examinant saith that the said James Silvester is the true father of the said child or children. And further saith not. The mark of Sarah Powell. Sworn at Chelsea, the day and year above written, before me, Thomas Lediard.

278. [p.62] Middlesex. Elizabeth Wingfield, widow, aged near 54 years, upon oath saith that she was married in the year 1720 to Edward Wingfield, deceased, at the parish of St Mary Magdalene, Old Fish Street, London. And that about four years ago her said late husband rented a house of £10 a year near the bridge belonging to Chelsea Waterworks, which is in the parish of St George Hanover Square in the county of Middlesex, where they continued not quite a year. But says that her said husband was charged for the said house towards the relief of the poor and that it was paid accordingly. And this examinant says that since the time of quitting the said house she, nor her said late husband, has not done any act to gain a settlement elsewhere. Elizabeth Wingfield. Sworn, 1 Nov. 1754, before us, Thomas Lediard, Benjamin Cox. Passed to St George Hanover Square.

279. [p.63] Middlesex. John Tovey, gardener, aged near 70 years, maketh oath and saith that about 20 years ago he rented a house and some land upon lease for the term of eleven years in the parish of Binstead in Hampshire at £16 a year rent, which he held for six years and paid all parochial taxes. After he quitted the said premises he, this examinant, lived a servant in two places, the last was with the Reverend Mr Rother at Chelsea for about five years. But says that he had a wife all the time he lived there who had lodgings near Chelsea. And this examinant says that since the time of his quitting the premises at Binstead aforesaid he has not rent[ed] any other house or paid any parochial taxes or otherwise done any act (to his knowledge) to gain a legal settlement. John Tovey. Sworn, 14 Dec. 1754, before Benjamin Cox.

280. [p.64] Middlesex. Richard Britton, aged near 48 years, upon oath saith that his late father (Thomas Britton) was a labouring man and lived in the parish of Dean in the county of Bedford. [And] says that he has often heard his said late father mention and declare (and he believes it to be true) that he, this examinant, was born in the said parish of Dean. And says he was brought up in the said parish and when he attained the age of 17 years he, this examinant, entered himself a soldier in the army. And says that he has not lived a year as a hired servant in any place, nor done any act (to his knowledge) to gain a legal settlement since his birth at the parish aforesaid, nor can give any other account with regard to his late father's settlement as aforesaid. And this examinant further says that about sixteen years ago he was married in the city of Dublin to Elizabeth, his present wife, by whom he has four children living; to wit, Elizabeth, aged 10 years, Richard, 6 years, Dina, upwards of 3 years, and Jane Leasy, an infant aged near 6 months. And this examinant says that he is not, nor has not been able to for some time past, to support his said family but by the charitable assistance and relief of several kind people. The mark of Richard Britton. Sworn, 18 Dec. 1754, before Thomas Lediard. All passed as vagrants to Dean.

281. [p.65] Middlesex. Margaret McGrigore, widow, aged near 60 years, upon oath says that she was born (as she hath been informed) about 20 miles of the town of Galway in the kingdom of Ireland. And says that before she was married she lived a hired servant for a year and upwards with one Mr [blank] French, a merchant in the said town of Galway. And says that she hath had two husbands (who were both soldiers) but cannot give any account of the place of settlement of either of them. And this examinant says and declares as to herself, she has not done any act, to her knowledge, to gain a settlement since she lived a servant with the said Mr French in Galway as aforesaid. The mark of Margaret McGrigore. Sworn, 18 Dec. 1754, before Thomas Lediard. Passed as a vagrant.

282. [p.66] Middlesex. Andrew Conningham, labourer, aged about 28 years, born in the parish of Rossnowleghe in the kingdom of Ireland, says that about nine years ago he lived a servant hired by the year with one John Stanley, a farmer in the parish of Powerscourt in Ireland aforesaid, with whom he continued and served fifteen months and received his full wages for the said time at the rate of £2 15s. a year, meat, drink, washing and lodging. And says that about three years ago he was married in the . . . liberty of the Fleet, London, to Sarah, his present wife. By whom he has a child living, named Sarah, aged near 15 months. And this examinant says that since the time of his living with the said John Stanley as aforesaid, he has not done any act (to his knowledge) to gain a legal settlement. Andrew Conningham. Sworn, 24 Dec. 1754, before Thomas Lediard.

283. [p.68] Middlesex. Mary Crooke, aged 65 years, upon oath says that she is the widow of Richard Crooke, deceased, who was an in pensioner of Chelsea hospital. [She] says that she cannot give any account of the place of her said late husband's settlement. But as to her own settlement, she declares and says that she has been often informed, and she believes it to be true, that she was born in the parish of Penn in the county of Buckinghamshire, she having been brought up and lived with her father (William Bowles) in the said parish till she came at the age of 20 years and upwards. After which she left her parents and for a livelihood says she has worked in different places in the fields and gardens, and has not been a hired servant a year in any place, or done any act (save and except her intermarriage) to gain a legal settlement since she came away from the said parish of Penn. The mark of Mary Crooke. Sworn, 4 Feb. 1755 before Samuel Bever.

284. [p.69] Middlesex. Thomas Robinson, aged 61 years, born as he has been informed in the parish of Kinross in Scotland, says that his late father, Archibald Robinson, was a tailor and lived in the said parish of Kinross, and that he, this examinant, lived with his said father till he entered for a soldier at the age of 23 years, and continued in the army till he was discharged, and is now an out pensioner of Chelsea Hospital. And this examinant says that he has not done any act (to his knowledge) to gain a legal settlement since the time of his birth and living with his father at Kinross in Scotland as aforesaid. And this examinant further says that about eleven years ago he was married to Jane, his present wife, in the liberty of the Fleet, London.

285. [p.70] Middlesex. Elizabeth Gordon (the wife of Roger Gordon), aged 39 years, upon oath says that about two years ago she, this examinant, was married to her said husband in the town of Leeds in Yorkshire. [She] says that he is an out pensioner of Chelsea Hospital, but cannot give any account as to the place of his legal settlement, only that he was born in some part of Scotland. As to her own settlement, [she] says that the last place she lived in as a hired servant by the year (before marriage) was with one Mr William Lonemore, a smith and farrier in the parish of Stockwell in the city of Glasgow in Scotland aforesaid, where she continued four years and received her wages for the said time, meat, drink, washing and lodging. Since which this examinant says she has not done any act, to her knowledge, (save and except her marriage aforesaid) to gain a legal settlement elsewhere. And this examinant further says that her said husband having been absconded and gone away from her for some months past, she has been so much distressed that she has been forced to ask for relief for her subsistence and support. [She] says that she has a son named Herbert Cole, aged near 3 years, a child by her first husband, John Cole, deceased, who was also a Scotsman, and was born in Glasgow aforesaid. The mark of Elizabeth Gordon. Sworn, 15 Jan. 1755, before Samuel Bever.

286. [p.71] Middlesex. The voluntary examination of Mary Morris, single woman, taken on oath before me . . . , 14 Jan. 1755. This examinant on her oath saith that on the night before King George's birthday last twelve month, she was delivered of a female bastard child in the dwelling house of one Mrs Hinton in the hamlet of Hammersmith in the parish of Fulham in the county of Middlesex aforesaid (which child is baptised and named Ann). And was unlawfully begotten on her body by one Thomas Howard of the parish of St Martin in the Fields in the county of Middlesex aforesaid, peruke maker, who had carnal knowledge of her body the first time in the room where this examinant lay in the dwelling house of the said Mr Howard, with whom this examinant lived about two months a hired servant. And [he] had carnal knowledge several times after in the said house. And this examinant says that the said Thomas Howard is the true father of the said female bastard child. And this examinant as to her own settlement says that about four years ago she lived a hired servant with her late uncle (Henry Blake) in Church Lane in the parish of Chelsea for a year and upwards, and received £3 a year wages, and has not done any act since to gain a settlement. The mark of Mary Morris. Sworn at Chelsea, 14 Jan. 1755, before Samuel Bever.

287. [p.72] Middlesex. The voluntary examination of Elizabeth Powell, single woman, taken before me, . . . [blank] Jan. 1755. Who upon oath says that on Sunday last, was five weeks, (which was 8 Dec. last) she, this examinant was delivered of a female bastard child in the apartment where her parents live in the stable yard behind Great Cheyne Row in the parish of Chelsea in the county of Middlesex. Which child is baptised and named Elizabeth and was unlawfully begotten on her body by one John Stansby, a journeyman barber in Chelsea, who had carnal knowledge of her body the first time in the garret at the house of Mr Bradley's in Chelsea aforesaid (where the examinant lived a servant) and several times after in the stable belonging to the said house. And the examinant says that the said John Stansby is the true father of the said female bastard child. The mark of Elizabeth Powell. Sworn at Chelsea the day and year above mentioned, before Samuel Bever.

288. [p.73] Middlesex. William Gentleman, aged 27 years, upon oath says that he lived in the last place a servant hired by the year with one Alexander Irwin at the Faulcon Alehouse in Pall Mall in the parish of St James, Westminster, in the county of Middlesex, where he continued and served six years, and received his wages for the said time. And says that since he quitted the said service [he] has not done any act (to his knowledge) to gain a settlement. And further says that about nine years ago he married Susannah, his present wife, at the parish church of St James in Westminster aforesaid. William Gentleman. Sworn, 15 Jan. 1755, before Samuel Bever.

289. [p.74] Middlesex. James Fox, aged near 60 years, upon oath says that he was often informed and does believe it to be true that he, this examinant, was born in the town of Galway in the kingdom of Ireland, and that he was removed from thence in his infancy (his father being at that time a soldier). And says that about 40 years ago he entered for a soldier in the army, in which station he continued always, and is now an in pensioner of Chelsea Hospital. And this examinant says that he has never rented a house of £10 a year, or paid any parochial taxes, or been a yearly hired servant or otherwise done any act (to his knowledge) to gain a legal settlement. And further says that he, this examinant, was married about four years ago to Ann, his wife, at Wisbech in the Isle of Ely in the county of Cambridge. The mark of James Fox. Sworn, 4 Feb. 1755, before Samuel Bever. [See **314**].

290. [p.75] Middlesex. William Storey, aged about 66, by trade a barber and peruke maker, maketh oath and saith that in the year 1724 he, this examinant, rented a house in Orchard Street facing St Ann's Lane in the parish of St Margaret, Westminster, in the county aforesaid. Where he continued two years and paid £13 a year rent and all parochial taxes for the same. [He] says that soon after he quitted the said house he rented an apartment of one Mrs Arundell in Hermin's Row in the parish of St Martin in the Fields in the said county of Middlesex, consisting of a shop and room behind with another room [up] two pair of stairs. But says that the way his customers came to and from his shop was through the entry or passage from the street in common with the other inmates or lodgers of the said house. And [he] paid £12 a year rent (but no taxes) and continued there one year. And this examinant says that he has never done any act, to his knowledge, to gain a legal settlement since he quitted the house in Westminster as aforesaid. William Storey. Sworn, 10 Feb. 1755, before us, Benjamin Cox, Francis Bedwell.

291. [p.76] Middlesex. Margaret Phillips, widow, aged about 37 years, upon oath saith that about eighteen years since she was married at the Fleet to John Phillips, an yearly servant to one Mr Bartholemew of Knightsbridge in the parish of St Margaret, Westminster, in the county of Middlesex, ass man. With whom he continued for the space of two years or thereabouts. And this examinant further saith that her said husband (as she has been often informed by him) never rented a house of £10 a year, or been an apprentice, or done any act to gain a settlement since the time of living with the said Mr Bartholemew. Nor has this examinant gained a settlement in any other parish since the death of her said husband. Margaret Phillips, her mark. Sworn, 18 June 1755, before us, Benjamin Cox, Saunder Welch. Passed.

292. [p.77] Middlesex. Matthew Sutton, aged about 56 years, born in the parish of St James in the liberty of Westminster, upon oath saith that about 9 Mar., which was in the year of our Lord 1716/7 he was bound apprentice to John DeSeret of the parish of St Ann in the liberty of Westminster, silver

95

smith, for the term of seven years, with whom he continued and served during all the said term of seven years. Since which time this examinant hath jobbed and done journey work but hath never lived as a servant hired by the year, or rented a house of £10 a year, or done any act (to the best of his knowledge) to gain a settlement since the serving his said apprenticeship. That on 5 Jan., which was in the year of our Lord 1753 he was married to Sarah, his present wife, in the liberty of the Fleet, London. And this examinant saith that he hath not done any act, to his knowledge, to gain a legal settlement since his apprenticeship. Matthew Sutton. Sworn, 26 July 1755, before us, Thomas Lediard, Benjamin Cox. Passed.

293. [p.78] Middlesex. The examination of Hannah Baker, who on her oath says that she is the widow of Edmund Baker, who hath been dead one year and better. Her said husband rented a house in Russell Court in the parish of St Martin in the Fields at the rent of £30 per annum and upwards, by whom she hath two children; vizt, Edmund, about 9 years of age, [and] Sarah, about 2 years of age and upwards. And [she] is now likely to become chargeable to the parish of Chelsea. The mark of Hannah Baker. Sworn before us, 29 July 1755, Samuel Bever, Benjamin Cox. Passed.

294. [p.79] Middlesex. The examination of Alice Barton, who on her oath says that she is the widow of Samuel Barton. That she hath heard her late husband declare that when he was a single man that he was a hired servant in the house of Mr Spencer, a brewer in the parish of Kensington by the year at the wages of £8 per annum, and lived with the said Mr Spencer about one year and a half, and also meat, drink and lodging. And then he lived in several places afterwards, but always was hired by the week. And about three years past he married this examinant, by whom she hath two children; vizt, John, aged about 17 months, and Samuel, aged about 11 weeks. And now is likely to become chargeable to the parish of Chelsea. The mark of Alice Barton. Sworn before us, 29 July 1755, Samuel Bever, Benjamin Cox. Passed.

295. [p.80] Middlesex. Arabella Rands, spinster, aged about 47 years, was born at Derby, upon oath saith that she was a hired servant for the space of two years and upwards to Mr John Ambler, a hop merchant in Tooly Street in the parish of St Olave, Southwark, in the county of Surrey, of whom she received the yearly wages of £5, meat, drink and lodging. That she quitted the said service about six years ago, since which time she, this examinant, hath not continued a year in any one place, nor hath she rented a house of £10 a year, or done any act to gain her legal settlement. And saith that by reason of sickness she has and continues likely to become chargeable to the parish of Chelsea. The mark of Arabella Rands. Sworn before us, 7 Aug. 1755, Thomas Lediard, Henry Fielding. Passed.

296. [p.81] Middlesex. The examination of Ann Jennings, who on her oath says that she is the wife of Lawrence Jennings, who is now a soldier in General Bragg's regiment, now in Ireland. Says that about eight years past she was married to her said husband in the Fleet. Says that her said husband is native of Ireland and born in the army, that he was in several regiments, and several times discharged, and when discharged used to wander about to look for work in any parish or place where he could find it, but the most part of the time was in the parish of Chelsea. And further says that she doth not know any thing of his legal settlement. This examinant says that she was born in the parish of Wimbledon in the county of Surrey, that her own father and grandfather was born and lived in the said parish all their times. And says that she, this examinant, hath been a hired servant by the year in several parishes, but never lived one whole year in any one place, or hath done any thing to gain any other settlement except the marriage. And says that she hath two children by her said husband; vizt, Ann, aged [p.82] about 3 years, and Elizabeth, aged about 1 year [and a] half, both which and this examinant is now chargeable to the parish of Chelsea. The mark of Ann Jennings. Sworn before me, 26 Aug. 1755, Samuel Bever. Vagrant pass.

297. [p.83] Middlesex. Examination of Mary MacDonald, who on her oath says that she is the wife of Donald MacDonald, who is now a soldier and in garrison at Plymouth, and was born in the Highlands of Scotland, but doth not know any thing of his legal settlement. And says that her maiden name was Mary Holt, born in the parish of St Andrew in town of Plymouth. And as it appears by a certificate dated 13 June 1749 under the hands of Oliver Gregory, lecturer of St Andrew in the said town, that this examinant was married to the said Donald MacDonald in the said parish, 5 May 1749, by whom she hath three children; vizt, Edward, about 5 years, and John, about 4 years, and James, about 12 months. And that she is not able to go to her husband, and is now obliged to ask relief and beg alms in the parish of Chelsea. The mark of Mary MacDonald. Sworn before me, 18 Sept. 1755, Samuel Bever. Vagrant pass.

298. [p.84] Middlesex, to wit. Examination of Martha Bracken, who on oath says that she is the widow of William Bracken, who was a pensioner in Chelsea College and died there about seven weeks past. That he was born in Ireland, but this examinant doth not know anything of his legal settlement. Says that her maiden name was Martha Amonet, born in the city of Waterford in Ireland as she hath been informed. That she was married to her said husband about seventeen years past in Ireland, and that she hath two children by her late husband; vizt, James, about 10 years 1/2, [and] Mary, aged about 8 years. And [she] is now obliged to ask relief in the parish of Chelsea. The mark of Martha Bracken. Sworn before me, 18 Sept. 1755, Samuel Bever. Vagrant pass.

299. [p.85] Middlesex, to wit. Examination of Thomas Harriss, who on oath says that he is now a pensioner in the Royal Hospital at Chelsea, that [he] is about 48 years of age, born in the parish of-Old Swinford in county of Worcester. And when he was about 20 years of age, he listed into the army. That about two years past he married Winnifred Perry, 29 May 1753, as appears by a Fleet certificate, and that his said wife is now chargeable to the parish of Chelsea, and is found wandering and begging. N.B. The examinant is blind. Sworn before me, 18 Sept. 1755, Samuel Bever. Vagrant pass.

300. [p.86] Middlesex, to wit. Examination of Margaret Jones. The examination of Peter Jones senior in relation to the settlement of the said Margaret. Vizt, Margaret Jones on her oath says that she is the wife of Peter Jones (the son of the above Peter Jones) who is lately pressed into His Majesty's service on board the Essex Man of War. That she hath now three children by her said husband; vizt, Robert, aged about 4 years, Sarah, aged at 3 years, and Jane, aged about 17 months, whom is now chargeable to the parish of Chelsea. Peter Jones senior, on his oath says that the above named Peter Jones junior, his said son, was born in the hamlet of Hammersmith, and that he, this examinant was, and now is, a certificate man from the said hamlet to the parish of Chelsea. That his said son served him as an apprentice, and hath not gain[ed] any other settlement than the settlement of this examinant, Peter Jones. The mark of Margaret Jones. The mark of Peter Jones senior. Sworn before me, 18 Sept. 1755, Samuel Bever.

301. [p.87] Middlesex, to wit. Examination of Mary Holder, who on her oath says that she is the widow of Luke Holder, by trade a chimney sweeper. Says that her late husband kept a house . . . in Pye Street in the parish of St Margaret, Westminster, at the rent of £12 or £14 per annum. That he was a hired servant by the year at the wages of £4 a year to Mr and Mrs Brown in the aforesaid house upwards of eight years before he rented the said house. He afterwards rented a house in the parish of Chelsea of £7 per annum, but never paid any parochial taxes. The mark of Mary Holder. Sworn before me, 18 Sept. 1755, Samuel Bever. Orders of removal. [See **388**].

302. [p.88] Middlesex, to wit. Examination of Elizabeth Forbes, who on her oath says that [she] was the widow of Richard Gidney, a barber and peruke maker, and that she was married to him in the town of Plymouth in the county of Devon, that he kept a shop there for some small time and then went to sea. And she never see or heard from him afterwards, till the ship come home and then she heard that he was dead. And in the year 1740 this examinant was married to Robert Forbes, a soldier, in the church of St Andrew in the said town of Plymouth, and [he] hath been dead about twelve months last past, then an out pensioner in Chelsea College. And she hath heard her late husband say that he was born in the city of Aberdeen in Scotland. And says that he was the son of Sir William Forbes in the said city. And [she] is now found begging and also chargeable to the parish of Chelsea, and hath two children by her late husband; vizt, John, aged about 10 years, and Honour, a girl about 5 years. Both which children is now provided for by her relations. The mark of Elizabeth Forbes. Sworn before me, 18 Sept. 1755, Samuel Bever.

303. [p.89] Middlesex. Examination of Walter Corbett, a in pensioner in Chelsea College, relating to the settlement of his wife Isabella. This examinant, on his oath says that he was born in the parish of Old Swinford in the county of Worcester, and was apprentice to Bennet Townsend, a nailer in the said parish. And when he was about 16 years of age, he listed into the army and hath continued ever since. And says that he was married to the said Isabella in the city of Ghent in Flanders about 46 years past, and that he is not able to provide for her. And she is now found wandering and begging in the parish of Chelsea. The mark of Walter Corbett. Sworn before me, 10 Oct. 1755, Samuel Bever. Vagrant pass.

304. [p.89 This item is crossed out in the original manuscript.] Middlesex. The voluntary examination of Lydia Bridgeman, single woman, taken before me, . . . [blank] Jan. 1756. Who upon oath saith that on Tuesday last, was five weeks (being 2 Dec. last) she, this examinant, was delivered of a male bastard child in the apartment of her sister, Mrs Kent, near the Swan Walk in the parish of Chelsea in the county of Middlesex (which child is baptised and named Robert). And was unlawfully begotten on her body by Robert Cooper, a brewer's servant in Chelsea aforesaid, who had carnal knowledge of her body for the first time at his own apartment in Robinson Lane in Chelsea aforesaid in the beginning of the month of March last, and at several other times after had carnal knowledge of her in the same apartment. And this examinant saith that the said Robert Cooper is the true father of the said child. And further saith not. [Blank]. Sworn at Chelsea, [blank] Jan. 1756, before us, [blank]. [See **305, 306**].

305. [p.90] Middlesex. The examination of Lydia Bridgeman, who on her voluntary oath says that she is a single woman, and that she was on 2 Dec. last, delivered of a male child in the parish of Chelsea. And that the said child is born a bastard, and is now likely to become chargeable to the said parish of Chelsea. And she doth charge Robert Cooper, a brewer's servant in the said parish of Chelsea with getting her with child of the said bastard, and no other person. And that the said bastard child hath been baptised in the said parish by the name of Robert. The mark of Lydia Bridgeman. Sworn before me, 22 Jan. 1756, Samuel Bever. Passed. [See **304, 306**].

306. [p.91] Middlesex. The examination of Lydia Bridgeman to her settlement, who on her oath says that she is about 25 years of age, and is a single woman, born in the parish of East Barnet in the county of Middlesex. That her father was [a] parishioner there. And she, this examinant, says that she hath been a hired servant in several places in London and in the parish of Chelsea, but never lived twelve months together in any one place, or ever was apprenticed, or hath done anything to gain any settlement since her birth. The mark of Lydia Bridgeman. Sworn before me, 22 Jan. 1756, Samuel Bever. Orders of removal. [See **304, 305**].

307. [p.92] Middlesex. Examination of Mary Hyde to settlement. Who on her oath says that she is about 35 years of age. Says that she hath been told by her mother that she was born in Lancashire, but doth not know the name of the parish, and that she was removed by her father and mother when this examinant was an infant into Shropshire, where she hath a mother now living and married to George Floyd in the parish of Dawley in the said county of Shropshire. With whom this examinant hath for fourteen or fifteen years past resided and lived with them in the winter season and hath usually come every year to or near London to work in the summer season, and hath constantly about Michaelmas gone to the said parish of Dawley aforesaid, of her own home. And should have done the same at Michaelmas last had she not been afflicted with sore eyes. And [she] hath lately been discharged out of St Georges Hospital, blind and incurable. And further says that she hath several effects of value in the said parish of Dawley aforsaid. The mark of Mary Hyde. Sworn before me, 22 Jan. 1756, Samuel Bever. Vagrant pass.

308. [p.93] Middlesex. Examination [of] Mary Phillips, who on her oath says that she was married to John Phillips, an out pensioner in Chelsea College about eight years past, that he was sent to garrison in the island of Jersey about four or five years past, and does not know whether he is dead or alive. And also that she doth not know any thing of his legal settlement. This examinant says that she is about 77 years of age, born in the parish of Little Glemham within two miles of Saxmundham in the county of Suffolk. That she was a hired servant to Elizabeth Coxell in the parish of Aldeburgh in the county of Suffolk, with whom she lived three years 1/4 at the wages of 40s. and 50s. per annum. And [at] about sixteen years of age she was married to Samuel Sparrow, born in the parish of St Michael Coslany in the city of Norwich, and learned the trade of a weaver of his father in the said parish of St Michael, and never did any thing to gain any subsequent settlement. And he died a pensioner in Chelsea College. The mark of Mary Phillips. Sworn before me, 27 Jan. 1756, Samuel Bever. [See **345, 381**].

309. [p.94] Middlesex. The examination of Elizabeth Shaw, who on her oath says that she is the wife of Charles Shaw, who is now gone and left her destitute, without any subsistence, with three small children; vizt, Charles, about 10 years old, Mary, about 8 years old, and John about 6 years old. This examinant says that her said husband, before he was married, was a hired servant by the year at the wages of about £7 or £8 per annum to Mr Wharton in the parish of St Michael Bassishaw in Basing Hall Street in the city of London, and lived with his said master about 20 months. And [he] was married to this examinant about seven or eight months before he left his said master. Then he rented a house in the parish of Chelsea at £7 per annum for about six years, and some other small houses, but never paid any parochial taxes, or served any office in the said parish. The mark of Elizabeth Shaw. Sworn before us, 5 Mar. 1756, Samuel Bever, Benjamin Cox. Passed.

310. [p.95] Middlesex. The examination of Elizabeth Symons, who on her oath says that she is the widow of William Symons, who was apprentice to

Stephen Bagshaw, a waterman in the parish of Chiswick, and who died [on] 23 Nov. last. This examinant was married to her said husband about ten weeks after . . . he was out of his time, and that he never rented any house of £10 per annum, or ever did any thing to gain any subsequent settlement. The mark of Elizabeth Symons. Sworn before us, 9 Mar. 1756, Samuel Bever. Passed.

311. [p.96] Middlesex. The examination of Mary Cottrell. Mary Cottrell, widow of Charles Cottrell, aged about 26 years, upon oath saith that she was married to the said Charles Cottrell on or about 27 June 1753 at the parish church of St Aldate in Oxford, by whom she hath had two children which are now both living; vizt, Elizabeth, aged about 2 years, and Sarah, aged about 7 months. And this examinant saith that she hath been informed by her said husband that he was bound apprentice some time about the year 1737, when he was about 14 years old, to John Ellis at Twyford in the parish of Hurst in the county of Berkshire, wheeler. And that he continued with his said master for the space of five years and upwards. [She] believes that her said husband never lived a twelve month in any place since, or hath rented a house of £10 a year, or done any act to gain a legal settlement since the said apprenticeship. And this examinant saith that by means of the death of her said husband, which happened about a month ago, she and her said two children are become chargeable to the parish of Chelsea in the county of Middlesex, and are likely to continue so. The mark of Mary Cottrell. Sworn before me, 31 May 1756, Benjamin Cox. Passed to Hurst.

312. [p.97 Blank.]

313. [p.98] Middlesex, to wit. A true copy of the examination of Mary Read, who on her oath says that she is the widow of George Read, who died about seventeen years past and left her with no child or any encumbrance. And this examinant, ever since, has been a hired servant by the year in several places. Says that the last place that she lived in was with Daniel Jones, a cobbler in Coventry Street in the parish of St James, at the wages of 20s. per annum, and lived with him about a year and a quarter after his wife's death, and that the said Daniel Jones died. And further says that she hath not done any thing to gain any subsequent settlement and is now like to come chargeable to the parish of Chelsea. Taken, 5 July 1756. The mark of Mary Read. Sworn before us, Samuel Bever. Passed to St James. N.B. She was before the wife's death hired to nurse her at 1s. per week, but after the wife died she was hired by the year.

314. [p.99] Middlesex. A true copy of the examination of James Fox, a pensioner in Chelsea College upon a vagrant pass from Camberwell in the county of Surrey, dated 7 July 1756. Who on his oath says that Ann Broadoake, who called her name Ann Fox in the said vagrant pass, is not his wife, nor ever was [he] married to her. And she, the said Ann Broadoake,

101

being present and doth acknowledge the same as witness both their hands. The mark of James Fox. Ann Broadoake. Sworn before me, 8 July 1756, Samuel Bever. N.B. Her settlement is in the parish of Chelsea. [See **289**].

315. [p.100] Middlesex. The examination of Mary Mascall taken 15 July 1756, who on her oath says she was passed by on order of two justices of this county about the year 1748 or 1749 to the parish of Gillingham in the county of Dorset from the parish of Chelsea. To which order no appeal hath been made to the best of her knowledge. But [by] her own request to the overseers of the poor for the parish of Gillingham aforesaid, she left the said parish and is now returned into the said parish of Chelsea. Mary Mascall. Sworn before me, Samuel Bever, and passed again per vagrant pass dated this day. [See **193, 196**].

316. [p.101] Middlesex. Examination of Elizabeth Lewis, who on her oath says she is the widow of John Lewis, who died lately an in pensioner in Chelsea College, by whom she hath three children; vizt, William, about 5 years, Thomas, about 3 years ¼, [and] Elizabeth, about 15 months. Says that her said husband was about 37 years old at his death, that he had been in the army about nineteen years, that he was by trade a sieve maker, born in the parish of Hanley near Bewdley in the county of Stafford, and that he never did any thing to gain any other settlement. Thus her said husband declared upon his death bed. The mark of Elizabeth Lewis. Sworn before me, 20 July 1756, Samuel Bever. Vagrant pass to Hanley aforesaid.

317. [p.102] Middlesex. Examination of Sarah Blunt, 15 July 1756. [Blank]. N.B. She pretended to have a husband, a pensioner in the college. The pensioner being present declared that she was not his wife. Sworn before me, Samuel Bever. To be entered in this book. Passed to St Andrew Holborn at the same time.

318. [p.103] Middlesex, to wit. The examination of Catherine Galleway, who on her oath says that she is the widow of John Galleway, lately deceased, an out pensioner of Chelsea College. By whom she hath one child named Margaret, about 8 years of age. This examinant has often heard her said husband declare that he was born in Ireland when his father was in the Royal Irish Dragoons. That as soon as he was fit for service he was entertained by the officers in the said regiment, and was listed into the said regiment. That he never did any thing to gain any settlement. This examinant further says that she was born in Ireland, and she never did any thing to gain any settlement in England. Is now found in the [blank]. The mark of Catherine Galleway. Sworn before me, 27 July 1756, Samuel Bever.

319. [p.104] Middlesex. The exam of Elizabeth Bullock, who on her oath says she is about 25 years of age, and is the wife of William Bullock, who is now a soldier in the Guards, born at Wolverhampton in the county of Stafford, and was apprentice to Mr Sparks, a buckle maker in the said town, and served out his said apprenticeship there. That she never heard him say that he did any thing to gain a settlement elsewhere, and hath been a soldier several years, and is now ordered away from her. And [she] hath by her said husband three children; vizt, Elizabeth, aged about 4 years, William, aged about 2 years, Thomas, aged about 2 months, all now residing in the parish of Chelsea. The mark of Elizabeth Bullock. Sworn before me, 11 Sept. 1756, Samuel Bever. Vagrant pass.

320. [p.105] Middlesex, to wit. Examination of William Jones, who on his oath says he is about 66 years of age, now an in pensioner at Chelsea College. Says that he was born near the town of Brecon in Brecknock, but cannot say what parish. That his father died when he was but 5 years of age. That his mother and this examinant used to stroll about the country a begging. That about 13 years of age he was a servant to a recruiting officer, who had no settled place of abode, and hath been in the army ever since, and hath now a wife named Catherine (maiden name Gill), born in Kinsale in the kingdom of Ireland. And this examinant was married to her 3 May 1722 in St Maltess Kinsale in the church of the said town. And she is now upwards of 60 years of age, and is now very infirm and is now chargeable to the parish of Chelsea. The mark of William Jones. Sworn, 11 Sept. 1756, before me, Samuel Bever. Passed. [See 322].

321. [p.106] Middlesex, to wit. Examination of John Green, who on his oath says he is about 58 years of age, born in the town of Chesterfield in the county of Derby, and apprentice to John Low, shoemaker in the said town. And [he] served out his apprenticeship. Soon after, he listed into the army, [and] never did any thing to gain any other settlement. And [he] is now a pensioner in Chelsea College, and hath now a wife named Margaret, whom he married in the parish church of St Andrews in the island of Guernsey, 24 May 1753. John Green. Sworn before me, 11 Sept. 1756, [blank]. Passed. [See 323].

322. [p.107] Middlesex. The examination of Catherine Jones, who on her oath says that she is the wife of William Jones, an in pensioner in the Royal Hospital in Chelsea, who is very old and utterly unable to provide for her. And the legal settlement of the said William is not to be found. This examinant says that she was born in Kinsale and was also married about 33 or 34 years past (as it appears on a certificate, the said William and Catherine Gill was married 3 May 1722) in St Maltess Kinsale in the kingdom of Ireland. That she is now very infirm and hath no lodging or place of abode. The mark of Catherine Jones. Sworn before me, 15 Sept. 1756, Samuel Bever. Vagrant pass. [See 320].

323. [p.108] Middlesex. The examination of Margaret Green, who on her oath says that she is about 40 years of age, that she is the wife of John Green, an in pensioner in Chelsea College . . . who is utterly unable to provide for her. And [says] that the legal settlement of the said John is in the town of Chesterfield in the county of Derby, where he was born and served an apprenticeship to John Low, a shoemaker in the said town

aforesaid, and soon after he entered himself in the army and hath never done anything to gain any other settlement. The mark of Margaret Green. Sworn before me, 15 Sept. 1756, Samuel Bever. Vagrant pass. [See **321**].

324. [p.109] Middlesex. The examination of Sarah Tomms, who on her oath says that she is the wife of Thomas Tomms, who is gone and left her with three children; vizt, Richard, about 5 years, Mary, about 2 years old, [and] Thomas, about 1 month. Says that her said husband was a hired servant by the year to [blank] Stooe in the parish of Swerford in the county of Oxford, with whom he lived two years, as this examinant hath heard him declare. And to this examinant['s] knowledge, her said husband was sworn to his settlement in the said county, which was adjudged to be in the said parish of Swerford. And [she] hath not done any thing to gain any other settlement, and is now found wandering in the parish of Chelsea. The mark of Sarah Tomms. Sworn before me, 27 Sept. 1756, [blank]. Vagrant pass.

325. [p.110] Middlesex. The examination of Ann Aylward, who on her oath says that she is a single woman. Says that in the year 1751 she was hired by the year at the wages of £6 to Dr Doyley in the parish of Chelsea, with whom she lived fourteen months, all under one hiring. And hath lived in several places since, but hath not been in any one for a year, and hath not done anything to gain any subsequent settlement. Ann Aylward. Sworn before me, 27 Sept. 1756, Samuel Bever. Passed.

326. [p.111] Middlesex. Examination of Mary Smith, who on her oath says that she is a single woman, about 64 or 65 years of age. That about five years past she was hired by the year to Mr John Davenport to be matron of the workhouse in St Martin Vintry in London, at the wages of £5 per annum, in which service she lived about three years, and hath not done any thing to gain any settlement since. And [she] is now reduced and likely to come chargeable to the parish of Chelsea. Mary Smith. Sworn before me, 15 Oct. 1756, Samuel Bever. Passed by an order, Philip Dyos.

327. Middlesex. Sarah Bellamy, an in pensioner wife. Vagrant pass to Newark in Nottinghamshire, 2 Nov. 1756, Samuel Bever.

328. [p.112] Middlesex, to wit. The examination of Amey Fuller, whom on her oath says that she is about 53 years of age, and is a single woman. That about four years and half past, she was hired by the year to Roger Life, a farmer in the parish of Acton in the said county, at the wages of £4 per annum. With whom she lived one year and half under one and the same hiring. That since she was hired to John Power in Bridges Street in the parish of Covent Garden, and lived with him about four months, and hath not been in any service since. And [she] is now come chargeable to the parish of Chelsea. The mark of Amey Fuller. Sworn before us, 9 Nov. 1756, Samuel Bever, Charles Cartrest.

329. [p.113] Middlesex, to wit. The examination of Mary Saunders, who on her oath says that she is the widow of William Saunders, a soldier in the guards who died in September last, by whom she hath one boy named William. Which boy was born in the parish of Chelsea and is now about 9 years and [a] half old. This examinant says that she did often enquire of her said husband where he was born and where his settlement was, but he never would tell her. Therefore [she] does not know any thing of his settlement. Says that . . . she, this examinant, was born in the parish of St Mary Whitechapel. Says that she was born at her grandmother['s] house in Red Lyon Street in the said parish. Says her name was Usshe Rippinker. Says her father's name was Thomas Wisles, that he was apprentice to a tailor in Blackfriars, but does not know his master['s] name, who died before he was out of time. That he was free of the Merchant Tailors Company in London. Further says that there is a butcher in Clare Market that used to call her husband school fellow, and that he told this examinant that her husband come from Aylesbury in Buckinghamshire. And this examinant and her son is now likely to become chargeable to the parish of Chelsea. Further says that she hath heard William Holloway, the aforesaid butcher, say that he knew that the said William Saunders lived about 20 years past a hired [p.114] servant to Rewland Bracebridge, a farmer in the parish of Aylesbury in the county of Bucks, with whom he lived a long time. And that he believed that he was born in the said town of Aylesbury. This examinant says that he, her husband, was in the army about nineteen years before he died. Mary Sanders. Sworn before me, 24 Nov. 1756, Samuel Bever. Vagrant pass to Aylesbury in Bucks.

330. [p.115] Middlesex, to wit. Examination of Martha Elliss, who on her oath says that she is about 77 years of age, born in the city of Canterbury in the parish of St Paul in the said city. That she never was apprentice, or any hired servant. Says that she was the daughter of Thomas White, a baker in the said parish of St Paul, [and] when she was about 21 years of age, she was married to Evan Elliss, a trooper in General Wood's horse, and was so for many years and hath been dead about eight years, and was an in pensioner in Chelsea College at the time of his death. She doth not know any thing of her said husband['s] settlement, and she is now destitute of any place of abode, money or maintenance. The mark of Martha Elliss. Sworn before me, 2 Dec. 1756, Samuel Bever. Vagrant pass to Canterbury.

331. [p.116] Middlesex, to wit. The examination of Elizabeth Cock, who on her oath says that she is about 16 years of age and was born in the parish of Chelsea, and apprenticed to Robert Ellis, a basket maker in the parish of St George Hanover Square, with whom she lived for some time until her said master removed into the parish of Chelsea. And there this examinant lived with her said master about one year and a half, and until that her said master went away and left her. Then this examinant went and lived with her own sister, a lodger in the parish of Fulham, without any hiring for a year, or any wages. And lived with her about one year and a half, and then came and applied herself to the overseers of the poor in the said parish of Chelsea. The mark of Elizabeth Cock. Sworn before me, 22 Dec. 1756, Samuel Bever.

332. [p.117] Middlesex. The examination of Mary Neat alias Bignall, who on her oath says that she is about 46 years of age, born at Earls Court in the parish of Kensington. That when she was about 16 years of age she was married to Joseph Neat, a woolcomber about her own age, but does not know where he was born, or apprentice, or any thing of his settlement, and was a soldier in the guards. That about six months after she was married to him, . . . he went to Philadelphia. That after he was gone about six or seven months, this examinant received a letter from her said husband dated from Philadelphia aforesaid. That this examinant soon after her said husband left her went to live about three years and half with [blank] Smith in the Haymarket in the liberty of Westminster, and then come from the said Smith about a fortnight, and then was married to John Bignall, who then was a servant to Mr Meriton to look after his gardens and house at Ealing, with whom he lived four or five years, and always lived in his house in the said parish of Ealing. And she hath (as she hopes) one child or son by the said Joseph Neat, [who] (if alive) is now about 26 years of age. [p.118] Further saith that she hath now living three children begotten on her body by the said John Bignall; vizt, Elizabeth, aged about 16 years, Marian, aged about 6 years, Ann, aged about 19 months. All three born at Earls Court in the parish of Kensington. Which two last is now in the parish of Chelsea. Says that the said John Bignall was in company with the said Joseph Neat at the house of Joseph Bounds in the parish of Kensignton, where the said Joseph Neat sold this examinant to the said John Bignall by writing, made by [blank] Miller, an attorney. Says that the said John Bignall arrested the said Joseph Neat about 16 years past for the maintenance of William Neat the son of the said Joseph. The mark of Mary Neat (alias) Bignall. Sworn before us, 28 Dec. 1756, Samuel Bever, Charles Wale.

Further says that before she was married she lived with Mr Wright at Earls Court about three years as a servant, and had meat, drink, washing and lodging and apparel, but no money. The mark of the above named.

333. [p.119] Middlesex, to wit. The examination of Mary Spittle, concerning the settlement of Thomas Robinson, a male child about 7 years of age. Says that he is the son of Thomas and Mary Robinson, whom she knoweth very well, but says that she doth not know any thing of the said Thomas or Mary where they are at this time. Says that the said Mary and this child were passed from St Giles in the county of Middlesex about two years 1/2 past to the town of Beverley in Yorkshire as the legal settlement of the said Mary and child. Which said child is now found wandering and destitute in the parish of Chelsea in the said county of Middlesex. The mark of Mary Spittle. Sworn before me, 6 Jan. 1757, Samuel Bever. Vagrant pass to Beverley.

334. [p.120] Middlesex. The examination of Hannah Burgiss, who on her oath says that she is a single woman and never was married. About 70 years ago [she was] born in the parish of Emley near Wakefield in the [blank] riding in the county of York. [Blank].

335. [p.121] Middlesex. The examination of Elizabeth Ann Booth, who on her oath says that she is about 20 years of age, and is the wife of Samuel Booth, an out pensioner of Chelsea College, belonging to the regiment [of the] late Colonel Durours, now at Antigua. That he is now gone and left this examinant with one male child, named James, about 2 years and 2 months old. Says that she was married to him in the Fleet 25 Oct. 1753. Says that her said husband was born in the parish of Over Alderley, and was apprentice to John Lovet, a miller in the parish of Prestbury in the county of Cheshire. And [after] about four or five year his said master died, and he soon after entered himself a soldier, and never gained any other settlement. The mark of Elizabeth Ann Booth. Sworn before me, 22 Jan. 1757, Samuel Bever. Vagrant pass.

336. [p.122] Middlesex. Examination of Mary Dean, who on her oath says that she is the wife of John Dean, who is now on board the Somerset Man of War, who has followed the trade of a sawyer as long as she hath known him. That he use to work for Mr Gomme, a carpenter at Hammersmith, and also for Mr Randall at Chelsea. Says that her husband was born in the town of High Wycombe in the county of Bucks, and that she never heard him say that he gained any subsequent settlement. That she hath two children; vizt, John, aged about 4 years, [and] Francis, aged about 2 years 1/2 old. Mary Dean. Sworn before me, 27 Jan. 1757, Samuel Bever. N.B. That the said child John is supported and maintained by the friends and relations; therefore is not sent with the mother.

337. [p.123] Middlesex. Examination of Elizabeth Austin, who on her oath says that she is the wife of Edward Austin who is now gone and left her. Says that her said husband and this examinant and three children was passed by an order of removal about Dec. 1751 to the parish of St Sepulchres in London, and there hath not been any appeal to the said pass from the parish of Chelsea. Further says that she, this examinant, and her children was provided for and maintain in the workhouse of St Sepulchres for nine months, and left the same about two years past. Says that she hath now one child with her, named John, aged about 7 years old, and one child named Elizabeth, about 10 months. And is now become chargeable to the parish of Chelsea without any certificate. The mark of Elizabeth Austin. Sworn before us, 2 May 1757, Samuel Bever, Henry Fielding. Passed by an order. [See **245**].

338. [p.124] Middlesex. The examination of Ann Knott, who on her oath says that she is the wife of George Knott, late an in pensioner in Chelsea College, but now in garrison at Plymouth. That she hath two children by him; vizt, Dorothy, age about 4 years, and Nicolas about one year 1/4. Says that her said husband was born in the city of Gloucester, and is about 48 years of age. And that he was apprentice to a barber and peruke maker in the said city. And says that she hath heard her said husband declare that he served his master about nine months and was discharged, and soon after entered himself into the army, and hath not done any thing since to gain

107

any other settlement. Says that she is not able to say in what parish that he was apprentice, and hath not any thing to support herself and her children. Ann Knott. Sworn before me, 7 July 1757, Samuel Bever. Vagrant pass.

339. [p.125] Middlesex. The examination of Jane Smith alias Miles, who on her oath says that she is a single woman and never was married, although she did for many years cohabit with Jonathan Miles. That she was a hired servant by the year to Mrs Goodalls in the parish of Chelsea, with whom she lived about thirteen months at the wages of £5 per annum, and never did any thing to gain any subsequent settlement. The mark of Jane Smith. Sworn before me, 19 July 1757, Samuel Bever.

340. [p.126] Middlesex. The examination of Mary Johnson, who on her oath says that she is the widow of Francis Johnson, who hath been dead about 19 or 20 years past, and who was permitted to reside in the parish of Chelsea from the parish of Milton Ernest in the county of Bedford. And [she] is now obliged to come chargeable to the said parish of Chelsea. The mark of Mary Johnson. Sworn before us, 21 July 1757, Samuel Bever. Orders to Milton Ernest.

341. [p.127] Middlesex. Examination of Rice Davies, who on his oath says that he is now an in pensioner in Chelsea College, and is about 79 years of age. That he hath a wife named Elizabeth, aged about 72, now residing in the parish of Chelsea, and is past her labour. And he, this examinant, is not able to support her and is now likely to come chargeable to the said parish of Chelsea. Further says that he was a hired servant by the year to the Lord Orkney, with whom he lived several years, and was married to Elizabeth, now his wife, while he was in the said service, which was on 20 Oct. 1709, and lived in the said service to the end of the year. Which year of service and wages expired the 5 Mar. following. And [he] is very sure that the last 40 days of servitude was in the parish of Taplow in the county of Bucks. The mark of Rice Davies. Sworn before us, 21 July 1757, Samuel Bever, Francis Tackman. Order to Taplow.

342. [p.128] Middlesex. The examination of Sarah Knapp, who on her oath says that she is the widow of James Knapp, an out pensioner from Chelsea College, formerly in Winyards regiment, and who died at Christmas last. By whom she hath one boy about 8 years old. Says that she hath heard her said husband declare that his father was a soldier and that he was born when his father was on duty in Ireland. And that her said husband came from Ireland when he was about 8 years old, and that he never knew any thing of his fathers settlement. Nor did he ever gain any settlement of his own, either in Ireland or England. This examinant further says that she is about 54 years of age, that her maiden name was Golding, born in the town of Abingdon in the county of Berkshire. Says that her father, whose name was Thomas Golding, . . . rented a house of £10 per annum and paid all parochial dues, next door but one to the Axe and Gate in the parish of Chelsea, and died there about seventeen years past. That she was a hired servant by the year to William Wells at the wages of £4 and £5 per annum, and lived with him about two years in the said parish of Chelsea, and never was any hired servant afterwards. The mark of Sarah Knapp. Sworn before me, 28 July 1757, Samuel Bever.

343. [p.129] Middlesex, to wit. The examination of Elizabeth Lovell (aged about 30 years), widow of Joseph Lovell, deceased, taken before us, . . . 8 Aug. 1757. Who on her oath saith that in the month of November, which was in the year of our Lord 1749 she was married at the sign of the Hand and Pen in the rules of the Fleet Prison to Joseph Lovell, her late husband, deceased. And in the month of May 1753, rented a house known by the sign of Lord Halford's Arms, victualling house, situate in a place called Grosvenor Passage or Little Grosvenor Street in the parish of St George Hanover Square in the said county of Middlesex, where he exercised the employ or business of a common victualler for the space of half a year and upwards, and paid rent and all parish taxes for the said house after the rate of £21 per annum. Saith that the said Joseph Lovell, her late husband, departed this life as she has been informed, about three years since, and has left only one child living, named Ann, aged about 7 years. That to the best of her knowledge and belief her said husband hath not done any act to gain a legal settlement since he rented the said house in the parish of St George Hanover Square aforesaid. Elizabeth Lovell. Sworn this day and year above mentioned, before us, Bartholomew Hammond, Theodore Lydenham.

344. [p.130] Middlesex. Examination of Elizabeth La Grove, who on her oath says that she is the widow of James La Grove, who died 8 Jan. 1757. And that she hath heard her said husband declare that he was a native of France, and when young he entered himself a soldier in General Briggs' regiment, then in Ireland. And at Cork, married this examinant, and in May 1756 was admitted an out pensioner in Chelsea College. And by whom this examinant hath three children with her in the parish of Chelsea; vizt, Elizabeth, aged 12 years, Griffith, aged about 9 years, [and] Katherine, aged about 7 years. This examinant further says that she was born in the city of Dublin, that Elizabeth, her daughter, was born in the parish of Kingston in the county of Surrey, and Griffith and Katherine was born in the Isle of Jersey. The mark of Elizabeth La Grove. Sworn before me, 9 Aug. 1757, Samuel Bever. Vagrant pass to Ireland, to rest at Bridewell.

345. [p.131] Middlesex. Examination of John Phillips, who on his oath says that he is an out pensioner of the College of Chelsea. That he hath a wife named Mary, to whom he was married about eleven years past. Says that he was apprentice to John Chipperfield, a baker in the parish of St Margaret in the liberty of Westminster, with whom he served about six years and then entered into the King's service, and never did any thing to gain a subsequent settlement, and is not able to maintain his said wife. John Phillips. Sworn before us, 9 Aug. 1757, Samuel Bever, Benjamin Cox. To be passed by an order. [See **308**, **381**].

346. [p.132] Middlesex. The examination of Frances Buckland, who on her oath says that she is a single woman, that she was a hired servant by the year to Mr Beddycoat in the parish of All Hallows Lombard Street in the city of London, and was passed by an order about four years past from the parish of Broadway in the county of Worcester to the said parish of All Hallows. And [she] was maintained there, and hath not done any thing since to gain any other settlement. That she hath lately applied herself to the said parish of All Hallows for relief, and hath been refused any relief without a pass. The mark of Frances Buckland. Sworn before me, 15 Aug. 1757, Samuel Bever, Benjamin Cox. Passed by an order.

347. [p.133] Middlesex. The examination of Ann Davey, 25 Aug. 1757, who on her oath says that she is a single woman about 20 years of age, born in the parish of Pattingham in the county of Stafford, was never apprentice, or any hired servant by the year. That six or seven years past she came to John Hutchins in the parish of Chelsea, and was hired by the week at 4s. 6d. or 5s. per week, and lay in his house, and paid him for her lodging for about ¾ of a year. Then she took another lodging in the said parish and continued to work for the said Hutchins at so much a week. [She] hath lately been in the Lock Hospital and is now in the workhouse at Chelsea, and says that the said Hutchins is willing to hire her by the year and to lodge in his house. The mark of Ann Davey. Sworn before me, 25 Aug. 1757, Samuel Bever.

348. [p.134] Middlesex. The examination of Sarah Grice, widow of Robert Grice, aged about 53, who on her oath saith that she was married in the year 1739 at the Fleet to her late husband, Robert Grice, deceased, who laboured for his livelihood. That they lived together about nine years in a small house in Barbican, but paid no taxes and never had any children. That she has been in several places at service since the death of her said husband. And about November or December, which was in the year 1754, this examinant was hired as a servant to Mr Edward Jones, a victualler at the sign of the French Horn and Half Moon in Strulton Ground in the parish of St Margaret in the liberty of Westminster, where she continued as a hired servant at the wages of £5 per annum. And was there provided with meat, drink, washing and lodging for the space of fourteen months. Since which time she, this examinant, hath not rented a house, or done any act to gain a legal settlement, and is now likely to become chargeable to the said parish of Chelsea. The mark of Sarah Grice. Sworn before us, 16 Sept. 1757, Benjamin Cox, John Goodchild.

349. [p.135] Middlesex. The examination of Ann Bingham, single woman, lodging with her mother, Elizabeth Bingham, in the Kings Road in the parish of Chelsea in the county of Middlesex, taken upon oath, 19 Sept. 1757. This examinant upon her oath saith that she is 19 years of age and never was married, bound an apprentice, kept house rented £10 by the year, or paid any parish taxes. But that she was a yearly hired servant to Mr Jarret, a publican at the Kings Arms in Compton Street in the parish of

St Ann within the liberty of Westminster in the county of Middlesex for the space of one year and nine months at the yearly wages of £4, diet and lodging, quitted the same about four months ago. And this examinant upon her voluntary oath further saith that she is now great with child or children, which is or are likely to be born a bastard or bastards. And that Michael Como, an upholster lodging at Mr Jarrett's aforesaid, had carnal knowledge of her body in the month of February last, upon a bed in the room up three pair of stairs forwards in the house of Mr Jarrett aforesaid, and several times afterwards at the same place. At which or one of which times he the said Michael Como did beget her with . . . the child or children she now goeth with and is pregnant of. And that he, the said Michael Como, is the true and only father thereof and no man else. Ann Bingham. Sworn the day and year above said, before me, Benjamin Cox.

350. [p.136] Middlesex. The examination of George Francis, one of the beadles of the parish of St Luke Chelsea in the county of Middlesex taken upon oath, 19 Sept. 1757. The examinant upon his oath saith that he very well knows Joseph Akerman, a poor child now in the workhouse of and in the parish of Chelsea aforesaid. And that the said Joseph Akerman was by the parish officers of Chelsea aforesaid bound out apprentice by indenture (dated 10 Nov. 1755) to Robert Wright, of Sugar Loaf Court in the parish of St Botolph Without Aldgate within the liberty of the city of London and continued with his said master for above twelve months in Sugar Loaf Court aforesaid. And further saith not. George Francis. Taken and sworn the day and year abovesaid, before Benjamin Cox, Henry Fielding. [See **376**].

351. [p.137] Middlesex. Examination of Mary Weaver, who on her oath says that she is a single woman about 19 years of age, born in the parish Whittington in the county of Salop. That when she was about 13 or 14 years of age she went to service in the said parish, and the last place that she lived in as a hired servant was with John Reaves in the said parish of Whittington near Oswestry in the said county of Shropshire, with whom she lived about 16 or 17 months at the wages of 40s. per annum and a shift. And [she] left the said Reaves in the month of May last, and then come to London and hath worked about in the fields and gardens in the parish of Kensington and Chelsea, laying about in barns and out houses and under the hedges in the parish of Chelsea aforesaid. The mark of Mary Weaver. Sworn before me, 10 Nov. 1757, Samuel Bever.

352. [p.138] Middlesex. Examination of William Boxall, who on his oath says that he very well knows a female. [See **260**].

353. Middlesex. Examination of Catherine Musgrove, who on her oath says that she is a single woman about 18 years of age, born in the hamlet of Hammersmith in the said county, and that her father was a parishioner there. That she never was apprentice, or hired servant and was supported in the workhouse of the said hamlet in March last, and hath ever since strolled about in the parish of Kensington etc. to get work. And is now found in the parish of Chelsea laying in the out houses of Mr Burchett in the said parish by his consent. And is now likely to become chargeable to the said parish of Chelsea. The mark of Catherine Musgrove. Sworn before us, 15 Dec. 1757, Samuel Bever, Charles Wale.

354. [p.139] Middlesex, to wit. Examination of Mary Pausley touching the settlement of Thomas Jefferys, a child about 8 years old, which she, this examinant, had by her former husband. Who on her oath says that she was formerly married to Robert Jefferys at the Fleet about nine years past. Says that when she first knew him he worked with Mr Silvester at Brompton in the parish of Kensington. Afterwards she says that he was a hired servant to Mr Field, a basket maker in the parish of Chelsea. Says that he did not live twelve months with Mr Field. Says that her late husband was maintained by his mother, who work[ed] with Mr Hutchins in Chelsea until she died, then he worked afterwards for the above Mr Silvester [and Mr] Field, but she doth not know any thing of his settlement. Says that she had this child by her late husband. Further says that she never did any thing to gain any settlement of her own. Says that her father John Jones was a certificate man from the parish of St Mary Magdalene, Bermondsey in Southwark to the parish of St Albans in Hertfordshire. The mark of Mary Pausley. Sworn before [me], 31 Jan. 1758, . . . Samuel Bever.

355. [p.140] Middlesex. The examination of Elizabeth Rowlett, who on her oath says that she is about 47 years of age, the widow of Jonathan Rowlett, a native of Ireland, and when she first knew him he was an in pensioner in Chelsea College. She hath heard her said husband declare that on or about the present King's coming to the crown, that he was discharged from General Hervey's horse. And after he was discharged he married a widow in Old Brentford and then he took a house of £10 or £12 per annum . . . and kept a distiller shop there, but does not know whether he paid any parochial taxes. And [he] lived there above 20 years and left the said Old Brentford about twelve years past, and then come and was an in pensioner in the said college, where he married this examinant, 31 Aug. 1750, at the Fleet, as appears by a piece of parchment to me produced. And she is now come chargeable to the parish of Chelsea. The mark of Elizabeth Rowlett. Sworn before me, 27 Feb. 1758, Samuel Bever. [The whole of the preceding paragraph is crossed out in the original.] Upon further inquiry it is found that the said Jonathan Rowlett gained no settlement at Old Brentford. [See **357**].

356. [p.141] Middlesex. The examination of Gilbert Termillin, brought before me in a cart by George Francis from Chelsea, who on his oath says that he was born in the parish of St Ervan in the county of Cornwall, that he was apprentice Thomas Bluy, a barber there, and never was a hired servant out of the said parish to live a whole year. [That he] is now about 40 years of age and is now a pensioner in Chelsea College, and hath lately received his pension from the said college. And is now in a sick and weak condition and hath spent all his money and is now chargeable to the parish of Chelsea and acting as a vagrant in the said parish, having neither house or home, but [is forced] to lay where he can and begging relief. The mark of Gilbert Termillin. Sworn before me, 27 Jan. 1758, Samuel Bever.

357. [p.142] Middlesex. The examination of Elizabeth Rowlett, who on her oath says that she is about 47 years of age, that she is the widow of Jonathan Rowlett, who was a native of Ireland and hath been dead near two years. That she doth not know anything of his settlement . . . . That she, this examinant, before she married the said Jonathan, she was the widow of Thomas Tucker who died and left her with no child or children. That she after his death was a hired servant to the Lady Howell in the parish of Aldermaston in the county of Berkshire at the wages of £6 per annum. With whom she lived one whole year and ten months, and received her full wages and did never hire her self afterwards by the year, but used to work by the day or week for her living. The mark of Elizabeth Rowlett. Sworn before me, 27 Feb. 1758, Samuel Bever. Passed per order. [See **355**].

358. [n.p.] Middlesex. The examination of Elizabeth Hender touching the settlement of Thomas her son, a bastard about 7 years of age. Who on her oath says that she is the widow of Abraham Hender, a soldier in the 3rd Regiment of Guards. And says that he was born and his friends and relations lived somewhere in Wiltshire, and that she was married to him, but knows nothing of his settlement, about two years past near Cricklade in the said county. And that he died the latter end of Aug. 1757, and that she is now with child by him. Says that she is now about 33 years of age, that she lived with Mr Harriss at the Prince Eugene Head in Jews Row when she was a single woman, once twelve month or better, and left the said service about twelve years. And then she kept company with one Joseph Evans, an out pensioner of Chelsea College, about ten or twelve years, and hath now two children by him; vizt, Mary, about 10 years of age, born in the parish of Little Wenlock in the county of Shropshire, now with Mary Hender in London, but does not know the place where she lives. The other child is named Thomas, born in the parish of Battersea in the county of Surrey and is about 7 years. Both bastards born of her body, for that she says that she never was married to the said Evans who is the father of both the said bastards. And says that the bastard Thomas was baptised in the said parish of Battersea, and that she hath applied herself to the parish of Battersea for relief, but they would not take the said child until he was passed from parish of Chelsea where it is now chargeable. The mark of Elizabeth Hender. [Sworn] before me, Mar. 1758. Passed the child to Battersea per order. N.B. It does not appear that she is the widow of Hender or ever married. Says that he was in Colonel Burges Company. . . Not foresworn, sent to Bridewell, 11 Mar. 1758.

359. [p.144] Middlesex. The examination of William Carr, 56 years old, who on his oath says that he is an out pensioner to Chelsea College [and] that he is now obliged to ask relief. Says that he has a wife named Mary and two children, Sarah, about 6 years, and Ann about 4 years. Says that he was born in the town of Liverpool in the county of Lancashire and he hath been in the army in North America about 34 years and never did any thing to gain any other settlement. [He] is now found wandering and begging in the said parish of Chelsea. The mark of William Carr. Sworn before me, 11 Mar. 1758, Samuel Bever. Vagrant pass.

360. [p.145] Middlesex. The examination of John Waite of the hamlet of Hammersmith touching the settlement of Katherine and John Ward, two children found in the parish of Chelsea, wandering there without father or mother, she being lately deceased. Who on his oath says that he, this examinant, is uncle by their mother['s] side to the aforesaid children. Who says that he was well acquainted with John Ward, who is the father of the aforesaid children, and further says that the said John Ward was born in parish of Great Torrington in the county of Devon, and that he hath heard by his sister, the mother of the said two children, that the said John Ward was apprentice to a saddler in the said parish of Great Torrington, and kept a house in the said parish several years, and never did any thing to gain any subsequent settlement that he knows. The children; vizt, John is about 8 years old, and Katherine about 2 years old. John Waite. Sworn before me, 11 Mar. 1758, Samuel Bever. By a letter that appears before me under the hand of the said John Ward, that he is now resident at Mr Richard Martins, saddler in Tavistock. Vagrant pass.

361. [p.146] Middlesex. The examination of Thomas Dixon, overseer of the poor of the parish of Chelsea in the said county, who on his oath says that George Babb, a child of about 13 years of age, is now come chargeable to the said parish of Chelsea, he, the said George, having lately intruded himself into the said parish. And as it appears unto us as well upon the oath of the said Thomas Dixon, that it also appears that the said George Babb is now an apprentice to James Bryerley, a weaver in the parish of St Matthew Bethnal Green in the said county of Middlesex, by an indenture dated 19 Jan. 1756. Thomas Dixon. Sworn before us, 16 Mar. 1758, Samuel Bever, Benjamin Cox. [See **376**].

362. [p.147] Middlesex. Examination of Thomas Cox, who on his oath says that he is a single man about 40 years of age, that the last place he lived as a hired servant was with Sir Peter Deline in Grosvenor Square. With whom he lived three years at the wages of £3 10s. and left the said service about six years past, and hath not been a servant by the year ever since. And [he] is now likely to come chargeable to the parish of Chelsea. The mark of Thomas Cox. Sworn before us, 10 Apr. 1758, Samuel Bever, Charles Wale. Passed To St George Hanover Square.

363. [p.148] Middlesex. The examination of Jane Rumbell, single woman, in the workhouse of and belonging to the parish of St Luke Chelsea in the county of Middlesex, taken upon oath 25 Apr. 1758. This examinant upon her oath saith that she is 22 years of age and never was married, and that she was on 20 Apr. 1757 delivered of a hale bastard child (since christened John) yet living, and become chargeable to the said parish of St Luke Chelsea. And that John Phillips heretofore of Lawrence Street in Chelsea aforesaid, had carnal knowledge of her body in the year 1754 upon a bed in a house near Charring Cross in London, and several times afterwards during the space of three years at different times and places. At which, or one of which, times he, the said John Phillips, did beget on her body the said male bastard child, and that he, the said John Phillips, is the true and only father thereof and no man else. Jane Rumbell. Taken and sworn the day and year above said, before me, Benjamin Cox.

364. [p.149] Middlesex. The examination of Elizabeth Steward, aged about 43 years, wife of Charles Steward, who on her oath saith she was married to her said husband at the Fleet in the year 1729, but hath been since informed that his real surname was De Champs, that he then was valet or servant hired by the year to one General Mackcaul who lodged in St Martins Lane in the parish of St Martin in the Fields in the county of Middlesex aforesaid. That this examinant's said husband informed her he was allowed by his said master after the rate of £18 per annum wages besides his lodging, which was in his master's in St Martins Lane aforesaid. And that he had resided there for the space of seven years before such his marriage with [this] examinant. That she hath two children now living, the one named James, aged about 26 years, and the other named Anna Maria, aged about 8 years. She believes her husband was born somewhere in the kingdom of Ireland, but where she knows not. That he left her many years ago in the parish of Chelsea, and where he now is she knows not. But as she was never informed of his death is rather induced to think him living than dead. She doth not know that her said husband ever rented [p.150] a house of £10 per annum or hath ever done any other act, except his service with General Mackcaul, to gain a legal settlement. And this examinant further saith she is informed by her mother and believes it to be true, that she was born in the parish of St Mary . . . Whitechapel in the county of Middlesex in the house of her grandfather. But never was in any service for a year together, or hath done any other act to gain a legal settlement except by her marriage as aforesaid. That she and her youngest child, Anna Maria, are now both become burdensome to the parish of Chelsea. The mark of Elizabeth Steward. Sworn, 18 May 1758, before me, Benjamin Cox, John Goodchild. Passed to St Martin in the Fields.

365. [p.151] Middlesex, to wit. Catherine Weaver, aged about 30 years, lodging with Mrs Little near Paradise Row in the parish of St Luke Chelsea, upon her oath saith she is the wife of Joseph Weaver (gone from her) to whom she was married at Loughborough in the county of Leicester about fifteen months ago. That her said husband was born at Newcastle, but the particular part this examinant cannot tell. That he never kept house, rented a tenement of £10 by the year, paid any parish taxes, or was a yearly hired servant in any one place for twelve months together as she ever heard. That she, this examinant was a yearly hired servant before her intermarriage to

Mr Keeling, who lodged at Mr Macklin's, a grocer in Pall Mall in the parish of St James within the liberty of Westminster, for the space of three years at the yearly wages of £6, diet and lodging, quitted the same about eighteen months before her intermarriage. That she never kept house, rented a tenement of £10 by the year, paid any parish taxes, nor hath been a yearly hired servant in any one place for twelve months together since. The mark of Catherine Weaver. Sworn, 3 June 1758, before Benjamin Cox. Passed to St James Westminster.

366. [p.152] Middlesex, to wit. Examination of Sarah Stubbington, alias Cook, who on her oath says that she was born at Croydon in the county of Surrey, her father and mother then residing there, and hath heard, by virtue of a certificate to the said parish of Croydon from the parish of Chelsea. That when she was about 3 years of age her father and mother died, and this examinant was brought to Chelsea to her grandmother, Prudent Stubbington, who kept a farm in the parish of Chelsea, with whom this examinant lived with until her grandmother died. Then about 12 or 13 years of age [she]. . . then went to service, but says that she never lived a year in any place. And when she was about 19 years of age she was married at the Fleet to Jonathan Cook, a soldier in the 2nd Regiment of Foot Guards, by whom she hath one child, named Elizabeth, aged about 4 years. And soon after she was married to him, this examinant heard that he had a wife and one child when he married her. And [she] lived with him about three years and hath not cohabited with him for four years past. Says that her husband, Jonathan Cook, declared upon his knees to this examinant that he was not married at that time he married this examinant, but acknowledged that he had a child by a woman, and knows nothing of the settlement of the said Jonathan Cook. The mark of Sarah Stubbington, alias Cook. Sworn before me, 11 July 1758, Samuel Bever.

367. [p.153] Middlesex, to wit. The examination of Anne Maynard, a single woman, who on her oath saith she is about 29 years of age, and that she was born in the parish of Hurst in the county of Berkshire, and came from thence with her father and mother when she was but 6 months old to the parish of St Luke Chelsea in the county of Middlesex, where (as she says) her father rented a house of £3 a year and lived there about nine years and a half and then died. After which this examinant went and hired her self as a yearly servant to Mrs Hall, who kept Salters Coffee House in the said parish of Chelsea, with whom she lived four years and a half at the wages of 50s., and after, wages at £4 a year. After which her mother gave a sum of money to Mrs Elizabeth Collins, a mantua maker in Watermans Court in the aforesaid parish of Chelsea, to teach her the art of mantua making. From thence she went to Deptford in the county of Kent, where she has followed her business as a mantua . . . maker ever since, but has gained no subsequent settlement since her servitude with Mrs Hall. Ann Maynard. Sworn before us, 13 July 1758, Samuel Bever, Charles Wale.

368. [p.154] Middlesex. The examination of Mary Sowell, who on her oath says that she is the wife of Alexander Sowell, who is now an invalid in garrison at Bristol, who was born in the parish of Ingatestone in Essex, and was in the army ever since he was 17 years of age. And she further says that she hath now a child named Thomas, about a year and 8 months old. That her husband's father's settlement was in the said parish of Ingatestone. The mark of Mary Sowell. Sworn before me, 27 July, 1758, Samuel Bever.

369. [p.155] Middlesex, to wit. Copy of the information of Mary Bingham, single woman, lodging at Mr Grace's near the Six Bells in the Kings Road in the parish of St Luke Chelsea in the county of Middlesex, taken upon oath this 7 Aug. 1758. This examinant upon her Oath saith that she is 19 years of age and never was married, bound an apprentice, kept house rented £10 by the year, paid any parish taxes, or been a yearly hired servant in any one place for twelve months together. That she was born in the said parish of Chelsea where her father Richard Bingham served his apprenticeship. And this examinant further saith that she is now great with child or children which is or are likely to be born a bastard or bastards and to become chargeable to the said parish of Chelsea. And Thomas Yerby, a ploughman to Mr John Hutchins, a farmer at Chelsea aforesaid, had carnal knowledge of her body in the month of January last upon a bed in a room up two pair of stairs forwards in the house of Mr Grace aforesaid, and several times afterwards at the same place. At which, or one of which times he, the said Thomas Yerby did beget her with . . . the child or children she now goeth with and is pregnant of. And that he, the said [p.156] Thomas Yerby, is the true and only father thereof and no man else. The mark of Mary Bingham. Taken and sworn the day and year above said, before me, Benjamin Cox.

370. [p.156] Middlesex, to wit. Richard Quelch, aged 47 years, lodging at Mr Howells, a dealer in coal near the Horse Ferry at Chelsea in the parish of St Luke Chelsea in the county of Middlesex, upon oath saith that he is a waterman and was bound apprentice by indenture for seven years to Mr Walter Nutt, a waterman who kept the ferry from Battersea to Chelsea aforesaid. And this examinant further saith that during all his apprenticeship he, this examinant, lay in his said master's house near the Twelve Acres in the parish of Battersea in the county of Surrey. And this examinant saith that his said apprenticeship expired about 27 years ago, since which time he has not kept a house rented £10 by the year, paid any parish taxes or been a yearly hired servant. That he was married to his present wife, Mary, at the Fleet about 25 years ago, by whom he hath no children living. The mark of Richard Quelch. Sworn, 19 Aug. 1758, before us, Benjamin Cox, Henry Fielding.

371. [p.157] Middlesex, to wit. Ann Sowton, aged 31 years, lodging at Mr Clark's in Lordship Yard, Chelsea in the parish of St Luke Chelsea in the county of Middlesex, upon her oath saith that she is the wife of Henry Sowton to whom she was married at Mr Keith's New Chapel, May Fair in the parish of St George Hanover Square and liberty of Westminster. That the said Henry Sowton is a painter and glazier and served his apprenticeship to one Edmund West in East Street in the parish of St Andrew in the city of Chichester in the county of Sussex, as she, this examinant, has been informed and verily believes. And since the said Henry Sowton hath been out of his time, he never kept house rented £10 by the year, paid any parish taxes, or been a yearly hired servant to this examinant's knowledge. That she hath one child by her said husband now living; to wit, Henry, aged about 6 weeks, now with this examinant. The mark of Ann Sowton. Taken and sworn, 22 Aug. 1758, before Benjamin Cox, Henry Fielding.

372. [p.158] Middlesex. Examination of Ann Farrant and her father, Daniel Farrant, touching their settlements. Who on her oath says that she is about 21 years of age and a single woman. Says that she was brought into the parish of Chelsea when she was about 1/2 year old by her father and mother and has been a hired servant in several places, but not for twelve months. The last place that she lived as a hired servant was with Mr Duffell in the parish of Chelsea, with whom she lived eleven months and ten days, and then went to her mother's sick in the said parish. She being very ill [she] told her said master that she was not able to do his work, and desired of him to let her go to her father and mother's house, and he answered her and said that she might stay there if she pleased or go, and accordingly she, this examinant, went home to her father and mother's house 21 days before her year's service was expired. And in two or three days after she was gone her said master sent her £2 11s., which money with £4 2s. 6d., which she was paid before, made £6 13s. 6d., being the money paid to her for the wages for the eleven months and ten days. And he also further made her a present of 12s. and also a further sum of 21s. for her Christmas box or vales. And then she thought herself quite discharged from her aforesaid service.

The aforesaid Daniel Farrant being present deposeth upon oath that his legal settlement is in the parish of South Weald near Brentwood in the county of Essex, from which said parish he, the [p.159] said Daniel, had a legal certificate from the aforesaid parish of South Weald about 24 years past, direct to the parish of Barking in Essex (or elsewhere). And was then a married man. And after some time his being in the said parish of Chelsea, he was summoned to swear to his legal settlement, at which time of summons he then produced to Justice Elers and the officers of the parish of Chelsea the above certificate. Which said certificate was received into the hands of Justice Elers, who ordered the clerk of the vestry to take care of it and to give a copy of the same to the said Daniel Farrant. By virtue of which said certificate he and his family hath resided in the said parish of Chelsea ever since to this time, and hath not rented any tenement of £10 per annum, or served any parochial office. Daniel Farrant. The mark of Ann Farrant. Sworn before me, 25 Nov. 1758, Samuel Bever, Charles Wale. Pass order. [See **462**].

373. [p.158] Middlesex, to wit. Lydia Reeves, destitute of lodging, upon [her oath] saith that she is 22 years of age and never was married, bound an apprentice, kept house or rented £10 by the year. But that she was a yearly hired servant [to] Joseph Thornhill, peruke maker in that part of Fleet Lane which [is] in the parish of St Sepulchre, London, for the space [of] four years at the yearly wages of 30s. a year, diet and lodging. [She] quitted the same about twelve months [ago] and hath not been a yearly hired servant in any one place for twelve months together since. The mark of Lydia Reeves. Taken and sworn, 8 Nov. 1758, before Benjamin Cox.

374. [n.p.] Mr Knowles at Lord George Benticks. She thinks the gentleman's name that her husband lived with in Chelsea was Davison. [See **378**]

375. [p.159] Middlesex. Benjamin Mappin, lodging at the White Horse near Chelsea church, upon his oath says that he was born and served his time at Sheffield in Yorkshire to his father Joseph Mappin, and that he is a baker by trade. That he never kept house, rented a tenement of £10 a year, nor paid parish taxes. And this deponent further maketh oath and saith that he was married to his present wife, Alice Mappin, at the Fleet about seven years ago, and that he hath one child living by his said wife, named Eleanor, about 4 months old, now with this examinant. Benjamin Mappin. Sworn, 21 Dec. 1758, before Benjamin Cox.

376. [p.160] Middlesex, to wit. The examination of George Francis, the beadle of Chelsea in the county of Middlesex, taken upon oath this 23 Dec. 1758. This examinant on his oath says that he hath been informed that George Babb, now in the workhouse of and in the parish of Chelsea aforesaid, was bound an apprentice (by the officer of the parish of Chelsea) by an indenture, until he should attain the age of 24 years, to James Bryerley, a weaver in the parish of St Matthew Bethnal Green in the said county of Middlesex, bearing date, 19 Jan. 1756. George Francis. Sworn, 23 Dec. 1758, before Benjamin Cox. Sent to St Matthew Bethnal Green. [See **350**, **361**].

377. [p.161] Middlesex, to wit. The examination of Jobb Cox, who on oath says that he is about 64 years of age and is now an in pensioner in Chelsea College, and whose wife, named Elizabeth, aged about 55 years,. . . died in July 1758. And [he] was married to her 33 years, and hath now by her, his late wife, three children; vizt, Susanna, aged about 11 years, and Mary, aged about 8 years, and Martha, the same age being twins. Which said children is now with him in the parish of Chelsea, and that he is not able to maintain them and is obliged to ask relief of the said parish of Chelsea. Further says that he was born and apprenticed in the parish of Sedgley in the county of Stafford, and that he never was a hired servant, or ever rented any tenement of £10 per annum, or paid any parochial taxes, but hath been in the army ever since he was 20 years of age. Mark of Jobb Cox. Sworn before me, 4 Jan. 1759, Samuel Bever.

378. [p.162] Middlesex. The examination of Ann Williamson, who on her oath says that she is about 22 years of age, . . . born in the parish of Ashby

De La Zouch in the county of Leicester. That when she was between 15 and 16 years of age she was hired by the year to Lord George Bentick, who then lived in Soho Square, and some times at Heston in the county of Middlesex. In whose service she lived almost two years, in which time aforesaid she came acquainted with Martin Williamson, to whom she soon after married at Chesterfield in the county of Derby, by whom she hath one child alive, 4 years old, named William, and is now with her uncle Ward in the parish of Rippon, a farmer. That about three years 1/2 past her said husband was pressed for a soldier and is voluntarily listed in Lord Heines' regiment now in Germany, and was shipped off from Cowes in the Isle of White, from the camp there. That before . . . her said husband was sent to Germany . . . he told this examinant that his settlement was in the parish of Chelsea in this county, which he gained by being a hired servant by the year to Mr Davies, or some such name, in the said parish of Chelsea, with whom he lived about sixteen months. [She] does not know at what wages, or where the said Davies was a house keeper or not, or what business he was of. And her husband never was a hired servant afterwards. The mark of Ann Williamson. Sworn before me, 11 Jan. 1759, Samuel Bever. [See **374**].

379. [p.163] Middlesex, to wit. Sarah Freelove, aged 60 years, lodged at Mr Clarke's in Lordship Yard in the parish of St Luke Chelsea, upon her oath saith she is the widow of Francis Freelove, who died about fifteen years ago, to whom she was married at Stratford Le Bow in the year 1713. That he was a brewer and lived in and rented an house at Wapping Wall in the parish of St Paul Shadwell in the county of Middlesex for the space of five years at the yearly rent of £40, besides taxes. [He] quitted the same about thirty years ago. That he never kept house, rented a tenement of £10 by the year, paid any parish taxes afterwards, nor hath she, this examinant, nor been a yearly hired servant in any one place since her said husband['s] death. Sarah Freelove. Sworn, 22 Jan. 1759, before Benjamin Cox. Passed to St Paul Shadwell.

380. [p.164] Middlesex, to wit. Bridget Cowley, aged about 34 years, in the workhouse of and in the parish of St Luke Chelsea, upon her oath saith she never was married, that she was a yearly hired servant to Mr James Fitzgerald at the Elephant and Castle in the Strand (near Temple Bar) in the parish of St Clement Danes in the county of Middlesex for the space of fourteen months at the yearly wages of £4, diet and lodging, quitted the same about thirteen years ago. That she never kept house, rented a tenement of £10 by the year, paid any parish taxes, nor been a yearly hired servant in any one place for twelve months together since. The mark of Bridget Cowley. Sworn, 22 Jan. 1759, before Benjamin Cox. Passed to St Clement Danes.

381. [p.165] Middlesex, to wit. Mary Phillips, aged 80 years, lodging in Jews Row in the parish of St Luke Chelsea, upon her oath saith she is wife of John Phillips, now in gaol, to whom she was married at the Fleet about fourteen years ago. That he served six years apprenticeship to John Chip-perfield, a baker in the parish of St Margaret in the liberty of Westminster. That he never did any thing to gain a subsequent settlement. The mark of Mary Phillips. Sworn, 22 Jan. 1759, before Benjamin Cox. [See **308**, **345**].

382. Middlesex and Westminster, to wit. The information of John Booth, a stone mason on Chaney Row in the parish of St Luke Chelsea in the county of Middlesex, taken upon oath, 1 Feb. 1759. The informant upon his oath saith that about six years ago he lived in and rented a house in Tufton Street which is in the parish of St John the Evangelist in the liberty of Westminster in the county of Middlesex, at the yearly rent of £9 10s. a year beside taxes. At which time one Ann Booth lived with the informant as a servant and was there delivered in the said house of a female bastard child named Sarah Hadley, now with the informant. [Preceding entry crossed out in the original.] [See **383**].

383. [p.166] Middlesex, to wit. The examination of John Booth, a stone mason in China Row in the parish of St Luke Chelsea in the county of Middlesex, taken upon oath 1 Feb. 1759. This examinant on his oath saith that he very well knows Sarah Booth, an infant aged 6 years, now with this examinant and is likely to become chargeable to the said parish of St Luke Chelsea. That the said Sarah was born of the body of Ann Booth, single woman, at this examinant's house, who then resided in Tufton Street in the parish of St John the Evangelist in the liberty of Westminster. John Booth. Sworn the day and year above said before Benjamin Cox. Sarah Booth passed to St John the Evangelist in the liberty of Westminster. [See **382**].

384. [p.167] Middlesex, to wit. Elizabeth Mercer, aged about 34 years, lodging at Mrs Carteris in Turks Row in the parish of St Luke at Chelsea in the county of Middlesex, upon her oath saith she is the wife of Thomas Mercer (gone to sea), to whom . . . she was married at the Fleet about thirteen years ago. That he was bound an apprentice by an indenture for seven years to James Hull, a waterman in the parish of Wandsworth in the county of Surrey, and there served one year and then went to sea and served the remainder of his said time at sea. That he never kept a house, rented a tenement of £10 a year, paid any parish taxes, nor been a yearly hired servant since the expiration of his said apprenticeship. That she hath three children living by her said husband; to wit, William, aged 10 years, Thomas, 8 years, and Richard, aged 9 months. All now with this examinant. The mark of Elizabeth Mercer. Sworn, 12 Mar. 1759, before Benjamin Cox. Elizabeth Mercer and her three children passed to Wandsworth, 13 March 1759.

385. [p.167] Middlesex. Examination of Charity Snell. On her oath says that she is about 47 years of age, that about nineteen years past she was married at the Fleet to her late husband John Snell who is lately dead. That the father, [blank] Snell, was an inhabitant in the hamlet of Hammersmith, and that her late husband was born in the said hamlet, and that the father's settlement was in the said hamlet, and when he died he left his wife, the mother of the said John Snell to the value of £300. She, the mother, married a 2nd husband whose name was John Lamborn, a poulterer, and further says that she hath often heard her late husband declare that he never was an apprentice or any covenant or hired servant to any one to live with one whole year, or ever rented a tenement of £10 per annum, or paid any parochial taxes, or served any office. And always declared that his settlement was in the hamlet of Hammersmith. That she hath now with her a girl named Ann, about 14 years of age, the child of her late husband. The mark of Charity Snell. Sworn before me, 24 May 1759, Samuel Bever. Passed to Hammersmith.

386. [p.168] Middlesex. The examination of Margaret Spears, who is sent to the parish of Chelsea from the parish of Thirsk in the county of Yorkshire in the North Riding, and was brought by [blank] Adams, the contractor for conveying of vagrants for the county of Middlesex by a vagrant pass. N.B. No order was made thereon to be delivered at Chelsea by any magistrate for the county of Middlesex. This examinant on her oath says that she is the wife of Andrews Spears, a cordwainer and a soldier in the 36th regiment of foot commanded by Lord Robert Maners. That as it appears by indenture . . . her said husband was apprentice to William Wallis of Castle Garth, a cordwainer in the town and county of the town of Newcastle upon Tyne in the county of Northumberland. And that he never did any thing by being a hired servant by the year, or renting any tenement of £10 per annum, or paid any parochial taxes, nor gained any other settlement. That she hath two children by him, Jane and John. That she left the said place of Castle Garth aforesaid about five weeks past to wander about to seek her husband, and was allowed by the said place of Castle Garth aforesaid, 1s. 6d. per week while she was there [as]. . . their own parishioner. The mark of Margaret Spears. Sworn before me, 28 June 1759, Samuel Bever.

387. [p.168] Middlesex. The examination of Winifred Wilson, alias Jones (Smith her maiden name), who on her oath says that she is about 63 years of age, born in the parish of Higham Green. That she never was apprentice, or a hired servant by the year. That when she was about 22 years of age she was hired to John Brown, a butcher in the parish of Woughton (near Harwich) in the county of Suffolk, and lived with him about two years at the wages of £3 per annum. And in the last year of her service she married William Jones, a sergeant upon duty in Langard Fort, and that the said Jones was a sergeant in the guards several years before, and kept an alehouse in Queen Ann's time at the Two Fighting Cocks in the parish of Chelsea. And she, this examinant, lived with him at the said house, but does not know what rent he paid, or ever paid any parochial taxes, or ever received any wages from him, she being then very young. That she was the wife of the said Jones about fifteen years, but knows nothing of his settlement. He listed in the guards when about 18 years of age and then died, leaving her one child, William Jones, who was lost with Admiral Baleten in the year

1734. As appears by a Fleet certificate she was married again to John Wilson, a pensioner in Chelsea College, and knows nothing of his settlement. And [he] left her one child named Sylvia Wilson, about 23 years of age, born in the parish of Chelsea, and who has not done any thing to gain a settlement of her own. And this examinant now comes and demands relief of the parish of Chelsea. The mark of Winifred Wilson. Sworn before me, 5 July 1759, Samuel Bever. Married at Badingham in Suffolk.

388. [p.169] Middlesex. The examination of Mary Holder, alias Johnson, who on her oath says that she was the widow of Luke Holder, and that soon after the said Holder died she was examined to her settlement, as appear by an examination in this book dated 18 Sept. 1755, and this examinant being now asked the question, if she is married to Timothy Johnson? To which said question this examinant is not willing, but refuses to testify upon oath. 5 July 1759, Samuel Bever. [See **301**].

389. [p.169] Middlesex, to wit. William Brasier, aged about 49 years, residing in the parish of Chelsea, upon his oath saith that he is a tailor by trade, that he never was bound an apprentice. That before his intermarriage and while single, he was a yearly hired servant to Mr Peter Dickson, a tailor in Kings Arms Court on Ludgate Hill in the parish of St Bridget, vulgarly St Brides, London, for the space of four years at the yearly wages of £2 for the second year, £3 for the third year, and £5 for the last year, diet and lodging. [He] quitted the same several years ago. That he never kept house, rented a tenement of £10 by the year, paid any parish taxes, nor hath been a yearly hired servant in any one place for twelve months together since. That he was married to his present wife, Mary, at Chelsea about three months ago. William Brasier. Sworn, 29 Oct. 1759, before Benjamin Cox. Passed them both to St Brides in the city of London.

390. [p.170] Middlesex sessions. The voluntary examination of Mary Glover, single woman, taken before me . . . Who being on oath saith that she is now with child, and that the said child is likely to born a bastard and be chargeable to the parish of St Luke Chelsea in the said county of Middlesex. And this examinant saith that in the month of March last one Richard Longford of the parish of St Martin in the city of Worcester, breeches maker, had carnal knowledge of this examinant's body diverse times. And this examinant saith that the said Richard Longford is the father of the child she is now pregnant with, and no other person whatsoever. Mary Glover. Taken and sworn before me, 19 Sept. 1759, Saunders Welch.

391. [p.171] Middlesex. The examination of William Haines. This examinant on his oath saith that he is 43 years of age and never kept house, or rented £10 per year. That he is a gardener by profession, but never was an apprentice. That he was married to his present wife Ann at the Abbey Church at St Albans in Hertfordshire, by whom he has two children living; Elizabeth, aged about 10 years, and Samuel, aged about 2 years. That this examinant's father lived in and rented a house for many years at Warminster in Wiltshire, where this examinant was born. William Haines his mark. Taken and sworn 12 June 1760, before Benjamin Cox.

392. [p.171; a numbering error in the original manuscript] Middlesex. The examination of Elizabeth Cox, who on her oath says that she is about 22 years of age and now a single woman, that she was born in the parish of Chelsea in the said county and is now troubled with the venereal disease. That she was apprentice to Robert Ellis in St George Hanover Square for seven years, and at the end of five years of her apprenticeship her said master removed to the town of New Windsor in the county of Berkshire. And this examinant went with him and served her said master the last two years at the said town of Windsor, whom this examinant left about twelve months past and hath not lived in any place since above three months, or hath been married to any man. The mark of Elizabeth Cox. Sworn before us, 4 July 1760, Samuel Bever, Thomas Rea. Pass by an order.

393. [p.172] Middlesex. The examination of John Shanno, who on his oath says that he is about 40 years of age, born in the parish of St Anne Soho, Westminster, and was apprenticed by indenture for seven years to Mrs Baronyn, a watch case maker in Bolt Court in the parish of St Dunstan in the West in the city of London, and served her the whole time (except a fortnight). [He] never was a hired servant, or rented any house of £10 per annum, but hath ever worked as a labourer since his apprenticeship. At or about nine years past he married Margaret Cox, his now wife, by whom he hath two children; vizt, John, aged about 7 years, [and] Abraham, aged about 3 years. All now likely to come chargeable to the parish of Chelsea. John Shanno. Sworn before us, 4 Aug. 1760, Samuel Bever, John Mackin. Pass by a order.

394. [p.172, a numbering error in the original manuscript] Middlesex, to wit. Anne Jobbins, aged about 35 years, lodging at Mr Richard Water's in Church Lane in the parish of St Luke Chelsea in the county of Middlesex, upon her oath saith that she is the wife of Thomas Jobbins (gone from her), to whom she was married at the Fleet about nineteen years ago. That her said husband is a farrier by trade and was bound an apprentice by indenture for seven years to Mr John Meares, a farrier in Wood Street in the parish of St John the Evangelist in the liberty of Westminster, and there served part of his time, but how long this examinant cannot tell. When his said master removed to the Horse Ferry in the said parish of St John, and this examinant's husband with him, and there served the remainder of his time out. But when his said time expired this examinant knoweth not. That he never kept house, rented a tenement of £10 by the year, paid any parish taxes, or was a yearly servant in any one place for twelve months together. That she hath three children living by her said husband; to wit, James, aged 8 years and upwards, Thomas, aged 5 years and upwards, and Joseph, aged 1 year and upwards. All now with this examinant. Ann Jobbins. Sworn, 15 Oct. 1760, before Benjamin Cox, Philip Dyos. Passed by order.

395. [p.173] Middlesex, to wit. The examination of Mary Wilkinson, lodging in the parish of Chelsea in the county of Middlesex, taken upon oath this [blank] Nov. 1760. This examinant, upon her oath saith that she is near 23 years of age, that she was born in the parish of Walton-on-Thames in the county of Surrey. That she was put out by the said parish of Walton as an apprentice to one Richard Henley, a weaver at Addlestone in the parish of Chertsey in the said county of Surrey. That she continued with her said master between six and seven years. That she never was married, that she never kept a house, or tenement of £10 by the year, paid any parish taxes, nor hath been a yearly hired servant in any one place for twelve months together since. This examinant upon her voluntary oath further says that she is now great with child or children which are likely to be born a bastard or bastards, and to become chargeable to the parish of Chelsea. And that Thomas Rayner, an in pensioner belonging to the sixth ward in his Majesty's Royal Hospital in the said parish of Chelsea had carnal knowledge of her body (and he only). That he and the examinant cohabited together going on three years, lastly in the house of one Richard Angier in or near Turk's Row in Chelsea aforesaid. By whom, the said Thomas Rayner, she now is great with child or children, she now goeth with and is pregnant of. And that he, the said Thomas Rayner, is the true and only father thereof, and no man else. [Blank]. Sworn the day and year above written. [The above statement is crossed out in the original.]

396. [p.173, a numbering error in the original manuscript] Middlesex, to wit. The examination of Hannah Bradly, lodging in the parish of Chelsea in the county of Middlesex, taken on oath, 8 Nov. 1760. This examinant upon her oath says that she is 28 years of age, that she was born in the parish of St Margaret Westminster in the county of Middlesex. That she was apprenticed to one Sarah Dyer in the said parish of St Margaret, purse maker. Since which time she lived as a hired servant (at the yearly wages of £5 10s. per annum) with Dr John Wilmer in Millman's Row in the parish of Chelsea in the county of Middlesex, with whom she lived three years and nine months. That she never was married, that she never kept a house, or tenement of £10 by the year, nor paid any parish taxes, nor hath lived in any one place for twelve [months] together since. This examinant upon her voluntary oath says that she is now great with child or children which are likely to be born a bastard or bastards, and are likely to become chargeable to the said parish of Chelsea. And that Thomas Leigh, an attorney's clerk or writer in the Roll's Office in Chancery Lane in the Precinct of the Rolls in or near the city of London had carnal knowledge of her body in the house of Mrs Ballester in Warwick Street near Golden Square in the parish of St James Westminster (with whom she was a servant, and there lived only five months). He, the said Thomas Leigh, being at the said time a lodger in the said house, and he having several times carnal knowledge of her body from the month of Feb. 1760 to May following, in the said Mrs Ballester['s] house, at which or one of which times, the said Thomas Leigh did beget her with [the] child or children she now goeth with and is pregnant of. And that he, the said Thomas Leigh, is the true and only father thereof and no one else. And further says she has applied herself to the said Thomas Leigh for aid and assistance for her lying-in, she not having wherewithal to maintain her self and the child. He answered, if one single half penny would save her and the child that he would not give it her, and pushed her out of his office. Hannah Bradley. Sworn before me, Samuel Bever.

397. [p.174] Middlesex, to wit. The examination of Isaac Richards. This examinant, aged upwards of 48 years of age, upon his oath says that he was born in the parish of Frome in Somersetshire. That his father put him out and bound him apprentice to one Arthur Spencer, a shoemaker in the parish of Bruton in the aforesaid county of Somerset. That he left his said apprenticeship when he was about 17 years of age and came up to London and worked in and about London as a journeyman some years. Afterwards he hired himself into the service of the Right Honourable the Earl of Wilmington as a helper or under groom. In which service he lived upwards of sixteen months at the rate of £4 per annum, meat, drink, lodging. That he was discharged in the parish of Bone and had his wages paid him at his lordship's house in the said parish of Bone in the county of Sussex. That he was in the said service in the said parish of Bone between two and three months when he was discharged from thence. And that he married his late wife Margaret about 25 years since, by whom he had sixteen children, four whereof are now living; vizt, William, about 14 years of age, Mary, about 13, Moses, about 7, and James, about 3. That never since he left the above said service (and discharged at Bone), which was before he was married, has not lived as a hired servant. That he never rented any house or land of £10 per annum, nor paid any parochial taxes, nor did any act to gain a settlement since, to the best of his knowledge. [Blank]. Sworn before me, [blank] Jan. 1761, [blank]. N.B. That this examinant was with the family some part of the sixteen months at St James Square, and some time in the parish of Chiswick. N.B. The last 40 days before he was discharged was at Bone.

398. [p.175] Middlesex, to wit. Elizabeth Smith, aged 33 years, lodging in the parish of St Luke at Chelsea, upon her oath saith that she is the widow of William Smith who died five weeks ago. To whom she was married at the Fleet fifteen years ago. That her said husband was a basket maker by trade. That he was bound an apprentice by an indenture for seven years to Mr Jackson, a basket maker at Southley in the parish of Datchet in the county of Bucks. And there served all his time out, which expired 40 years ago. That he never kept house, rented a tenement of £10 by the year, paid any taxes, nor was a yearly hired servant in any one place for twelve months together, to this examinant's knowledge. That she hath one child living by her said husband; to wit, John, aged four years and upwards, now with this examinant. The mark of Elizabeth Smith. Sworn, 18 Feb. 1761, before Benjamin Cox, Henry Fielding. Passed to Datchet, 19 Feb. 1761.

399. [p.176] Middlesex, to wit. Ann Carrack, single woman, aged near 69 years, lodging in the parish of Chelsea, maketh oath that about 39 years ago she with one Mrs Mary Erick took a house in Christ Church parish in or near the city of London. And there followed the business of milliners, in joint partnership with the said Mary Erick. And there paid £30 per annum and all parochial taxes for the said premises. From thence they both removed and lived in a house in Bull Head Court of £16 per annum in the said parish of Christ Church, and there lived about four years and paid there likewise all parochial taxes for the said house, share and share alike. Business not answering there, they then dissolved their partnership and lived separate for several years. She, this examinant, since that time has got her livelihood by work at her needle (not as a hired servant) till about 20 years since. She then growing lame and infirm applied her self to her old friend Mrs Mary Erick, who took a house and followed business at Chelsea, who is now also reduced. With whom she has lived ever since as a friend and relation, not as a hired servant. And this examinant further says that she never was married, rented any house, or paid parochial taxes, or has lived as a hired servant since she left Bull Head Court (as above mentioned). Nor has done any act, to the best of her knowledge, to gain a settlement elsewhere. And is now become burdensome to the parish of Chelsea. Ann Carrack, her mark. Sworn, 25 Mar. 1761, before me, Benjamin Cox . . . Passed to Christ Church, London, 25 Mar. 1761.

400. [p.177] Middlesex. The voluntary examination of Ann Crockford, single woman, taken before me, . . . 22 June 1761. Who on her oath says that on Tuesday, 26 May last she, this examinant, was delivered of a male bastard child in the workhouse belonging to the parish of Chelsea in the county of Middlesex (which said child is baptised and named John). Was unlawfully begotten on her body by John Spooner, who keeps a public house known by the sign of the Swan and Scotch-Grey in Jews Row in the said parish of Chelsea, with whom she lived as a hired servant in the said house. And in the bed where she lay in his said house, [he] had carnal knowledge of her body several times. And this examinant further says that the said John Spooner is the true father of the said child, and no other person. Ann Crockford, her mark. Sworn the day and year above written, before Henry Fielding. [See **439**].

401. [p.178] Middlesex. Elizabeth Hall, the wife of Abel Hall, aged near 39 years, upon her oath says that on 27 July 1746 she, this examinant (as also appears by a certificate), was married to her said husband in the parish of St Sepulchre in the liberty of the Fleet, London. Says that her said husband was born at Highgate in the parish of Hornsey in the county of Middlesex. And there lived and worked with his father, Nathaniel Hall, a mason who was a man of credit, with whom he lived to the time of his death. Then he was about 20 years of age. And about twelve months after, was married to her (as aforementioned). She does not know whether he was apprenticed by indentures to his said father or no. By whom she has had eight children, and only one child now living, whose name is Nathaniel, aged near 20 months, which the father has taken away with him. That he never lived as a yearly hired servant, rented a house of £10 per annum, or paid parochial taxes since his said father's death. And this examinant further says that her said husband, Abel Hall, has absconded and left her. That she is not able at this present to provide for her self without relief, and is now likely to come chargeable to the parish of Chelsea. The mark of Elizabeth Hall. Sworn, 6 July 1761, before us, Samuel Bever, Benjamin Cox. Passed to Hornsey, 8 July 1761.

402. [p.179] Middlesex, to wit. Charles Whitesides, aged about 52 years, upon oath says he was born in the parish of St James Clerkenwell in the county of Middlesex. That when he was about 13 years of age, he was put out and bound apprentice for seven years to one Thomas Docket, a shoemaker who lived in Cursitor Street in the parish of St Dunstan in the West in the Precincts of the Rolls in or near the city of London. With whom he lived and had his meat, drink, washing and lodging as an apprentice for about six years and no longer. For when he was about 19 years of age he enlisted for a soldier and is at this time a sergeant in Colonel Tonyn's regiment of foot. And that he was married to Ann, his present wife (who now lodges in the parish of Chelsea), as appears by certificate, on 11 July 1753 in the Fleet. By whom he has now four children living; vizt, Ephraim, about 6 years, Thomas, near 5 years of age, Daniel, about 3 years of age, Hester, about 10 months. And that his said wife is pregnant at this time by him. And this examinant on his oath further says that he never since he left his said apprenticeship lived with any person as a hired yearly servant, nor rented a house of £10 per annum, nor has done any thing, to the best of his knowledge, to gain a subsequent settlement. [See **413**].

403. [p.180] Middlesex, to wit. Mary Jones, spinster, 48 years of age and upwards, was born in the town of St Davids in Pembrokeshire in Wales. Upon oath says that she was a hired yearly servant to Dr Smollet in the parish of Chelsea in the county of Middlesex, of whom she received £5 per annum, meat, drink, washing and lodging. In whose service she lived upwards of fourteen months, all under one living. And has not since she left the above said service (which is about six years since) lived in any service twelve months together, or ever rented a house of £10 per annum, or hath done any thing (to the best of her knowledge) to gain any other settlement since. Mary Jones. Sworn, [blank] Oct. 1761, before me, Benjamin Cox.

404. [p.181] Middlesex. The examination of John Adams. This examinant on his oath says that he is about 45 years of age, by profession a labourer, was born in the parish of Shepshed in Leicestershire. [He] got his livelihood by labouring work or jobbing about till about seven years ago, and then he hired himself as a yearly servant to one Mr James Brady in the parish of Mile End Old Town in the county of Middlesex. With whom he lived two years and received £8, victuals, drink, washing and lodging. And this examinant further says that since he left the above service, [he] never lived as a hired servant in one place a twelve months, or rented a tenement or land of £10 per annum, nor done any act since to gain a settlement. And now is a vagrant, and become burdensome to [the] parish of Chelsea. [Blank.] Sworn before, [blank]. [See **405, 406**].

405. [p.182] Middlesex, to wit. The information of John Gardner, an inhabitant of the parish of St Luke Chelsea in the county of Middlesex, taken on oath, 13 Nov. 1761. This informant on his oath saith that he did the eleventh instant apprehend John Adams, a rogue and vagabond, in the parish aforesaid, lodging in the open air contrary to the statute in that case made and provided. The mark of John Gardner. Sworn the day and year above said, before Benjamin Cox. [See **404, 406**].

406. The examination of John Adams, a rogue and vagabond apprehended by John Gardner, an inhabitant of the parish of St Luke at Chelsea in the county of Middlesex, and brought before me, . . . and taken before me, 13 Nov. 1761. This examinant on his oath saith that he is 40 years of age and upwards, that he never was married, that he was a yearly hired servant to Mr James Brady in the hamlet of Mile End Old Town in the parish of Stepney in the county of Middlesex for the space of two years, at the yearly wages of £7, diet and lodging. That he hath not done any act to gain a subsequent settlement. The mark of John Adams. Sworn the day and year above said, before Benjamin Cox. Passed to Stepney. [See **404, 405**].

407. [p.183] Middlesex. John Edenbury, aged about 55 years, born in Plaistow in the county of Essex, upon his oath says that he was bound out an apprentice to Mr Thomas Harris, a gardener in Plaistow in the parish of West Ham in the county of Essex. After he served out his said apprenticeship, the last place he lived in as a yearly hired servant before he was married was with the Right Honourable Earl Cowper, at his lordship's house at Cole Green in the parish of Hertingfordbury in the county of Hertford, four years and a half or thereabouts as his principal gardener at the rate of £17 per annum, lodging and diet all the said time. Soon after he left the said service, he married his present wife, Ann, by whom he has six children living. And further this examinant says upon his oath that since his said marriage he never rented any house, garden, or tenement of £10 per annum, or paid parochial taxes or ever did any act since to have gained a subsequent settlement, to the best of his knowledge. Sworn, 9 Jan. 1762, before me, Samuel Bever.
Hannah, about 19 years, in service, Mary, about 17 years, in service, Sarah, about 15 years, in service, John, about 13 years, apprentice to Thomas Blanch in St Margaret, Westminster, William, about 10 years, Francis, about 7 years. Both the two last at home with him. [See **408**].

408. [p.184] Middlesex. Examination of John Edenbury taken 9 Jan. 1762. Who on oath says that he is about 55 years of age, born. [Crossed out in the original manuscript.] [See **407**].

409. [p.185] Middlesex. Ann Holland, wife of William Holland, aged about 58 years of age, formerly the wife of Thomas Davies the elder. On her oath says that she was married about 40 years ago to one Thomas Davies the elder, since deceased, who often told her that he served his apprenticeship in the parish of St Gregory by St Paul's in the city of London. Which parish of St Gregory's had given to the parish of St Luke Chelsea in the county of Middlesex a certificate acknowledging and confirming the same. And further this examinant says that her said husband, Thomas Davies, with her and six children were passed by the officers of the aforesaid parish of Chelsea to the said parish of St Gregory's upwards of 20 years since (about the time of the hard frost). And at this time she had living six children by the said Thomas Davies; vizt, 1st Amelia, the wife of James Powell, 2nd Mary, the wife of Samuel Suckley, 3rd Ann, unmarried, 4th Thomas, the younger, who is gone for a soldier [and] whose wife is lately dead. By her the said Thomas has two children now living; vizt, Ann, about 7 years of age, and Thomas, about 5 years of age. Which said two children he has left in the parish of Chelsea, and is now become burdensome and chargeable to the said parish. 5th Eleanor, unmarried, 6th and youngest at this time, an apprentice (whose name is John) to a waterman at Hungerford in the parish of St Martin in the Fields, Westminster. And lastly this examinant on her oath further says that her said husband, Thomas Davies, nor her said son, Thomas Davies, to her knowledge, never rented any [p.186] house or tenement of £10 per annum, or paid any parochial taxes, or served any parish office whatever, nor has gained any settlement than as aforesaid, other than what appears by the certificate mentioned. The mark of Ann Holland. Sworn before us, 18 Jan. 1762, Samuel Bever, Benjamin Cox. Passed the two children, 19 Jan., to St Gregory's. [See **410**].

410. Middlesex. Mary Suckley, inhabitant of the parish of Chelsea in the county of Middlesex, aged about 32 years of age, on her oath says that she was married to one Samuel Suckley about fourteen years since in the liberty of the Fleet in the parish of St Brides (alias St Bridget), London. And that her said husband before he was married was a hired [a] yearly servant to one Mr Bond, a gardener in the parish of Chelsea aforesaid. With whom he lived upwards of two years at the rate of £5 per annum, meat, drink, washing and lodging. And that he never since he left the above said service was a hired servant by the year, or rented any tenement of £10 per annum, nor paid any parochial taxes, nor since, to her knowledge, has gain any subsequent settlement. The mark of Mary Suckley. Sworn, 18 Jan. 1762, Samuel Bever. [See **409**].

411. [p.187] Middlesex. Eleanor Healy, single woman, aged about 45 years, upon her oath says her father, Thomas Healy, served his apprenticeship of seven years with one Mr Norton, a vintner in the parish of St James, Westminster, who afterwards kept a public house in the said parish. She further says that she was born in the said parish and that she never lived in any other parish as a hired yearly servant. And that her last place of service was with one Mrs Mary Davis, a laundress in Great Windmill Street in the aforesaid parish of St James in the liberty of Westminster in the county of Middlesex, with whom she lived seven years and upwards, and had great part of the said time £5 a year, diet and lodging. And that she says that she was passed by an order about two years ago from St George's to St James parish. That she never was married, nor done any act (to the best of her knowledge) to have gained a subsequent settlement. And that she has been chargeable to Chelsea. Eleanor Healy, her mark. Sworn before us, 23 Jan. 1762, Benjamin Cox, Thomas Kynaston. Passed to St James.

412. [p.188] Middlesex. Catherine Wheeler, single woman, aged 23 years, upon her oath says that she was born near St Margaret's church in the city and liberty of Westminster. And that both her father and mother were poor labouring people. And that the parish officers of St Margaret aforesaid put her out and bound her an apprentice to one Joseph Baker, at Walham Green in the parish of Fulham in the county of Middlesex, gardener, till she was 21 years of age. But her said master and her mistress became so poor that they had all their goods and effects seized on by their landlord, at which time she had her indenture of apprenticeship returned to her after living with them upwards of five years. With whom she had apparel, diet and lodging, and then was about 18 years of age. Since which time she never lived in any place twelve months as a yearly servant, nor never was married to any man, nor done any act whatever since her said apprentice-ship (to the best of her knowledge) to gain any subsequent settlement. And that she is become chargeable to the parish of Chelsea. Catherine Wheeler, her mark. Witness Robert Higden. Sworn before us, 5 Feb. 1762, William Spinnage, Benjamin Cox. Passed to Fulham, 15 Feb. 1762.

413. [p.188, a numbering error in the original manuscript] Middlesex, to wit. Ann Whitesides, aged about 34 years, lodging in the parish of St Luke Chelsea in the county of Middlesex, upon her oath says that she is the wife of Charles Whitesides, and that she was married to him in the liberty of the Fleet in the city of London on 11 July 1753 (as appears by a certificate). And that her said husband has often told her that he was bound out as an apprentice at the age of 13 years to one Mr Thomas Duckett, a shoemaker in or near Cursitor's Street in the Precinct or liberty of the Rolls (in the county of Middlesex in the parish of St Dunstan in the West) with whom he lived until he was 19 years of age. And then he left his said master and entered himself into the army and ever since has belonged to it. By whom she now has living five children; vizt, 1st Ephraim, 6 years of age and upwards, 2nd Thomas, 5 years of age and upwards, 3rd Daniel, about 3 years of age, 4th Hester, about 15 months old, 5th Nicholas, about 6 weeks old. And that her said husband has left her and her said children without any support or sustenance. And this examinant further on her oath says that she never heard or ever knew that he, since he left his said master with whom he was an apprentice, ever lived as a hired servant, or ever rented a tenement of £10 per annum to gain a subsequent settlement, to the best of her knowledge. And that they are all become chargeable to the above said parish of Chelsea. Ann Whitesides, her mark. Sworn before us, 2 Apr. 1762, Benjamin Cox, Thomas Kynaston. Passed her and her five children to the Rolls, 2 Apr. 1762. [See **402**].

414. [p.189] Middlesex, to wit. The examination of Jean Mcquestin relating to the settlement of Catherine Robinson her niece, at this time a lunatic. Jean Mcquestin, living in the parish of Chelsea in the county of Middlesex, single woman, aged about 36 years, on her oath says that she was born in the said parish of Chelsea, as was also her only sister Elizabeth (who now is dead). And as soon as they both were capable of getting their maintenance they went out to service. And the last place her said sister Elizabeth lived in as a yearly hired servant was with Mr Thomas Street, a hosier near Somerset House in the parish of St Mary le Strand within the Duchy of Lancaster in the county of Middlesex. With whom she lived upwards of a year and received wages, meat, drink and lodging. And about six weeks after she left her said service, she was married to one Thomas Robinson, by trade a leather breeches maker. [He was] born and also served his time of apprenticeship (as she often heard him say) was in Scotland, which she verily believes to be true, but at what place in Scotland, she knows not. And this examinant further says that after her said sister was married her husband took the lesser part of a shop to follow business in, and also a second pair of stairs room in the said house in Russel Court in the parish of St Martin in the Fields in the county of Middlesex, for which together [he] paid £12 per annum, but no taxes whatever, for as the other (greater) part of the shop and also all the other parts of the house was occupied by the landlord himself. He and he only paid all taxes whatever. And that her said sister lived with her said husband about ten years and then died, leaving behind her one child whose name is Catherine Robinson, now aged about 18 years, who was born in Russel Court, and at this time [is] not capable to get her maintenance, being a lunatic. Soon after her sister's death he returned to Scotland and sent for his daughter Catherine to be taken care of, and there lived near six years. He, the said Thomas Robinson, her father, went into his Majesty's service and left her. She then come up to London a few months since. And to the best of her knowledge and belief this examinant says her said niece, Catherine Robinson, never lived a year as a yearly hired servant in one place, never was an apprentice, or ever was married, or ever gained her self any [p.190] settlement in any place. And that the said poor girl, her niece, is become chargeable to the parish of Chelsea. And lastly this examinant on her oath further says that the said Thomas Robinson, father of the said Catherine, during the whole time of his living in England, ever rented a distinct tenement of £10 per annum, or ever paid parochial taxes, or ever gain[ed] a subsequent settlement since he first left Scotland, to the best of her knowledge and belief. Jean Mcquestin. Sworn before us, 7 June 1762, George Wright, Saunders Welch. Passed by an order to St Martin in the Fields, 7 June 1762.

415. [p.191] Middlesex, to wit. The examination of Mary Younge. Mary Younge, widow of Alexander Younge, an in pensioner of Chelsea Hospital, lately deceased, aged now about 30 years, upon her oath says that she was married to the said Younge about twelve years since in the Fleet. And that he was born in Scotland, but in what part thereof she knows not. And that she now has three children living by her said husband, all born in the parish of Chelsea; vizt, Jane, about 7 years of age, Mary, about 5 years of age, and Elizabeth, about 3 years of age. And this examinant on her oath further says that she was the daughter of one James Thompson who also was an in pensioner of Chelsea Hospital (but he has been dead 24 or 25 years). And that her said father was born and also served his time of apprenticeship in the city of Norwich, but in what parish there she never heard. And that her mother lived in the parish of Chelsea when her father married her, and that she herself was born in the parish of Chelsea in the county of Middlesex. And lastly on her oath says that neither her aforesaid husband, Alexander Younge, or her father or mother ever rented a house or tenement of £10 per annum, or ever paid parochial taxes in any place whatever (to the best of her knowledge and belief). And that [she] herself never lived as a hired servant in any one place twelve months. Mary Younge, her mark. Sworn before me, 9 July 1762, William Spinnage.

416. [p.192] Middlesex, to wit. The examination of Frances Taylor. Frances Taylor, aged about 42 years, on her oath says that she was married to John Taylor, her husband, by licence in the parish church of St James in the liberty of Westminster in the year 1748. Soon after her said husband took a public house known by the sign of the Goat at Four Tree Hill in the parish of Enfield in the county of Middlesex, and they kept the same for near four years, paid £20 per annum for the same, and also all parochial taxes. Business not answering, was obliged to quit the said house and being so reduced, both were obliged to go to labouring work. And that [he] never kept any house or tenement of £10 per annum, or ever paid any parochial taxes since they left the said parish of Enfield. And to the best of her knowledge never has done any thing since to gain a subsequent settlement. And further says her said husband, about six weeks since, left her poor and destitute, and is now become chargeable to the parish of Chelsea in the county of Middlesex. Frances Taylor, her mark. Sworn, 9 July 1762, before us, William Spinnage. Passed to Enfield, 9 July, by an order.

417. [p.193] Middlesex, to wit. The examination of John Woodcock. John Woodcock, an out pensioner of Chelsea Hospital, at this time in the workhouse in the parish of Chelsea in the county of Middlesex, aged about 57 years, on his oath says he was born in the parish of Bardwell, near Bury St Edmunds in the county of Suffolk, in which said parish of Bardwell he was put out apprentice to one Mr Thomas Cox, a miller for seven years. With whom he lived about five years of his apprenticeship (his mother bought out the other two years of his time from his master). Soon after he enlisted himself for a soldier and has ever since belonged to the army. That about 31 years ago he was married to his present wife, Elizabeth, in Belfast, in the North of Ireland. And that by her (his said wife who now is about 56 years of age) has had several children. Two whereof he believes are now living; vizt, James, aged about 25 years, now a soldier in Jamaica, also a daughter, Mary, aged about 23 years, married to one Philip Owen, an invalid soldier at Portsmouth. And that on his oath this examinant further says he was passed about four years ago by a vagrant pass from Barnet in

Hertfordshire to his aforesaid parish of Bardwell. And further says since his said apprenticeship he never lived in any place as a yearly hired servant twelve months, nor never rented any house or tenement of £10 per annum, nor ever paid parochial taxes, nor ever did any thing, to the best of his knowledge, to gain a subsequent settlement. John Woodcock, his mark. Sworn before us, 9 July 1762, William Spinnage. Died in our workhouse.

418. [p.194] Middlesex. The voluntary examination of Sarah Baldwin, single woman, taken upon her oath before me, William Spinnage esq. . . . Who saith that she is pregnant of a bastard child or children which was or were unlawfully begotten on her body by one Thomas Ball, who keeps the sign of the Flask, near Avery Farm in the parish of St George Hanover Square in the liberty of Westminster. With whom she lived for the space of nineteen months as a hired yearly servant. And this examinant says he frequently and often times lay with her in her bed in the house aforesaid, and had carnal knowledge of her body diverse times. And that the said child or children is or are likely to be chargeable to the parish of Chelsea in the county of Middlesex. And this examinant saith that the said Thomas Ball is the true father of the said child or children she is now pregnant with, and no other person whatsoever. [Blank]. Taken and sworn before me, [blank] Aug. 1762, [blank]. The said Sarah Baldwin was passed by an order to us from St George Hanover Square, on our appeal at Hick's Hall, the pauper was to go to them.

419. [p.195] The voluntary examination of Elizabeth (whose maiden name was Carpenter) now the wife of Stephen Dodd of Brentford in the county of Middlesex, taken before me, William Spinnage esq. . . . Who on her oath says that before she was married and at the time she was a single woman she lived with James Worthington esq., a hired servant at his house in Pall Mall in the parish of St James within the city and liberty of Westminster. At which time in the said house lived Richard Dickinson, a hired servant also to the said James Worthington esq. During the time of their living there he, the said Richard Dickinson, several times and often lay with her, the said Elizabeth Carpenter (now Dodd), in her bed and had carnal knowledge of her body several times. By whom she was got with child. And when her time of delivery grew near, lodgings was taken for her in the house of John Pearse in Turk's Row in the parish of Chelsea in the county of Middlesex, in which said house or lodging she was delivered of a daughter on 1 Oct. 1759, and that the said child was baptised in the parish church of Chelsea by the name of Hannah. And that the said child is now living in the parish of Chelsea and is become chargeable to the said parish, and that it is not in her power or capacity to provide and support her said child. And further this examinant says on her oath that the aforementioned Richard Dickinson is the true and real father of the said child, Hannah Carpenter, and no man else. And that on 23 Sept. 1761 she was married (since the birth of the said child) to Stephen Dodd, with whom she lives in [p.196] New Brentford in the county of Middlesex. Elizabeth Dodd. Sworn before me, 25 Aug. 1762, at Knightsbridge, William Spinnage.

420. Middlesex. Ann Whitman, single woman, aged about 60 years, on her oath says that she is the daughter of Thomas and Elizabeth Whitman, late of the parish of Chelsea in the county of Middlesex, gardeners. Who kept a house and gardens in the King's Road (leading to Fulham), in which house she heard her mother say she was born. And that when she was about 20 years of age, she went and lived as a servant with one Mr William Burchett, a farmer in Little Chelsea in the parish of Chelsea in the county of Middlesex, deceased. With whom she lived near five years together, and received £5 per annum, meat, drink and lodging. And after she left her said service she has travelled about the country selling fruit etc. for to get her livelihood and maintenance. And this examinant on her oath further says that she never lived in any one place as a hired servant since she left Mr Burchett aforesaid twelve months together. And that she never was married to any man, and that she never rented any tenement or land of £10 per annum, nor paid any parochial taxes, nor has done any act since (to the best of her knowledge) to gain a subsequent settlement. [Blank]. Sworn before me, [blank] Aug. 1762, [blank].

421. [p.197] Middlesex. The examination of Robert Ridhall. Robert Ridhall, aged about 33 years, on his oath says he was born in the parish of Painswick in the county of Gloucester. And that he served seven years apprentice-ship to his father, John Ridhall, a carpenter in the said parish of Painswick. And as soon as he had served the full time of his apprenticeship, he worked journey work and has continued so ever since. And that about three years ago he was married to Ann Barton, a widow, in St Margaret's church, Westminster (who lately died). By whom he has a child living near eighteen months old, named William. And that he never lived as a yearly hired servant, never rented any tenement or land of £10 per annum, or ever paid any parochial taxes, or ever did any thing (to the best of his knowledge) to gain a subsequent settlement. Robert Ridhall. Sworn before us, 6 Oct. 1762, Thomas Kynaston. Went with his said child to the place of its nativity. Voluntary.

422. [p.198] Middlesex. The examination of Joannah Philips. Joannah Philips, aged about 61 years, wife of William Philips, to whom she was married as appears by a certificate on 11 Oct. 1751, on her oath further says that she has often heard her said husband say that his friends bound him out an apprentice to the trade of a wine cooper (his master's name she forgot), near the church in Botolph Lane (the said house her husband has shown her, which she well knows and remembers) in the parish of St George Botolph Lane within the city of London. With whom he lived between two and three years an apprentice until his master died. And [he] was never after turned over to any other person, but went home and lived with his friends in Buckinghamshire. And that he never was after his said master died a covenant or yearly hired servant to any person whatever, never rented any house or land of £10 per annum, or ever paid any parochial taxes, or ever done any act since his said apprenticeship, to the best of her knowledge, to gain a subsequent settlement. And that her said husband is gone and left her in a poor, distressed condition, and that now she is become chargeable to the parish of Chelsea. Joannah Phillips. Sworn before [blank] this 20 Oct 1762, Thomas Kynaston, J. Miller. Passed by an order to St George Botolph Lane, 20 Oct.

423. [p.199] Middlesex. The examination of Mary Painter. Mary Painter, aged about 32 years, single woman, on her oath says that she was born in the parish of Goring in Oxfordshire, in which said parish her father, Matthew Painter (who now is living), was also born, as was also her grandfather, as she oft times had heard her said father say. And this examinant on her oath further says that she never was married, that she never lived with any person as a yearly hired servant, nor ever rented any land or tenement of £10 per annum, or ever did any act, to the best of her knowledge, to gain any subsequent settlement since her birth. Mary Painter, her mark. Sworn before me, 20 Oct. 1762, Thomas Kynaston. Passed away by a permit, 20 Oct. 1762.

424. [p.200] Middlesex, to wit. The voluntary examination of Jane Tapsell taken on oath the [blank] Nov. 1762. This examinant on her oath says that she is near 28 years of age, that she has lived in the parish of Chelsea in the county of Middlesex upwards of three years last past. The first two years thereof she lived as a yearly hired servant with Miss Elizabeth Storey in Paradise Row in Chelsea. That as soon as she left that service she hired her self and lived in the service of James George Douglas esq., at his house in the King's Road, Chelsea aforesaid. There she lived a full and complete twelve months together. From which house she was discharged 29 Aug. 1762 (or then about). And there also she received her wages, £7 per annum and 7s. per week board wages. And this examinant on her oath further says that she never was married, that she never rented any house or tenement of £10 per annum, or ever paid parochial taxes, or ever did any act, to the best of her knowledge, to gain a settlement than as is aforesaid. Sworn before me the day and year above written, [blank]. [See **425**].

425. [p.201] Middlesex. The voluntary examination of Jane Tapsell, single woman, taken 12 Nov. 1762, before me, Thomas Kynaston esq. . . . Who on her oath says that she is pregnant of a bastard child or children which was or were unlawfully begotten on her body by one Richard, whose surnames she knows not, a bricklayer who works at the said trade or business in the parish of Chelsea in the county of Middlesex. Who had carnal knowledge of her body the first time, was the latter end of April last, in the house of James George Douglas esq. in the King's Road in the parish of Chelsea aforesaid. At which time and in the said house she lived a yearly hired servant. And says that the said Richard [blank] had carnal knowledge of her body several times after in the said house, and that the said Richard [blank] is the true and only father of the said child or children that she is pregnant with, and no other man else. And that she is in distress, and is become chargeable to the parish of Chelsea. Jane Tapsell, her mark. Sworn before me, the day and year above written, Thomas Kynaston. N.B. Richard Brittain was the man's name. He made satisfaction. The child [is] since dead. [See **424**].

426. [n.p.] Middlesex, to wit. The examination of Isabella Mills, widow. Isabella Mills, aged about 65 years, the widow of John Mills, late a pensioner of Chelsea Hospital, deceased, upon oath saith that she was married to her said late husband on 10 Dec. 1732 in the liberty of the Fleet within the city of London (which also appears by certificate). And at that time he was a soldier belonging to the army. And this examinant further says that she often heard him say that he, her said husband, was born in Scotland, but in what part or parish she never heard, and that he enlisted in the army when he was young. That he . . . [had] no trade, never lived with any person as a hired yearly servant, nor ever rented any house or tenement of £10 per annum, or ever paid parochial taxes. By whom she had eight children, seven of which are dead. Her only now child living is Sarah, unmarried, aged about 21 years and lives in London. And this examinant further says that before her said husband was married to her, she got her livelihood by going to service, and that the last place she lived in for a twelve month together before she was married was with one Mr Hazard, a shoemaker in Bow Lane in the parish of St Mary Le Bow within the city of London, with whom she lived thirteen months together, and had £5 per annum, board etc. and lodging. And that after she left her said service [she] never lived in any one place twelve months and since, has done no act to gain a subsequent settlement, to the best of her knowledge, and that she is become chargeable to the parish of Chelsea. [Blank]. Sworn before us, [blank] Feb. 1763, [blank].

427. [p.203] Middlesex, to wit. The examination of Thomas Wythe. Thomas Wythe, aged about 39 years, on his oath saith that when he was about [blank] years of age he was put out and apprenticed to one Mr Nebot in the parish of St Giles in the Fields in the county of Middlesex, limner and painter, for the term of seven years. Which said term he served as an apprentice, lodged and boarded in the said house with his aforesaid master. And that after he was out of his said apprenticeship he got his livelihood by working at his trade, sometime as a journeyman and sometime by piece work. And that about ten years ago he was married to his present wife, Mary, by whom he has now three children living; vizt, Montilla, his eldest daughter, aged near 9 years, the 2nd daughter, Mary, aged near 7 years, 3rd George, his son, aged about 2 months. And this examinant further says that he never lived a twelve month together in any place as a yearly hired servant since his said apprenticeship, nor ever rented any house or tenement of £10 per annum, or ever paid any parochial taxes, or ever did any kind of act since to gain a subsequent settlement, to the best of his knowledge. And that he and his family are become chargeable to the parish of Chelsea. [Blank]. Sworn before us, [blank] Feb. 1763, [blank].

428. [p.204] Middlesex, to wit. The examination of Philadelphia Ford, single woman. Philadelphia Ford, single woman, aged 20 years and upwards, on her oath saith that the last place she lived in for a 12 month together was in the service of the Right Honourable the Earl of Peterborough at Parson's Green in the parish of Fulham in the county of Middlesex, in which place she lived twelve months and about seven weeks as a dairymaid, and received £5 per annum, lodging board etc. And that she left the said service about four months ago. And this examinant on her oath further saith that she never was married, never rented any tenement of £10 per annum, or ever paid any parochial taxes, or has ever done any act to gain a settlement since she left her aforesaid service, to the best of her knowledge. And that she is become chargeable to the parish of Chelsea in the county of Middlesex. Philadelphia Ford, her mark. Sworn before us, 5 Mar. 1763, Richard Glyn, Thomas Kynaston. Passed to Fulham.

429. [p.205] Surrey and Middlesex, to wit. The voluntary examination of Christian Dew, wife of Edward Dew, taken 20 April 1763 before me, Sir John Fielding knight . . . . Who on her oath says that she is about 36 years of age and that about thirteen years ago she was married to Edward Dew, and that upwards of five [years] ago he left her. Since which time she never once have seen him, but by a letter (which was near three years since), which informed her that he, her said husband, was gone or going abroad in one of his Majesty's ships of war as a marine or sailor, but which she cannot tell. And on her oath this examinant further says that she is now pregnant of a bastard child or children, which was or were unlawfully begotten of her body by one Philip Gibson of the parish of Richmond in the county of Surrey, bricklayer, who had carnal knowledge of her body several times in his own dwelling house in the parish of Richmond aforesaid. And that she reckoneth that she now has about six or seven weeks to go before she is delivered. And that the aforesaid Philip Gibson is the true and real father of the said child or children that she is pregnant with, and no man else. And that she has now become chargeable to the parish of St Luke Chelsea in the county of Middlesex. And that she has not been married to any man since her said husband Edward Dew left her. Christian Dew. Sworn before me, 20 April 1762, John Fielding. Vide 209. [See **433**].

430. [p.206] Middlesex, to wit. The examination of Thomas Matthews. Thomas Matthews, aged near 39 years, on his oath saith that he was born in the parish of Buxton in the county of Norfolk, that he was bound apprentice to his father, Robert Matthews, a smith, and served out his full time of apprenticeship for his said father in the parish of Buxton aforesaid. And that he never since lived with any person as a hired yearly servant, nor ever rented any house, tenement or land of £10 per annum, or ever paid any parochial taxes, nor never since he came out of his apprenticeship done any act (to the best of his knowledge) to gain a subsequent settlement. And further says that he at this time is not married to any woman whatsoever. Thomas Matthews. Sworn before me, 29 April 1763, Richard Glyn.

431. [p.207] Middlesex, to wit. The voluntary examination of Sophia Maria Saint, single woman, taken before me, . . . 31 May 1763. This examinant on her oath says that on Sunday 10 April last past she, this examinant, was delivered of a female bastard child in the house of John Verney in Jews Row in the parish of Chelsea in the county of Middlesex. Which said child is baptised by the name of Henrietta, [and] was unlawfully begotten on her body by William Bared De' Costa who lodges in the house of Mr Bowsey in Newport Street near Leicester Fields in the parish of St Martins in the Fields, with whom she lived as a hired yearly servant. In which said house he had carnal knowledge of her body several times. And this examinant further says that the said William Bared De' Costa is the father of the said child, and no man else. And that she now is become chargeable to the parish of Chelsea in the county of Middlesex and that she has no thing to support her and the said child. Sophia Maria Saint. Thomas Kynaston.

432. [p.208] Middlesex, to wit. The examination of Diana Granger, widow. Diana Granger, widow, aged about 58 years, on her oath says that she was married about 19 years ago to one John Granger who was several years an inhabitant in the parish of Chelsea. And that he rented a house in the parish, but not with any certainty knows whether he ever paid taxes for the same. But further on her oath says that she has often been told that he, her said husband, when he first came to live in Chelsea was with one Mr Thomas Fleet, a gardener, with whom he lived some years as a yearly hired servant. Soon after he left his said service he was married. That her said husband died in Chelsea about twelve years ago. And further says that she has not been married since, nor done any act to get a subsequent settlement (to the best of her knowledge). Diana Granger, her mark. Sworn before me . . . 15 June 1763, Thomas Kynaston. Sent to the work house.

433. [p.209] Middlesex, to wit. The examination of Christian Dew, who on her oath says that she is about 36 years of age, and is the wife of Edward Dew (if living), a soldier who has been gone abroad about three years and hath not been in England since, to the best of this examinant's knowledge and belief. And further on her voluntary oath says that on Thursday 16 June 1763 she was delivered of a female bastard child in the workhouse in and belonging to the parish of St Luke Chelsea in the county of Middlesex (since christened by the name of Sarah). Which said child is now living and chargeable to the said parish of St Luke Chelsea. And that Philip Gibson, a bricklayer in the parish of Richmond in the county of Surrey unlawfully begot on her body the said female bastard child so born of her body aforesaid. That the said Philip Gibson is the only true and real father thereof and no other person whatever. Christian Dew. Sworn before us, 3 July 1763, Richard Glyn, Thomas Kynaston. N.B. Satisfaction made to the parish of Chelsea. The child since dead. [See **429**].

434. [p.210] Middlesex, to wit. The examination of Martha Elms, single woman. This examinant, Martha Elms, single woman, aged about 22 years, on her oath saith that she never was married, that she maintains and supports her self by going to service and that the last place she lived in for a twelve month together was with Mr John Glass at the Swan Tavern in the parish of Chelsea in the county of Middlesex, with whom she lived about eighteen months as a yearly hired servant. And that she had wages [of] £5 per annum, board and lodging etc. and that she left the said service in the month of Feb. 1763 on account that she was far advanced in her pregnancy of a bastard child. And this examinant voluntary maketh oath that the said bastard child, as before mentioned, [was] born of her body, and [she] was delivered of the said child in the house of Mrs Mary Adams near the Physic Gardens in the parish of Chelsea in the county of Middlesex on 10April 1763, since christened by the name of Matthew. And on her voluntary oath further saith that Matthew Murphy, who was a waiter or servant with Mr John Glass, had carnal knowledge of her body several times in the house of Mr Glass, and that the said Matthew Murphy is the only and true father of the said bastard child and no man else. And further says that the said bastard child is now living and is still supported and kept at the sole expense of the parish of Chelsea. Martha Elms. Sworn before me, 4 July 1764, Thomas Kynaston. The child [is] in our workhouse.

435. [p.211] Middlesex, to wit. William Hawker, aged about 55 years, born in the parish of St Andrew Holborn in the county of Middlesex, who on his oath says that when he was about the age of 14 years he was put out and bound apprentice by the parish officers of the aforesaid parish to one Pattrick Hammond, a necklace maker who lived in the liberty of Saffron Hill within the said parish of St Andrew Holborn in the county of Middlesex, with whom he continued and lived with as an apprentice near five years of his time. But as his said master Pattrick Hammond, having frequently beat and abused him, he thereupon absconded and left his said master. After which this examinant says he got his living by labouring work and going on errands in different places for several years, and that he was soldier in the army some years till he was discharged in the year 1749. And on his oath says that in the year 1753 he was passed by an order from the parish of St Luke Chelsea in the county of Middlesex to the parish of St Andrew Holborn in the county of Middlesex. And lastly this examinant says that he never in his life time rented any tenement or land of £10 per annum, or ever lived with any person as a hired yearly servant, or ever paid any parochial taxes since his said apprenticeship, or ever done any act to gain a subsequent settlement since (to the best of his knowledge). And that he is now become chargeable to the parish of St Luke Chelsea in the county of Middlesex. The mark of William Hawker. Sworn, 17 Dec. 1763, before us, Benjamin Cox, Thomas Kynaston. Passed him to St Andrews. [See **256**].

436. [p.212] Middlesex, to wit. The examination of Dorcus Edmunds, single woman. This examinant on her oath says that she is about 30 years of age, and that she never was married to any man, and that she got her livelihood by going out to service. And that the last place she lived in a twelve month together was with one Mr John Keen in Beach Lane near Cripplegate in the parish of St Giles in the city of London. With whom she lived until he died, which was near two years. And that her said master Keen died about twelve months ago. And on her oath further says that she never since lived in any place whatever as a hired servant a twelve month, nor ever rented any house, ground or tenement of £10 per annum, or ever paid any parochial taxes, or done any subsequent act to gain a settlement, to the best of [her] knowledge. This examinant, Dorcus Edmunds, on her voluntary oath says that the female child born of [her] body, from which said child she was delivered on Tuesday last in the house of Mrs Mary Vias near Ranelagh House in the parish of Chelsea in the county of Middlesex, which said child has been baptised by the name of Mary, was born a bastard, for that she never was married to any man whatever. And lastly on her oath says that one John Brown who lived with a gentleman as a servant was the real and true father of the said female bastard child and no man else. And that the said Brown (as she has heard say) left England to go to the West Indies, and that he is since dead. Dorcus Edmunds. Sworn before me, 16 April 1764, Thomas Kynaston. The child was sent to our workhouse and there died.

437. [p.213] Middlesex, to wit. The information of Elizabeth Hatt of the parish of Fulham in the county of Middlesex, widow, touching the settlement of Ann Hatt, her daughter (now a lunatic) by William Hatt her late husband. Who on her oath says that the said Ann Hatt, her daughter, is about 27 years of age and never was married. And that the last place she lived in for a year as a yearly hired servant was with one Mr Francis Smith and his wife in the parish of St Luke Chelsea in the county of Middlesex. With whom she lived two years. And that her said daughter never since lived in any one place one year as a hired servant, nor ever did any act whatever (to the best of her knowledge) to gain a subsequent settlement since she left Mr Smith's service, which is about seven years and a half ago. Elizabeth Hatt, her mark. Sworn before me, 18 April 1764, Thomas Kynaston. N.B. The above Ann Hatt is in our workhouse.

438. [p.214] Middlesex. The examination of Susannah Jones, who says that she is about 40 years of age and on her oath says that about nineteen years since she was married in the liberty of the Fleet in the city of London to Thomas Jones, who was at that time an apprentice to one Mr Partridge, a barber and periwig maker at the Gore in the parish of Kensington in the county of Middlesex. And that when he had served upwards of six years of his said apprenticeship he enlisted himself for a soldier. And when discharged from the army [he] became an invalid in pensioner of Chelsea Hospital [and] therein lived some years. And as she has heard say, he dismissed himself from the said hospital at Chelsea and went away. And that she has now living two children; vizt, a son and a daughter. George Smith, [the] eldest child was born on 24 Mar. 1757, and the youngest child, Sarah Smith, was born the latter end of August 1762. And on her oath further says that her said husband never since his apprenticeship aforesaid has done any act whatever (to the best of her knowledge) to gain a subsequent settlement. Susannah Jones her mark. Sworn before us, 31 May 1764, Thomas Kynaston, Paul Vaillant. All passed to Kensington.

439. [p.215] Middlesex, to wit. John Spooner of the parish of Chelsea in the county of Middlesex maketh oath and says that he was well acquainted and knew John Davis and also his wife Mary who is at this present time not perfect in her understanding. And that he believes them to be married to each other, and that they lived together as man and wife for several years. And that they kept together a public house, the sign of the Scotch Grey, in the parish of Kensington in the county of Middlesex, but being reduced has left his said wife. And at this time she is not capable to maintain herself and is burdensome to the parish of Chelsea. And this examinant on his oath further says that since they left the aforesaid public house, that they have not gained (to the best of his knowledge) any subsequent settlement. John Spooner. Sworn before us, 30 May 1764, Thomas Kynaston, Paul Vaillant. Passed to Kensington. [See **400**].

440. [p.216] Middlesex, to wit. The examination of Elizabeth Davis, single woman. This examinant on her oath says that she is about 28 years of age, and that she never was married to any man, and that she got her livelihood by going out to service, and that the last place she lived in a twelve month together as a hired servant was with one Mrs Hannand, a green grocer in St Albans Street in the parish of St James in the liberty of Westminster in the county of Middlesex. With whom she lived four years and a half and had £3 per annum wages. Which place she left about two years and a half ago. Since which time she went to live at Chiswick with one Mr Holland, a baker with whom she lived about four months, which place she left on account being with child. And that to the best of her knowledge [she] never did any act to gain a settlement since she left her service as above mentioned in St Albans Street. This examinant, Elizabeth Davis, on her voluntary oath says that the female bastard child . . . she now has with her, was born on her body, and that the said child is now about 10 months and a fortnight old. And that she was delivered of the same in a house in Watermans Court in the parish of Chelsea in the county of Middlesex, since baptised by the name of Sarah. And that at the time she lived at Chiswick as a servant, Moses Gibson, a journeyman to her master had carnal knowledge of her body several times. And on her oath says that the said Moses Gibson is the true and real father of the said bastard child, and no man else. Elizabeth Davis her mark. Sworn before me, 13 July 1764, Thomas Kynaston. N.B. The said Moses Gibson was taken up and made satisfaction to the parish of Chelsea. The girl was sent to our workhouse and is since dead.

441. [p.217] Middlesex, to wit. William Horder, aged about 68 years, on his oath says that about 33 years ago he lived with Captain Richard Culliford in Laurence Street in the parish of Chelsea in the county of Middlesex. With whom he lived twelve months and 11 days as a yearly hired livery servant. Soon after he left the said service he went to Lymington in Hampshire, and there and thereabouts he worked as a labourer at the brick kilns ever since. And about 28 years ago there he was married to his now present wife, Hannah, who is now aged about 62 years of age. And this examinant on his oath further says that since he left his aforesaid service with Captain Culliford, he never lived as a yearly hired servant a year in any place whatever, nor rented any house or land of £10 per annum, or ever did any act since (to the best of his knowledge) to gain a subsequent settlement. Nor has he at this time any child or grandchild living. William Horder, his mark. Sworn before me, 2 Oct. 1764, Thomas Kynaston. N.B. The above William Horder and his wife Hannah were sent to the parish of Chelsea per an order from Lymington. But at the request and by permission of the officers of Lymington they both went back again on the promise of the officers of Chelsea to allow each of them one shilling each. Which is to be sent to them half yearly.

442. [p.218] Middlesex, to wit. The examination of Thomas Waters taken 18 Oct. 1764. This examinant, Thomas Waters, who is now about 42 years of age, on his oath says that he served his apprenticeship to his father, Joseph Waters, in the parish of St Margaret Lothbury within the city of London, to learn the art and mystery of a tailor. Soon after he served his said apprenticeship he entered into the army, and in or about the month of Sept. 1763 was discharged from the army as an invalid, and was recommended to the Royal Bounty of Chelsea. And [he] was admitted on the books of the said hospital as an out pensioner in the said month of September. Some little time after he goes to the parish of St Katherine by the Tower and lodged in the house of one Thomas Lewis in the court called Hansons Gain in the said parish of St Katherine, where he was taken ill of a fever (so ill that it is now much doubted whether he will recover). And that the said Thomas Lewis and his wife Mary, with the assistance of a waterman (whose name he knows not), did put him in a boat on the Thames about 4 o'clock in the morning on Tuesday 16 Oct. 1764. Forcibly and against his consent [they] did convey him to Chelsea and did leave him in the said parish of Chelsea in the county of Middlesex in the above said illegal manner. And that he is now become chargeable and expensive to the said parish of Chelsea. And this examinant on his oath further says that since he came out of his said apprenticeship [he] never has done any act, to the best of his knowledge, to have any other settlement. Thomas Waters. Sworn before me, 18 Oct. 1764, Thomas Kynaston. N.B. The above said Thomas Lewis was taken up by a warrant and made satisfaction.

443. [p.219] Middlesex, to wit. The voluntary examination of Elizabeth Edwards, single woman, taken 18 October 1764, before Thomas Kynaston esq. . . . This examinant, Elizabeth Edwards, aged about 20 years, on her oath says that she never was married, and that she lived with Mr Thomas Reynardson in the parish of Chelsea in the county of Middlesex as a hired servant upwards of fifteen months. And that she left her said service about 35 days since. And on her voluntary oath says that she is now pregnant of a bastard child or children which was or were unlawfully begotten on her body by one Thomas Reynardson, nephew to her above said master, who did and now does live with her said master in Chelsea aforesaid. And that he had carnal knowledge of her body several times in her bed in her said master's house. And further on her oath says that the said Thomas Reynardson, nephew to her said master, is the real and true father on the said child or children, and no man else. And that she is now chargeable to the parish of Chelsea on account of her being so far advanced in her

143

pregnancy. Elizabeth Edwards, her mark. Sworn before me the day and year above written, Thomas Kynaston. N.B. Thomas Reynardson made satisfaction. The child [is] since dead.

444. [p.220] Middlesex, to wit. The examination of Elizabeth Smith. This examinant, Elizabeth Smith, aged about 42 years, on her oath says that she was married to her husband, Richard Smith, upwards of fourteen years ago in the parish of St Brides in London (which also appears by a certificate of the same). By whom she has now a daughter living, whose name is Elizabeth, aged about twelve years and upwards. Since which her said husband has left her, but whether he is living at this time she knows not. And this examinant on her oath further says that she had oft times heard her said husband say that he had lived with Lord Percival as a footman at his Lordship's house in Pall Mall in the parish of St James in the liberty of Westminster upwards of two years. From which house and service he was discharged. Since which time he never lived with any person a twelve month as a yearly hired servant, nor have done any act whatever (to the best of her knowledge) to have gained a subsequent settlement. Elizabeth Smith, her mark. Sworn before us, 11 April 1765, Thomas Kynaston, Paul Vaillant. Passed both to St James parish.

445. [p.221] Middlesex, to wit. The voluntary examination of Mary Brown, taken 8 May 1765, before Thomas Kynaston esq. . . . . This examinant, Mary Brown, aged about 37 years on her oath says that she was married in London to her husband, James Brown, about fifteen years since, and that about twelve years ago they both went to Ireland, and there lived together about two years. After which time he left her big with child, and on her oath says that she has never once seen her said husband James Brown or ever heard from him since he deserted her in Ireland, which is ten years ago and upwards. And on her voluntary oath further says that she was delivered of a male bastard child born of her body, since baptised by the name of William Walter Grimbleson. That the said child was born 18 Jan. last in the house of William Jackson in Jews Row in the parish of Chelsea in the county of Middlesex. And that William Walter Grimbleson, who at this time keeps a house in Silver Street, facing the end of great Pulteney Street, by trade a carver and gilder, had carnal knowledge of her body several times, and that he is the real and true father of the said bastard child, and no man else. And that the said bastard is become chargeable to the said parish of Chelsea. Mary Brown. Sworn before me, 8 May 1765, Thomas Kynaston.

446. [p.222] Middlesex, to wit. Samuel Gatehouse, aged about 45 years, upon oath says that at the age of about 14 years he, this examinant, was bound apprentice to one Mr William Hancock in or near Grosvenor Street in the parish of St George Hanover Square in the liberty of Westminster in the county of Middlesex, barber and peruke maker, for the term of seven years. And that he served his said master the said term. And on his oath further says about ten years ago he was married to his present wife,

Elizabeth, at Perth in North Britain, by whom he has three children now living; vizt, Sarah, the eldest, near 8 years old, Ann, near 4 years old and Jane, the youngest, near 8 months old. And this examinant on his oath further says that he never lived with any person since he came out of his apprenticeship (as is above mentioned) as a yearly servant, nor rented any house, land or tenement of £10 per annum, or ever paid any parochial taxes, or done any subsequent act to gain any other settlement, to the best of his knowledge. Sam Gatehouse. Sworn before us, 30 Oct. 1765, Richard Glyn, Thomas Kynaston. Passed to St George Hanover Square, the whole family.

447. [p.223] Middlesex, to wit. Elenor McDonold (otherwise Kilbourn), aged about 26 years, who on her oath says that she was married between six and seven years ago to one Thomas Kilbourn, by trade a peruke maker, by a Romish priest in her own apartment in a private house in the parish of St Martin in the Fields in the liberty of Westminster in the county of Middlesex, and in no other manner was she married. By which said Thomas Kilbourn (who is now dead) she has living at this time two children; George, the eldest, near 2 years old, Margaret, the youngest is 8 months old. Which said two children were both born in Hedge Lane in the parish of St Martin in the Fields aforesaid, and that the said Thomas Kilbourn was the real and true father of her said two children. And on her oath further says that she never was married to any other man whatever, nor in any other manner than what is above mentioned. Elenor McDonold. Sworn before us, 6 Dec. 1765, Richard Glyn, Paul Vaillant.

448. [p.224] Middlesex, to wit. The examination of Sarah Dequester, single woman. This examinant says that she is about 64 years of age and that she was the daughter of one Mr Jacob Dequester who kept the Naggs Head Tavern in Cheapside in the city of London, where she was born. Who on her oath says that her father bound her an apprentice to one Mrs Nelson, a milliner in the Old Jewry in the city of London for the term and space of seven years. And that when she had served about five years of her said apprenticeship her said mistress failed and left off trade. And as her father was desirous she should serve her full time, on her oath further says, that she was bound again as an apprentice for the remaining two years to one Mrs Davage in Tavistock Street in the parish of St Paul Covent Garden in the liberty of Westminster in the county of Middlesex, milliner, which two years she faithfully served as an apprentice. Since which time she never lived with any person whatever as a yearly hired servant, nor rented any house or tenement of £10 per annum, or ever paid any parochial taxes. Neither was she ever married to any man, or ever done any act since she served her time as apprentice as is above mentioned, to the best of her knowledge, to have gained a subsequent settlement. And that she now is become chargeable to the parish of Chelsea in the county of Middlesex. Sarah Dequester, her mark. Sworn before us, 20 Dec. 1765, Thomas Kynaston. Passed to St Paul Covent Garden.

449. [p.225] Middlesex, to wit. The examination of Thomas Baker. Thomas Baker, aged about 53 years, who is at this time an inhabitant of the parish

145

of St Luke Chelsea in the county of Middlesex, labourer, . . . on his oath says that about 30 years ago he lived with one Mr Tooley who then kept the White Horse Inn in Church Lane in the parish of Chelsea aforesaid. With whom he lived near eighteen months at the said inn as a hired yearly servant and did receive £4 per annum wages, meat, drink, washing and lodging. And this examinant on his oath further says that he has not since he was discharged from the service of the above mentioned Mr Tooley in Chelsea lived with any person whatever for a twelve month together as a yearly hired servant, nor rented any house, land or tenement of £10 per annum, or ever paid any parochial taxes, or ever done any kind of act whatever since to have gain[ed] a subsequent settlement, to the best of his knowledge. And that he is become poor and wants relief. Thomas Baker his mark. Sworn before me, 25 Jan. 1766, Thomas Kynaston.

450. [p.226] Middlesex, to wit. The examination of Elizabeth White, widow. This examinant, Elizabeth White, aged near 40 years, on her oath says that about 17 years ago she lived with Sir George Pocock as a yearly hired servant at his house [at] the upper end of St James Street in the parish of St George Hanover Square in the liberty of Westminster in the county of Middlesex for the space of near two years, as did also her husband, John White, at the said time live with the said Sir George Pocock in the said house for the space of near six years as a yearly hired servant. In which service they both married together. But soon after they quitted it on account she being with child. And that her said husband, John White, has been dead about four years since and left four children born on her body. . . . James, the eldest, near 16 years of age, is now a servant. Elizabeth, near 13 years of age, and Robert, near 10 years of age, were apprenticed out by the officers of the parish of the aforesaid parish of St George Hanover Square. Mary, the youngest, near 6 years of age, is now living with her. This examinant on her oath further says that she nor her husband since they were married did rent any house, land or tenement of £10 per annum, or did ever pay any parochial taxes. Neither has she since her said husband['s] death done any act, to the best of her knowledge, to have gained a subsequent settlement since their marriage as aforesaid. And on her oath further says that she has not been married to any man since her said husband, John White's death. And that she herself and her said child Mary is in great want, and is become chargeable to the parish of St Luke Chelsea in the county of Middlesex. Elizabeth White, her mark. Sworn before us, 11 Feb. 1766, Thomas Kynaston, Thomas Balack. N.B. It is to be observed that Sir George Pocock at the time I then lived with him was called Captain George Pocock. Passed she and her child 11 Feb. 1766 to St George Hanover Square.

451. [p.227] Middlesex, to wit. The examination of William Wedell. This examinant, William Wedell, aged 52 years, on his oath says that when about 18 years of age he was hired as a yearly servant to live with the late Earl of Burlington, in which service he continued for about nineteen years, until he married his late wife, who was at that time also a servant in the same family, who has been dead near fifteen years past. On his oath further says that most of the time he was in the said service was in his Lordship's House called Burlington House in Piccadilly in the parish of St James in the liberty of Westminster in the county of Middlesex. And that the last 40 days and upwards of his said service, before he was married or dismissed from his Lordship's service, was at Burlington House in Piccadilly aforesaid. And further on his oath says that since he left the said service he never rented any house, land or tenement of £10 per annum, or ever paid any parochial taxes, or done any act whatever (to the best of his knowledge) to have gained any subsequent settlement. And that he is now sick and become chargeable to the parish of St Luke Chelsea in the county of Middlesex. William Wedell, his mark. Sworn before us, 18 Feb. 1766, John Fielding, J. Lonsdale. Passed him to the parish of St James Westminster, 18 Feb. 1766.

452. [p.228] Middlesex, to wit. The voluntary examination of Elizabeth Boxall, single woman, taken upon oath before me, Thomas Kynaston esq. . . . Elizabeth Boxall, aged about 32 years, widow of Thomas Boxall, late an inhabitant and parishioner of the parish of Chelsea in the county of Middlesex, smith, by whom she has now living a boy named James, aged 5 years, who on her oath says that since her said husband's death she has not been married to any man, nor has she done any act whatever to have gained a settlement since (to the best of her knowledge). This examinant, Elizabeth Boxall aforesaid, on her voluntary oath says that she is at this time pregnant of a bastard child or children which was or were unlawfully begotten on her body by David Edwards, who by trade is a baker, and works as a journeyman with Mr Christopher Holm, a master baker in the parish of St Paul Shadwell in the county of Middlesex, in whose service she herself did live. And that he has had several times carnal knowledge of her body since she left the said service. And she on her said oath says that he, the said David Edwards, is the true and real father of the said child or children that she is now pregnant with, and no man else. And she now believes she has about two months to go before she shall be delivered. And that the said child or children is or are likely to become chargeable to the parish of Chelsea in the county of Middlesex. And that she is become chargeable to the said parish of Chelsea on account of her pregnancy. Elizabeth Boxall. Sworn before me, 16 Apr. 1766, Thomas Kynaston. [See **260, 261**].

453. [p.229] Middlesex, to wit. The examination of Anne Desborow. Anne Desborow, aged about 63 years, maketh oath that she is the widow of Captain Dasigney Desborow, to whom she was married about 25 years at the time of his death. And that he died at his house in Manor Street in the parish of Chelsea in the county of Middlesex about 15 years since. And this examinant on her oath further says that since her said husband's death she has not been married to any man, nor rented any house, land or tene-ment of £10 per annum, or paid any parochial taxes, or ever lived in any place since a twelve month together as a yearly hired servant, or ever done any act whatever, since her said husband's death (to the best of her knowledge) to have gained a subsequent settlement. And that she now is in great necessity and want and is become chargeable to the parish of Chelsea aforesaid. Anne Desborow. Sworn before me, 12 April 1766, Thomas Kynaston.

454. [p.230] Middlesex, to wit. The examination of Ann Legattee, widow of James Legattee. Ann Legattee, aged about 61 years, on her oath says that she was legally married about 30 years ago in the parish of St Brides (otherwise St Bridgets) in the city of London to James Legattee, a parishioner and an inhabitant of the parish of Chelsea in the county of Middlesex, husbandman, he being at that time a single man, and she herself a spinster. And that he, her said husband, has been dead about 4 years, and that since his death she has not been married. And on her oath further says that while her said husband was living he never rented out of the parish of Chelsea any land or tenement, or ever paid any parochial taxes. Neither has she since his death, nor done any kind of act (to the best of her knowledge) to have gained any other subsequent settlement. Ann Legattee, her mark. Sworn before me, 24 April 1766, Thomas Kynaston.

455. [p.231] Middlesex, to wit. The examination of Elizabeth Sharpless. Elizabeth Sharpless, single woman, aged about 35 years, on her oath says that she is the daughter of Richard Sharpless, who was born and lived and followed the trade of a shoemaker in the parish of Hungerford in the county of Berkshire. In which place he kept house and paid parochial taxes. And that she herself was also born in the parish of Hungerford aforesaid. And that she never was married to any man, nor ever lived in any place or service whatever as a yearly hired servant a twelve month together (except to Lady Whitlock which was in the said parish of Hungerford with whom she lived about a whole year), nor ever rented any house, land or tenement of £10 per annum, or ever paid any parochial taxes, or done any kind of act (to the best of her knowledge) since she left the parish of Hungerford aforesaid to have gained a subsequent settlement. [Blank]. Sworn before me, [blank] May 1766, [blank].

456. [p.232] Middlesex, to wit. The examination of Samuel Abbott. Samuel Abbott, an out pensioner of Chelsea Hospital (from the 12th Regiment of Foot), aged about 44 years, on his oath says that he was born in the parish of Battlesden near the town of Bedford in Bedfordshire, and that he got his livelihood as a husbandman before he went for a soldier. And that the last place he lived in as a yearly hired servant was with one Mr Laurence Peak a farmer in the parish of Thurleigh in the county of Bedford, with whom he lived a whole year as a yearly hired servant and did receive £4 wages, meat, drink and lodging. And on his oath further says that he never lived in any place whatever since he left Mr Peak's service aforesaid, a 12 month, nor rented any house, land or tenement of £10 per annum, or ever paid any parochial taxes, or ever done any kind of act since (to the best of his knowledge) to have gained a subsequent settlement. And on his oath further says he was married to his wife, Elizabeth, about three years ago in St Michael at Thorn church in the city of Norwich, by whom he has now living one child, named Samuel, aged about 23 weeks. And that he himself, wife and child are become chargeable to the parish of Chelsea in the county of Middlesex. [Blank]. Sworn before us, [blank] June 1766, [blank].

457. [p.233] Middlesex, to wit. The examination of Ambroshea Mottrom, widow. Ambroshea Mottrom, aged about 63 years, on her oath says that she was married to Joseph Mottrom about 37 years ago, who was a carpenter and lived and followed the said business in the parish of Chelsea in the county of Middlesex until the time of his death, which was about 30 years since. That he her said husband rented a house of £10 per annum and paid parochial taxes for the same in the parish of Chelsea aforesaid. And on her oath further says that she never was married to any man since the death of her said husband Joseph Mottrom, nor rented any house or tenement of £10 per annum, or ever paid any parochial taxes, nor ever done any act since (to the best of her knowledge) to have gained a subsequent settlement. Ambroshea Mottrom. Sworn before me, 2 Sept. 1766, Thomas Kynaston.

458. [p.234] Middlesex, to wit. The examination of Mary Bird. This examinant, Mary Bird, single woman, aged about 90 years, on her oath says she was born in the city of Dublin in the kingdom of Ireland. And that about 35 years ago she was there hired to be a house servant to Major John Cottrell and his family, with whom she came over to England where the Major died. She still continued to live with Mrs Cottrell, his widow, in several parts of England, particularly about 10 years in the parish of Chelsea in the county of Middlesex. And that about two years ago her said mistress, Mrs Cottrell, left the parish of Chelsea and lived at a place called [blank] in Oxfordshire, with whom she still continued and lived as a servant. And [she] was not once discharged from her said service since she first came to live with them in Ireland as is aforementioned, till about 22 Dec. last past, on which day or there about her said mistress discharged her, and sent her to the house of Mr John Greenhead in Millman Row in the parish of Chelsea in a post-chaise under the care of the gardener of the family. With whom she lived and boarded till 8 July last (being somewhat more than six months). On which day Mr Greenhead brought this examinant to the parish workhouse and lodged her there on a promise and undertaking to pay for her board the time she lived there, for as this deponent further says that he had a note or draft of £30 value in his hands towards the support and maintenance of her. This examinant . . . on her oath further says she never was married to any man, nor never rented any house or tenement of £10 per annum, or ever paid any parochial taxes, or done any kind of act to have gain[ed] a subsequent settlement since she left her said Mrs Cottrell's service in Oxfordshire as aforesaid. [Blank]. Sworn before me, [blank] Sept. 1766, [blank].

459. [p.235] Middlesex, to wit. The voluntary examination of Lucy Robinson, single woman, taken 11 Sept. 1766, before Thomas Kynaston esq. . . . This examinant, Lucy Robinson, aged about 21 years, on her oath says that she never was married and that she lived with Mr David Deacon and his wife who keep the sign of the Five Bells in the parish of Chelsea in the county of Middlesex upwards of a year as a yearly hired servant, and received £4 wages per annum, board and lodging. And that she left her said service the latter end of October last past, and that she has not since she left her said service in Chelsea done any act (to the best of her knowledge) to have gained a subsequent settlement. And on her voluntary oath says that she is now pregnant of a bastard child or children which was or were unlawfully begotten on her body by one James Randall, who is by trade a painter and glazier, who worked as a journeyman with Mr David Deacon, her master, at the time she lived with him at Chelsea. And that the said James Randall and this examinant have cohabited and lived together, and that he has had carnal knowledge of her body several times, and that the said James Randall is the real and true father of the child or children that she is now pregnant with. And that she reckoneth that she has about two months to go before she shall be delivered. And that she is now become chargeable to the parish of Chelsea aforesaid on account of her being so far advanced in her pregnancy. Lucy Robbinson her mark. Sworn before me, 11 Sept 1766, Thomas Kynaston.

460. [p.236] Middlesex, to wit. The examination of Mary Rycroft. Mary Rycroft (whose maiden name was Whitaker), aged about 31 years, on her oath says that she lived between six and seven years ago with Mrs Villers on the King's private road in the parish of Chelsea as a yearly hired servant. At which time lived Benjamin Rycroft, who was a hired servant also and coachman to the said Mrs Villers, in which service he lived upwards of fourteen months before they were married together. And that he, the said Benjamin Rycroft, and this examinant were married to each other about six years since in the parish of Chelsea aforesaid. By whom she has now two children living; vizt, Mary-Elizabeth, about 5 years old, and Benjamin-Henry, about 18 months. And that her husband has deserted and left her and her two children, and that she is become poor and destitute. They, her said two children, were with her friends in Yorkshire, who are also very poor, and unless they have relief or some allowance from their father's parish they must become chargeable. And this examinant further says that she never was married to any other man, neither did she ever knew or heard that her said husband was married before, and that they never rented any house, land or tenement of £10 per annum, or ever paid any parochial taxes, or done any kind of act to have gained a subsequent settlement since they were married together (to the best of her knowledge). Mary Rycroft. Sworn before me, 7 Nov. 1766, Richard Glyn.

461. [p.237] Middlesex, to wit. The examination of Ann Roberts, single woman. Ann Roberts, aged about 63 years, on her oath says that she never was married, and that she got her livelihood by being a servant, and that the last place she lived in was with Mrs Aylworth, who kept a boarding-school near Chelsea Common, with whom she lived as a yearly hired servant 22 years and received £6 per annum wages, boarding and lodging. And that since she left Mrs Aylworth[ès] service she has not been in any service whatever, nor rented any house, land or tenement of £10 per annum, or ever paid any parochial taxes, or done any act (to the best of her knowledge) to have gained a settlement since. And that she has lived in the parish of Chelsea upwards of 40 years, and that at this time is an inhabitant thereof. And that she is become poor and destitute and desires relief from the parish. Ann Roberts. Sworn before me, 20 Nov. 1766, Thomas Kynaston.

462. [p.238] Middlesex, to wit. The examination of Daniel Farrant. Daniel Farrant, aged about 63 years, who on his oath says that he was born in the parish of Barking in the county of Essex, never was apprenticed to any person, got his livelihood by service, and that the last place he lived in a yearly hired servant was with one Mr Joseph Roberts, a plumber in the parish of South Weald near Brentwood in the county of Essex, with whom he lived one whole year as a yearly hired servant, and received and £7 7s. per annum, board and lodging. And that about nine months after he left the said service he was married to his late wife, by whom he has three daughters now living. And on his oath further says that Ann Farrant, one of his said daughters, was passed by an order near upon eight years since from the parish of Chelsea to the aforesaid parish of South Weald in the county of Essex, upon it being his parish or place of settlement. And further that the said parish of South Weald did, to him this examinant, give a proper certificate about 32 years ago, which said certificate he brought with him to the parish of Chelsea, by virtue of which he was permitted with his family to reside there. That the said certificate was put in the hands of the then vestry clerk of Chelsea. All which more fully appears by a former examination on his oath taken 25 Nov. 1758, which is in this book. Lastly he maketh oath that since he received the above certificate to this time, he never rented any house, land or tenement of £10 per annum, or ever paid parochial taxes, or served any parochial office. And that he is very poor and is now at this time become chargeable to the parish of Chelsea in the county of Middlesex. Daniel Farrant, his mark. Sworn before us, 20 Nov. 1766, Thomas Kynaston, Jonathan Durden. Passed to South Weald in Essex, [blank] Nov. 1766. [See **372**].

463. [p.239] Middlesex, to wit. The examination of Jane Temple. This examinant, Jane Temple, aged about near 30 years, on her oath says that she is a single woman, and that she never was married to any man whatever in her life, and that she lived with John Browning esq. in the parish of Chelsea about fourteen months as a yearly hired servant and did receive £6 6s. per annum wages, boarding and lodging. And that she was discharged from the said service in Chelsea between four and five years since, and that since she left the said service she never lived any place as a yearly hired servant twelve month, nor rented any house, land or tenement of £10 per annum, or paid any parochial taxes. This examinant further on her voluntary oath says that she kept company with a man by whom she had a child born of her body and is now living and with her. And that the said child was born a bastard, and that she was delivered of the said child in a house in or near to the corner of the place called Leeches Passage near

Church Street in the parish of Greenwich in the county of Kent about thirteen months ago. And the said child is baptised by the name of Esther Temple. And that she was not married to the father on the said child, nor never was married to any man whatever, and that the father of the child is dead, whose name was John Bates who had carnal knowledge of her body several times. Jane Temple, her mark. Sworn before us, 20 Nov. 1766, Thomas Kynaston, Jonathan Durden. Passed the child to Greenwich. [See **464**].

464. [p.240] Middlesex, to wit. Edward Ellis, master of the parish workhouse in and for the parish of Chelsea in the county of Middlesex, maketh oath that one Jane Temple, who was passed by an order of removal bearing the date 18 Nov. 1766 from the parish of Greenwich in the county of Kent to the parish of Chelsea in the county of Middlesex, was received and sent into the parish workhouse of Chelsea aforesaid, where the poor of the said parish are maintained and kept. That she brought also with her (as she said) her bastard child, aged about 13 months, called by the name of Esther Temple, which said child was born of her body in the parish of Greenwich in the county of Kent. And that the above said Jane Temple is gone from the said parish workhouse and left her said bastard child, Esther Temple, chargeable to the parish of Chelsea. And further, this deponent knows not where the said Jane Temple is gone since she deserted her said child. Edward Ellis. Sworn before me, 6 Dec. 1766, Thomas Kynaston. [See **463**].

465. [p.241] Middlesex, to wit. The examination of Ann Pugh. Ann Pugh, aged about 49 years, widow of Thomas Pugh, on her oath says that her said husband was an invalid soldier at Chelsea garrison and there died near seven years ago. That she was married to him at Shrewsbury about 28 years ago. That she has now living by him two children; vizt, a son, near 27 years of age who is by trade a weaver and rents a house in the parish of Bethnal Green, also a daughter, whose name is Amelia, aged about 14 years. And that she has often heard her said husband say that he served seven years apprenticeship to Mr Richard Hosier in the parish of St Ann Blackfriars London, a glover by trade. That her said daughter Amelia was born in the parish workhouse belonging to the said parish of St Ann, and that she has been several times relieved by the officers of that parish. And on her oath this examinant further says that her husband never was a hired yearly servant, nor did he ever rent any house, land or tenement of £10 per annum, or ever paid any parochial taxes, nor done any kind of act, to the best of her knowledge, to have gain[ed] a settlement since she was married to her said husband. And since his death she has not been married to any other man. And that she and her daughter are become chargeable to the parish of Chelsea in the county of Middlesex. Ann Pugh her mark. Sworn before us, 28 Nov. 1766, Thomas Kynaston, Thomas Balack. Passed them both to St Ann Blackfriars London, 28 Nov. 1766.

466. [n.p.] Middlesex, to wit. The examination of Mary Redford, single woman, a rogue and vagabond apprehended by Daniel Browne, an inhabitant of the parish of Chelsea in the county of Middlesex, and brought before me, . . . and taken before me, 28 Dec. 1766. This examinant, Mary Redford, aged about 20 years, who on her oath says that she was born in the parish and town of St Ives in the county of Huntingdon, in which said parish she lived a year as a yearly hired servant with Mr William Whittam, a farmer, and that she never was married, and that she has not done any act to have gained a subsequent settlement since she left her aforesaid service in St Ives. Mary Redford, her mark. Sworn the day and year above written, Thomas Kynaston. [See **467**, **468**, **469**].

467. Middlesex, to wit. The information of Daniel Browne, an inhabitant of the parish of Chelsea in the county of Middlesex, taken on oath 28 Dec. 1766. This informant on his oath says that he did, the sixth instant December, apprehend Mary Redford, a rogue and vagabond, in the parish of Chelsea aforesaid lodging in the open air contrary to the statute in that case [made] and provided. Daniel Browne. Sworn the day and year above written, Thomas Kynaston. [See **466**, **468**, **469**].

468. [n.p.] Middlesex, to wit. The examination of Elizabeth Redfern, single woman, aged about 28 years, a rogue and vagabond, apprehended by Daniel Browne, an inhabitant of the parish of Chelsea in the county of Middlesex, and brought before me, . . . and taken before me, 28 December 1766. This examinant, Elizabeth Redfern, who on her oath says that she is about 28 years of age, and that she never was married. And that the last place she lived in a yearly hired servant was with one Mr Andrew Cockan, who kept the sign of the Talbot Inn in the parish of Ashbourne in the county of Derby, with whom she lived a year and a half at the yearly wages of £4, diet and lodging. And that she has not done any act to have gained a settlement since. And that about two years ago she was passed as a vagrant to the aforesaid parish of Ashbourne in Derbyshire. Elizabeth Redfern, her mark. Sworn the day and year above written, Thomas Kynaston. [See **466**, **467**, **469**].

469. Middlesex, to wit. The information of Daniel Browne, an inhabitant of the parish of Chelsea in the county of Middlesex, taken on oath 28 Dec. 1766. This informant on his oath says that he did, the sixth instant December, apprehend Elizabeth Redfern, a rogue and vagabond in the parish of Chelsea aforesaid [lodging] in the open air contrary to the statute in that case made and provided. Daniel Browne. Sworn the day and year above written, Thomas Kynaston. [See **466**, **467**, **468**].

INDEX

This index covers persons, places and some subjects. In compiling it the following rules were used: 1. Families have been listed under the name of the examinee rather than the male head of household. Family members with different surnames are listed under those names as well. Fathers of bastard children are listed under their own names. 2. Place names have been indexed by parish for London and Middlesex, by county for the rest of England, and by country for everywhere else. Street names and references to places smaller than a parish located in London, Westminster, Middlesex and Southwark have also been indexed individually. 3. Occupations have been standardized under the most useful specific category, so 'in service as cook' has been indexed under 'cook' rather than 'servant'. 4. The outcomes of examinations (such as 'passed') have been indexed where known.

160

Low/Lowe
    Mr, 209
    John, 321, 323
Lowry, Hannah, 129, father John, mother
    Margaret, 129
Lubler, Jonathan, 264, wife Elizabeth, 264
Ludgate Church, London, 91
Ludgate Hill, London, 389
Lukey, Charles, 218, father John, wife Mary,
    children Charles, Frances, 218
Lumbey, Margaret, 158, bastard child Anne
    Johnson, *alias* Lumbey, 158
Lunn, Mary, 187, husband Daniel, child
    Mary, 187
Lydenham, Theodore, JP, 343
Lynn, Edward, father of bastard child, 34

MacDonald/McDonald
    Elenor *alias* Kilbourn, 447
    Mary, 297, husband Donald, children
        Edward, John, James, 297
McGrigore, Margaret, 281
Mackall, David, 83, brother James, wife
    Sarah, child Mary, 83
Mackcaul, General, 364
Mackenny, Anne, 5, 39
Mackin, John, 393
Macklin, Mr, 365
Mcquestin, Jean, 414
Main, Edward, 239, bastard child Ann
    Main, 239
Mainwaring, Boulton, JP, 222
maltman, 251
Mann, Robert, JP, 33, 44, 56, 58, 59, 81, 82,
    84, 91–4, 99, 104, 105, 111, 112, 118,
    120, 123, 124
Mansar, Revd Dr, 273
mantua maker, 367
Mappin, Benjamin, 375, wife Alice, child
    Eleanor, father Joseph, 375
Margettson, Michael, JP, 64
markets: Clare, 329; Covent Garden, 154,
    328; Hungerford Market, 57, 172
marriage: false, 317; Roman Catholic, 206;
    see also Fleet, Liberty of
Marris, Mrs, 180
Martin, Catherine, 36, father John, 36
Martins, Richard, 360
Mascall
    Mary, 193, 315, husband Charles, father
        Edward Mascall, 193
    William, 196, uncle Charles, 196
mason, 238, 382, 383, 401
Mason
    Alice, 205, husband Dennis, children
        Dennis, John, Hester, Elizabeth, 205
    Elizabeth, 209, husband Daniel, child
        Mary, 209
Matthew, Thomas, 430, father Robert, 430

Maver, Margaret, 48, 54, bastard child
    Elizabeth, 54
May Fair, Westminster, 371
Mayfair Chapel, Westminster, 227, 234, 371
Mayheau, Mr, 79
Mayhow, Elizabeth, 40, husband Samuel,
    40, 41, children Elizabeth, Samuel,
    Mary, Sarah, 40
Maynard, Anne, 367
Mealman's Row, Chelsea, *see* Milman's Row
Meares, John, 394
medical complaints and injuries: bad sore
    leg, 127; blindness, 92, 299, 307;
    consumptive disorder, 273;
    convulsions, 156; fever, 246, 442;
    fractured arm, 42; hurt in her back,
    194; ill, 264, 269, 270, 372; incurable,
    307; infirm, 276; lame, 57, 101,165;
    lunacy, 64, 73, 98, 179, 209, 414, 437,
    439; palsy, 257; pleurisy, 183;
    rheumatism, 56, 85; sick, 295, 356;
    sore eyes, 307; swelled foot, 218;
    wound in back, 199
Medley, John, 139
Medlycott, Charles, 14
Mercer
    Elizabeth, 223, 384, husband Thomas,
        children William, Thomas, Richard,
        233, 384
    John, JP, 30, 31
Merchant Taylors' Company, 329
merchant, 59, 79, 115
Meriton, Mr, 332
midwife, 114
migration, xvii–xviii
Mile End Old Town, Middlesex, 404, 406
Miles
    Jonathan, 339
    Rachel, 46, husband Michael, 46
milk woman, 242
Millbank, Westminster, 193
miller, 335, 417
Miller
    Mr, 230
    J., JP, 422
    William, JP, 45, 72, 73, 115
Milliard
    Anne, 61, child Anne, 61
    Mary, 61, 95, husband William, 61, 95,
        children William, 61, Maria, 95,
        stepchild Anne, 61
milliner, 339, 448
Mills, Isabella, 426, husband John, child
    Sarah, 426
Milman's (Mealman's, Millman's) Row,
    Chelsea, 20, 117, 396, 458
Mincing Lane, London, 59
minister, 70
Mint, The, Southwark, 76

LONDON RECORD SOCIETY

President: The Rt. Hon. the Lord Mayor of London

Chairman: H.S.Cobb, MA, FSA, FRHS
Hon. Secretary: H.J.Creaton, BA, MPhil, ALA
Hon. Treasurer: G.G.Harris, MA
Hon. General Editors: V.A.Harding, MA, PhD, FRHS
S.O'Connor, BA, PhD

The London Record Society was founded in December 1964 to publish transcripts, abstracts and lists of the primary sources for the history of London, and generally to stimulate interest in archives relating to London. Membership is open to any individual or institution; the annual subscription is £12 ($22) for individuals and £18 ($35) for institutions. Prospective members should apply to the Hon. Secretary, Miss H.J.Creaton, c/o Institute of Historical Research, Senate House, London WC1E 7HU.

The following volumes have already been published:
1. *London Possessory Assizes: a calendar*, edited by Helena M. Chew (1965)
2. *London Inhabitants within the Walls, 1695*, with an introduction by D.V.Glass (1966)
3. *London Consistory Court Wills, 1492–1547*, edited by Ida Darlington (1967)
4. *Scriveners' Company Common Paper, 1357–1628, with a continuation to 1678*, edited by Francis W. Steer (1968)
5. *London Radicalism, 1830–1843: a selection from the papers of Francis Place*, edited by D. J. Rowe (1970)
6. *The London Eyre of 1244*, edited by Helena M. Chew and Martin Weinbaum (1970)
7. *The Cartulary of Holy Trinity Aldgate*, edited by Gerald A. J. Hodgett (1971)
8. *The Port and Trade of early Elizabethan London: Documents*, edited by Brian Dietz (1972)
9. *The Spanish Company*, edited by Pauline Croft (1973)
10. *London Assize of Nuisance, 1301–1431: a calendar*, edited by Helena M. Chew and William Kellaway (1973)
11. *Two Calvinistic Methodist Chapels, 1748–1811: the London Tabernacle and Spa Fields Chapel*, edited by Edwin Welch (1975)
12. *The London Eyre of 1276*, edited by Martin Weinbaum (1976)
13. *The Church in London, 1375–1392*, edited by A. K. McHardy (1977)

14. *Committees for the Repeal of the Test and Corporation Acts: Minutes, 1786–90 and 1827–8*, edited by Thomas W. Davis (1978)
15. *Joshua Johnson's Letterbook, 1771–4: letters from a merchant in London to his partners in Maryland*, edited by Jacob M. Price (1979)
16. *London and Middlesex Chantry Certificate, 1548*, edited by C. J. Kitching (1980)
17. *London Politics, 1713–1717: Minutes of a Whig Club, 1714–17*, edited by H.Horwitz; *London Pollbooks, 1713*, edited by W.A. Speck and W.A. Gray (1981)
18. *Parish Fraternity Register: Fraternity of the Holy Trinity and SS.Fabian and Sebastian in the parish of St. Botolph without Aldersgate*, edited by Patricia Basing (1982)
19. *Trinity House of Deptford: Transactions, 1609–35*, edited by G.G.Harris (1983)
20. *Chamber Accounts of the sixteenth century*, edited by Betty R. Masters (1984)
21. *The Letters of John Paige, London Merchant, 1648–58*, edited by George F. Steckley (1984)
22. *A Survey of Documentary Sources for Property Holding in London before the Great Fire*, by Derek Keene and Vanessa Harding (1985)
23. *The Commissions for Building Fifty New Churches*, edited by M.H.Port (1986)
24. *Richard Hutton's Complaints Book*, edited by Timothy V. Hitchcock (1987)
25. *Westminster Abbey Charters, 1066–c. 1214*, edited by Emma Mason (1988)
26. *London Viewers and their Certificates, 1508–1558*, edited by Janet S. Loengard (1989)
27. *The Overseas Trade of London: Exchequer Customs Accounts, 1480–1*, edited by H.S.Cobb (1990)
28. *Justice in Eighteenth-century Hackney: the Justicing Notebook of Henry Norris and the Hackney Petty Sessions Book*, edited by Ruth Paley (1991)
29. *Two Tudor Subsidy Assessment Rolls for the City of London: 1541 and 1582*, edited by R.G.Lang (1993 for 1992)
30. *London Debating Societies, 1776–1799*, compiled and introduced by Donna T. Andrew (1994 for 1993)
31. *London Bridge: selected accounts and rentals, 1381–1538*, edited by Vanessa Harding and Laura Wright (1995 for 1994)
32. *London Consistory Court Depositions, 1586–1611: list and indexes*, by Loreen L.Giese (1997 for 1995)
33. *Chelsea settlement and bastardy examinations, 1733–66*, edited by Tim Hitchcock and John Black (1999 for 1996)

Most volumes are still in print; apply to the Hon. Secretary, who will forward requests to the distributor. Price to individual members £12 ($22) each, to non-members £20 ($38) each.